Financial Mail
on Sunday

Complete Guide
to Investment

*Financial Mail
on Sunday*

Complete Guide
to Investment

Andrew Leach

RANDOM HOUSE
BUSINESS BOOKS

Published by Business Books in 2002

1 3 5 7 9 10 8 6 4 2

Copyright © 2001 by Andrew Leach

Andrew Leach has asserted his right under the Copyright, Designs and Patents Act, 1988 to be identified as the author of this work

First published by Business Books in 2002.

Business Books
The Random House Group Limited
20 Vauxhall Bridge Road, London, SW1V 2SA

Random House Australia (Pty) Limited
20 Alfred Street, Milsons Point, Sydney,
New South Wales 2061, Australia

Random House New Zealand Limited
18 Poland Road, Glenfield,
Auckland 10, New Zealand

Random House (Pty) Limited
Endulini, 5a Jubilee Road, Parktown 2193, South Africa

The Random House Group Limited Reg. No. 954009

www.randomhouse.co.uk

A CIP catalogue record for this book
is available from the British Library

Papers used by Random House
are natural, recyclable products made from wood grown in sustainable forests. The manufacturing processes conform to the environmental regulations of the country of origin

ISBN 0 7126 8082 9

Typeset in Sabon by MATS, Southend-on-Sea, Essex
Printed and bound in Great Britain by
Mackays of Chatham PLC, Chatham, Kent

This book is dedicated to Bessie and Alfred Leach, Mary and Larry Grenham and Annie Blight.

Contents

Introduction

Financial security for you and your family is a priority and a job; savings, insurance and pensions are often at its core.

Although Britain still has a free National Health Service and an education system that ranks among the finest in the world, the state pension is coming under increasing pressure from an ageing population. Realising that the state cannot be relied on to help provide in old age, people are increasingly looking to protect their future through savings and investments. They are waking up to the potential of investment for increasing their returns and protecting themselves against one of their greatest enemies: inflation.

The stock market, where shares in companies are traded, is the natural place to look for the type of returns that can outpace any others. Each year investment bank Barclays Capital publishes a guide that compares the returns of shares, which are also known as equities, with gilts, which are government bonds, and cash on deposit. To understand the comparison it is important to remember that companies listed on the stock market usually return some of their profits to shareholders in the form of dividends. The government issues bonds, called gilts because they are gilt-edged in being certain to be repaid, to fund shortfalls in public expenditure.

Barclays Capital Equity Gilt Study

Published annually since 1956, the 2001 edition of the *Equity Gilt Study* looks at the returns achieved by shares, government bonds and cash over the 101 years from the end of 1899 to the end of 2000.

The year 2000 was one of the worst ever for shares and contrasted sharply with 1999, which was one of the best. However, as the table below shows, shares have consistently offered better returns than gilts and cash over the last 101 years.

Real Investment Returns (% per annum)

Last	2000	10 years	20 years	50 years	101 years
Equities	−8.6	11.8	11.8	7.7	5.5
Gilts	6.1	9.4	7.7	1.2	1.1
Cash	3.2	4.2	4.7	1.4	0.9

According to the Barclays study £100 invested in shares in 1899, with the dividend income reinvested, would have grown in value to £1.21 million by the end of 2000. The importance of reinvesting dividend income is shown by the fact that without it the investment in shares would have grown to just £12,329. A £100 investment in gilts in 1899, with income reinvested, would be worth just £15,350 by the end of 2000 and £100 put on deposit in 1899 would be worth £13,601. Allowing for inflation, a £100 investment in shares would have grown to £22,817, while the gilts investment would be worth £289 and cash £257.

Shares are traditionally viewed as being a hedge against inflation, but index-linked bonds are truly a hedge since they offer a guaranteed yield above the inflation rate. Investing in shares carries a risk because, unlike bonds, you could lose all your money and therefore investors need an extra incentive to put their cash into equities rather than gilts. They must expect a superior rate of return from shares, which is defined as their dividend plus their likely capital growth. The difference between this figure and the return offered by gilts is called the equity risk premium. According to Barclays, over the last 101 years as a whole the equity risk premium was 4.4 per cent, although in the last decade this narrowed to 2.4 per cent.

Even though the gap is closing with the safer returns offered by gilts, investing in shares still offers superior returns. Taking the 97 overlapping five-year periods over the last 101 years, shares have outperformed cash in 75 of them and outperformed gilts in 77 of them. The strong historic performance of shares relative to bonds and cash is a fact not lost on the growing number of small investors.

Shares for all

Once, the stock market was viewed as a world where only an elite group of professionals were able or even allowed to operate. It was a club where membership was virtually impossible because most people did not know the rules.

Today people are realising that the stock market is a less daunting place than they feared and with a little time and effort they can compete with professional investors in buying and selling shares.

Individuals used to be the only investors in shares, but in the last 100 years, with the rise of institutional shareholders such as pension funds and professional investment companies, individuals have become minority owners of stock market-listed companies and are therefore often referred to as small or private shareholders.

In the last 20 years there has been something of a renaissance in private share ownership, mainly on the back of the privatisation programme introduced by the then Conservative government. Shares in companies such as British Telecom, BP, British Gas and regional electricity and water businesses were sold cheaply as part of a massive privatisation programme partly aimed at creating wider share ownership in Britain.

Then, in the late-1990s, the ranks of private shareholders were swelled by the demutualisation of many building societies and insurance companies such as the Halifax, Woolwich and Norwich Union. In fact, Halifax still has more individual shareholders than any other UK stock market-quoted company.

Unlike with privatisations, these companies were already owned by their members who received free shares when the companies joined the stock market. For many people these windfall shares, which cost them nothing, were their first introduction to the stock market.

On the back of demutualisation the number of private shareholders in Britain, which was only about 3 million at the end of the 1970s, peaked at 15 million in 1997 and even after some have sold their shares it remains today at about 12 million. Although privatisation and demutualisation shares have enjoyed some mixed fortunes, they have whetted peoples appetite for stock market investment. Statistics from ProShare, an organisation that promotes wider share ownership, show that 16.5 per cent of shares are owned by individuals and 27 per cent of the UK adult population own shares.

Take stock

However, investing in shares, or equities as they are sometimes called, is not for everyone and even those thinking of taking the plunge should observe a few ground rules. Before even contemplating buying shares you should make sure that you are happy with your general finances. These will include having adequate pension provision. If you do not have a pension join your company's scheme, if it has one, and you are eligible to join. Even if you are already a member you could top up your payments in the form of additional voluntary contributions as long as combined with the company, overall payments do not come to more than 15 per cent of your salary. If your company does not have a scheme or you are not qualified to join, you should take out a personal pension. You can put up to 17.5 per cent of your salary into a personal pension plan up to the age of 35, beyond which the amount gradually rises by stages.

Other financial priorities should include making sure your mortgage payments are up to date, your debts are paid off and you have sufficient insurance for your property and health.

Finally, it is important to have a pot of rainy-day money, which is easily accessible, perhaps in a higher-rate deposit account with a building society. No one knows when an emergency will strike and to be able to get your hands on money quickly is a prudent move.

There is no rule of thumb for how much cash you should keep in the pot, but a rough guide would be the equivalent of three months' salary.

Only after you are confident that your current finances are sound should you consider taking the plunge into the stock market and even then, never invest money you cannot afford to lose.

The history of the stock market, as we shall see, is a roller-coaster affair and while over time it has risen strongly it has also occasionally fallen sharply and individual companies can fail altogether. Always remember that share prices can go down as well as up. That is why putting money into shares instead of other forms of investment is all about weighing up the risks against the potential rewards.

If you put your money in a bank account the interest it earns, the return, is low because your money is very safe since it is unlikely the bank will go bust. But while the amount of money in the account will grow gradually with interest, its real spending power is probably being destroyed by inflation. Beating the ravages of inflation is one reason why other forms of investment are attractive but they are not without risk, particularly if it is buying a share in an individual company. That is why the return needs to be high compared with, say, the bank account to compensate for the risk. With shares, investors can often enjoy two types of return. The first is capital growth – an increase in the share price. The second is a dividend – a sum of money paid to shareholders by the company, usually twice a year.

The guide

Judging risk is at the core of investing in the stock market and this guide will explain how to measure risk and pick winners rather than losers. It will also tell you whether you should be investing at all and, if you choose to do so, what type of investments might be best suited for you. My main aim, though, is to explode the myth that stock market investment is a closed world and only for the few. Anyone with some spare cash and a little time and motivation to increase their wealth can buy and sell shares.

We will look at the history of stock market investment and explain why, over time, nothing can beat the returns which can be achieved from shares. The guide will cover how the stock market works, why companies join it and how you can take part, how to value companies and how to choose a stockbroker. There is practical advice on investment techniques and choosing strategies that suit your own personal attitude towards risk and reward.

While investment decisions are a personal choice, we will also look at the secrets behind some of the most successful stock market investors and the lessons they can offer. This book will point out what type of shares to buy, when to buy them and, more important, when to sell them since cutting losses and taking profits is a vitally important way to increase your wealth. We will find out how to invest effectively without giving too much or anything to the taxman and share investments that offer something a little different, such as shareholder perks.

By the end of the book you should have a good idea whether you should invest at all, how much you should invest, how you should invest and, most important, when to harvest the fruits of your investment.

Follow the guide and your biggest headache should be how to spend the profits from your successful investments.

1

Stock Markets and the History of the London Stock Exchange

STOCK MARKETS

Stock markets simply bring sellers of shares together with buyers of shares. In this respect they are no different from fruit and vegetable markets or antiques sales. And just like any market they have certain characteristics, which enable them to work. The most successful markets bring plenty of sellers and buyers together, making trading easy and in stock market terms this is called liquidity. In a liquid market each person should have a choice of people they can sell to or buy from and the bigger the choice the more liquid the market. Markets also need to be secure and therefore people must have confidence that the organisation running the market will ensure that goods are properly exchanged for money.

Stock markets perform a regulatory role to ensure that when deals are struck they are honoured and that everyone within the market behaves according to set rules. Finally, just as a fruit vendor will open a stall somewhere else if the market charges too much for their pitch, stock markets have to ensure they are low-cost and convenient to use.

UK

The London Stock Exchange is the main stock market in the UK and it comprises a main market, where most shares are listed, and a junior market, the Alternative Investment Market known as AIM.

The main market is home to just under 2000 UK companies and more than 500 international companies, which tend to be long-established businesses that range in value from £1 million to many billions of pounds. These companies have to meet various listing rules to join the main market including having a trading record.

Those companies that do not have a trading record, perhaps because they are new start-up businesses, can list their shares on AIM and more than 500 businesses are listed on the market. Because they tend to be less established than those on the main market they often have low market values that can make them harder shares to trade and therefore riskier investments for shareholders.

The London Stock Exchange has three very important roles for both companies and investors. It enables companies to raise cash, allows buyers and sellers to trade shares and creates a framework of rules to govern these activities.

1 Companies can raise funds by offering shares in themselves and joining the stock market through a process known as an Initial Public Offering. They have to provide a range of details such as trading history and information about directors in a set of listing particulars or a prospectus. They can later raise more money by issuing new shares.

2 The Exchange's trading services provide a marketplace for buyers and sellers. Although government bonds, known as gilts, company bonds and other financial instruments such as options are all traded on the Exchange, its main function is for trading shares, which is the focus of this book.

3 Finally, the Exchange is responsible for regulating the marketplace to ensure it operates smoothly by vetting traders and companies, and dealing with breaches of its rules, although in recent years it has lost some of its functions to the Financial Services Authority, which has overall responsibility for policing investment business in the UK.

History

To get a feel for how the Stock Exchange operates and why it does what it does it is worth considering where it has come from since its origins 450 years ago. Today, the concept of a company selling a share in itself in order to raise money to fund its business is commonplace, but it was not always so.

The idea first began in 1553, when the owners of a business called the Muscovy Company, which was founded in London, decided to sell part ownership of the business to other investors. Muscovy was headed by explorer Sebastian Cabot who wanted cash to fund an expedition to try to locate a north-east sea passage, which would make trading with the Far East faster and cheaper. The company had three ships, which planned to find the passage and return with riches from the East to pay back shareholders, but in the event the expedition failed.

However, the Muscovy Company made its mark through being the world's first joint-stock company because its original investors brought on board new investors to own the business jointly.

This idea of selling a share in a business to new investors as a way of raising funds took off, and sellers and buyers started to get together initially on an informal basis in coffee houses in the City of London, also known as the Square Mile because of its size. The coffee house market began to take on a formal structure when middlemen emerged as brokers to bring buyers and sellers together. Brokers bought and sold shares on behalf of their clients and the people they sold the shares to or bought from were called jobbers.

In 1760 the Royal Exchange had replaced most coffee shops as the main meeting place for the brokers and jobbers. However, that year they were kicked out of the Royal Exchange because they were too rowdy and a group of about 150 brokers formed a club at Jonathan's Coffee House where they met to buy and sell shares in companies. In 1773 the members of this club voted to change the name of the coffee house to the Stock Exchange Subscription Room which, on the back of a formal set of rules, developed into the London Stock Exchange. The Exchange and the market it housed grew rapidly, and in 1801 the members took over a derelict building in Capel Court where it has remained to this day, albeit now a City skyscraper built in 1972.

During the Industrial Revolution the Exchange expanded fast and played a crucial role in financing companies. Its success encouraged other markets to spring up around the country and by the middle of the nineteenth century there were more than 20 exchanges in most of Britain's biggest cities. These regional exchanges were independent and thrived, but the increasing sophistication of the stock market in the twentieth century meant they operated better as whole and in 1973 they all joined together and became part of the London Stock Exchange. It was also in 1973 that the Exchange began to shed its image as a gentleman's club and the first women members were admitted.

Big Bang

By the early 1980s the Stock Exchange had operated in much the same way for over 100 years, but it was about to change radically. Although it was the world's biggest stock market, its title was under threat because of the growing influence of and competition from overseas markets. In 1979 the government abolished foreign exchange controls, which made it a lot easier for the big institutional investors, like pension funds, to invest abroad. The government also took the Exchange to court, claiming that some of its rules, such as minimum commission charges, stifled competition.

While all this was going on, technology was beginning to make obsolete the need for traditional face-to-face meetings of brokers and jobbers on the floor of the Exchange. With pressure growing from all sides the Exchange initiated a programme of sweeping reforms that came into effect on 27 October 1986 – a day known in the City as Big Bang.

- The new look London Stock Exchange allowed member firms to be owned for the first time by outside organisations. Many were bought by UK and foreign banks, which gave them the funds needed to compete against overseas competition.

- The roles of brokers and jobbers were merged, with jobbers becoming known as market-makers, allowing firms to buy and sell shares on behalf of clients without the need to use a third party.

- Minimum scales of commission were abolished and members became free to negotiate commission charges with clients.

- Trading moved away from the single Exchange trading floor to being performed via computer and telephone from separate dealing rooms.

- The Exchange introduced two computer-based dealing systems: Stock Exchange Automated Quotations (SEAQ) for UK shares and SEAQ International for overseas shares. These enabled share prices to be displayed in brokers' offices anywhere in the UK.

Electronic trading

Before electronic trading, brokers met on the floor of the Stock Exchange to transact business and while it was normally a civilised affair, occasionally, when news broke or a new share was issued, there would be chaotic scenes as people rushed to buy and sell shares. In these times deals were struck verbally, with brokers and jobbers trusting each other as they all adhered to the slogan: 'My word is my bond'. However, with the advent of electronic trading all this changed and the Stock Exchange floor was emptied as computer screens took the place of face-to-face dealing.

At the heart of this new system was SEAQ, which is a quote-driven system. This means a user can call up a computer screen for each company share and will be shown a bid price (buying price) and an offer price (selling price). The best bid price, i.e. the lowest, and the best offer price, i.e. the highest, are automatically highlighted on screen. Market-makers make their profit on the difference between the two prices, which is known as the spread.

All market-makers who are registered by the Exchange to trade a share must quote prices for it during normal trading hours, so as long as the Exchange is open you can always buy and sell shares. A broker then places an order to buy or sell shares either by phone or directly by computer.

In October 1997 the Exchange introduced a new system called the Stock Exchange Electronic Trading Service (SETS) to trade shares in the UK's top 100 stock market-quoted companies, which are members of the FTSE 100 index. This index, more commonly called the Footsie, comprises the 100 companies with the largest stock market value, based on their share price multiplied by the number of shares they have in issue. The FTSE 100 is one of several indices compiled by FTSE International, a firm owned by the London Stock Exchange and the *Financial Times* newspaper. While SEAQ was a quote-driven system because it showed a price at which someone was prepared to buy or sell a share, SETS is an order-driven system because it matches buyers and sellers. Someone who wants to sell a share puts the number of shares and the price they want on screen and the computer finds someone willing to buy them. Because SETS does not need a market-maker it is much cheaper to use than SEAQ, which has made it popular with investors who, once a buy or sell order has been carried out, transfer their money or their shares to complete the transaction.

Proof of ownership of shares used to be entirely through possession of a paper share certificate, but since 1997 most transfers have been conducted through an electronic settlement and registration system called CREST. This provides a computer record of who owns the shares in the same way as your bank account details are held electronically. CREST brought London into line with other major overseas stock markets and was designed to make settlement cheaper, faster and more secure.

The future

As dealing in shares becomes more popular and technology such as the Internet makes global markets more accessible, the Stock Exchange is once again having to embrace change in order to retain its status as one of the top three stock markets in the world next to New York and Tokyo.

In 2000 the Exchange gave up its mutual status and handed out shares in itself to its 300 member firms who owned it, opening the way for outside investors to buy shares in it for the first time. In 2001 it broke with tradition by appointing Clara Furse as its first female chief executive and in July 2001 Mrs Furse listed the Exchange's shares on its own main market.

The implications for small investors from all these changes may take some time to appear but, as the Stock Exchange has found throughout its history, unless it produces a market that works investors will take their trade elsewhere.

2
Risk

You now have some idea how the stock market works and you are probably eager to start investing, but patience is a vital virtue for investors and it is important to put in some groundwork rather than plunge head first into shares. Some of the most important foundation stones to lay are to decide exactly why you want to invest, how much you have to invest and just how much risk you are prepared to take on with your investments.

THE END GAME

Investment has a fun side in that you can pit your wits against the stock market and professional investors. But do not be fooled – it is a serious business.

It could involve losing as well as making money – since shares can go down as well as up – and therefore should not be taken lightly. In order to ensure that you are focused on the job it is essential to have a reason for investing. Simply to make money is not a reason. You need to have an aim, which making money will help you achieve. This could be a general aim, such as increased financial security or an improved quality of life, or it could be more specific, such as to make enough money to buy a car or a holiday. Others may want to make money in order to give it to friends and family or favourite charities.

It does not matter what your reason is for investing, as long as you have one. Only with a valid reason for investing will you put in even the small effort necessary to keep watch on your investments and be able to take decisions without sentiment in order to achieve your goals. Investing should be an unemotional business and many of the most important trading principles go against human nature, such as running with profits when they are being made but cutting losses. It takes conviction to sell underperforming shares at a loss, but unless you do they will destroy gains you make elsewhere. Only if you have a strong enough purpose to invest will you be able to grasp the nettle when you have to.

How Much Should I Invest?

Deciding how much you are prepared to invest in shares depends entirely on your personal circumstances and your income and outgoings. The important thing to remember is never to overstretch yourself since, unlike a bank account where it does not matter when you withdraw money, timing is a crucially important part of investing. It is no good being forced to sell shares because you need the money since the timing may be poor in terms of the share price.

The first thing you should consider is your level of income and how much money you need to meet monthly bills such as a mortgage and loan repayments, food, gas, electricity and car running costs. You will also have pension contributions, insurance, general savings and perhaps specific savings such as for a holiday to consider. Make a list headed by your salary figure and subtract from it all your expenditure so the amount of money you have left should be your spare cash. You may try to increase the amount of spare cash through budgeting, shopping around for better mortgage and insurance rates and even asking your boss for a pay rise. This pool of spare money is yours to spend how you wish and you should decide how much you want to use on quality of life and how much you are willing to risk improving your quality of life. Eating out at restaurants, going to the pub, visiting theatres or cinemas, shopping for designer clothes, watching football and even gambling on the horses or the National Lottery will all take a toll of your spare cash and it is up to you how important these things are in your life. This discretionary spending, so called because it is not essential, can use up all your surplus money, but by planning your expenditure carefully you can still be left with cash to invest.

Investments can cover a massive range of activities from collecting antiques to buying Premium Bonds, but this book focuses on shares as an investment and even if you have no more than £20 a month in spare cash the stock market is open to you. Just what sort of stock market investment you choose and how long you are prepared to tie up your money is all down to your risk profile. As we have discussed earlier, risk and the stock market go hand in hand and it is worth considering the history of their relationship.

How Risky Is the Stock Market

The history of the stock market is the history of financial risk with the first companies to offer shares in themselves exploring and trading businesses, which had no guarantee of success. Investors risked their money in buying shares in the companies in the hope of earning big rewards if they succeeded.

To underline the risks associated with the stock market it is worth taking a short look at what can and has gone wrong with investments in the past. Among the most notorious examples of investments going awry were Tulipmania and the South Sea Bubble, both of which have passed into investing folklore as cautionary tales.

Tulipmania is the name given to Europe's first ever investment crash, which occurred in the 1630s in Holland when tulip bulbs, which had been introduced 40 years earlier from Turkey, starting to become collectors items. High prices were paid for unusual varieties and by January 1637 prices were almost doubling every day. A month later prices were so high that more people decided to sell than buy and that is when the rot set in. With sellers outstripping buyers, prices began to fall, gradually at first but then, as demand evaporated and panic set in, they went into free fall and eventually tulip bulbs once worth the equivalent of hundreds of thousands of pounds were selling for less than the price of an onion. Many people lost fortunes, both real, because they had sold their assets to buy bulbs, and imagined, because their stockpiles of bulbs proved worthless and the whole affair even left Holland in recession. Tulipmania is chronicled by Charles Mackay in his well-named book *Memoirs of Extraordinary Popular Delusions* and serves as reminder of what can happen when investors lose their grip on reality.

Another example of speculation running out of control occurred closer to home in the early eighteenth century and has become known as the South Sea Bubble. The South Sea Company was formed in London in 1711, a time when England was prosperous and many people had large savings but few investment outlets. The company took on £10 million of government debt in return for being given a monopoly of all trade in the South Seas. Investors, including King George I, believed such a monopoly would open the way to huge profits and piled into the shares, which rose in value from about £100 each at the start of 1720 to more than £300 when the law was passed allowing it to take over Britain's entire national debt of £31 million. By the middle of 1720 the shares were trading at £1050 each.

Following the South Sea Company's success, a flood of new companies came to market to meet the public's appetite for investment and despite the absurdity of some of the ventures, which became known as bubble companies, people piled in with their cash. There were companies that imported jackasses from Spain despite a ready supply in England, a designer of perpetual motion machines and traders in human hair. The most notorious new share issue, though, was for 'A company for carrying on an undertaking of great advantage, but nobody to know what it is'. The entrepreneur behind that particular venture raised £2000 in one morning from investors and promptly disappeared, never to be heard of again.

It might have appeared obvious that with so many bogus schemes raising money the writing was on the wall for disaster. However, some investors even realised this but chose to buy on what could be termed 'the greater fool theory', since they believed there would always be someone else to buy their shares from them.

As with all bubbles, it had to burst eventually and the explosion came when directors of the South Sea Company started selling shares, triggering a panic reaction and a tumbling share price. Among the big losers was Sir Isaac Newton who lost £20,000 and said, 'I can calculate the motions of heavenly bodies, but not the madness of people.' Investors saw the figurehead South Sea Company's share price crash and sold shares in the companies that had followed in its wake, prompting the government to pass the Bubble Act which banned the issuing of stock certificates by companies and was not repealed until 1825.

In case all this seems too much like an ancient history lesson, there are far more recent examples of investors getting carried away with the stock market. At the end of the 1920s the stock market in the United States had boomed on the back of speculative buying, a great deal of which was done with borrowed money that investors planned to repay from their profits. This period became known as the Roaring Twenties. When the bubble burst there was a double whammy of people losing money as share prices fell and having to pay back the money they borrowed, which meant they had to sell more shares to meet their debts, driving down prices even lower. This led to the Wall Street Crash in October 1929, which was followed by the worst economic depression in the history of the US.

In 1998 there was a stock market madness akin to Tulipmania or the South Sea Bubble with the rise and rise of technology stocks. The belief that the Internet was a force that would revolutionise the business world led to a spate of new so-called dotcom companies – named after the ending for an Internet address – joining the stock market and lifting stock market values to record highs. The United States' top banker, Alan Greenspan, chairman of the US Federal Reserve central bank, referred to the soaring stock market as 'irrational exuberance' several years ago, but still values kept rising. In 1999 and early 2000 a raft of new businesses tagged with the dotcom label rushed to join the stock market in a wave reminiscent of the bubble companies in the eighteenth century. Investors backed the new share issues and while some believed in the companies the greater fool theory was also in operation and worked well until a major fall in technology stocks in March 2000.

The pace of technological change means there will be money to be made from the Internet, but it appears investors who initially got carried away are now more aware of the risks involved. They have woken up to the fact that investing in shares is a risky business, but this is not to deny that with careful planning it can also bring big rewards.

TYPES OF REWARD AND RISK

Rewards

In general, the riskier a share the higher the potential reward from investing in it, while the lower the risk, the lower the return. There are two main rewards you can hope for from investing in shares, cash dividends and capital gains, and the combination of the two is called total return.

- Dividends are generally paid at six-monthly intervals from that part of a company's after-tax earnings that directors decide to return to shareholders and provides investors with an income. Not all companies pay dividends, however: for example, fast-growing companies which prefer to use all their cash to invest in the business or start-up businesses, such as technology companies, which have yet to earn profits.

- Capital gain is something all shares offer the prospect of and it is simply an increase in the share price above what you originally paid.

Risks

The risk with dividends is that they are not paid automatically nor are they guaranteed. The pay-outs can be reduced in size or missed altogether at the discretion of the company's directors. Although many companies still pay dividends, there is a debate about just how long such pay-outs are likely to last since in recent years companies have increasingly chosen to use spare cash to buy up some of their shares through a process called share buy-backs rather than provide big increases in dividends. The share buy-back reduces the number of shares in issue and as long as the value of the company at least stays the same, because it is divided between fewer shares the share price will increase.

Because of the growth in share buy-backs companies themselves have shown that they regard capital gain as the most important measure of reward, but it has several types of risk associated with it.

- Company risk – the share price could fall because of a situation specific to the business such as poor sales or profits, a strike or management problems. At worst the company could go bust, leaving the investor with nothing.

- Industry risk – the price of your share and those of other similar companies could drop because of events affecting the whole of the sector in which the company operates. For example, a slump in oil prices would bring down shares in all the oil companies.

- Market risk – also known as systematic risk. If the whole stock market falls, as it did in the US in October 1929 or more recently on both sides of the Atlantic in October 1987, every share is likely to be dragged down. General stock market slumps can occur for many reasons including economic recession.

- Liquidity risk – this is a particular problem with small companies, which have a relatively low market value and where the shares are tightly held, perhaps by a large family shareholding. As a result only a few investors may trade in the shares, which can make it difficult to sell your shares for the price you want.

- Interest rate risk – generally low interest rates encourage big institutional investors and others to invest in the stock market because returns are seen to be higher than keeping money on deposit. It is also good for companies since it costs them less to borrow money and their lower interest bill means more cash turns into profits. However, if interest rates rise the safer haven of keeping money on deposit can become more attractive and as a result money moves out of shares, and because demand is lower the price falls.

- Exchange rate risk – if you invest in foreign shares you could fall foul of the exchange rate moving against you, reducing your returns however well the shares perform.

- Political risk – although more likely to be problem if investing in shares in overseas companies, particularly in emerging economies such as South America and the Far East, political changes can impact on share price. In the UK political attitudes to regulation of sensitive industries such as banking and the media can also hit share prices.

There are ways of protecting against some of these risks, which we will consider in a later chapter, but now you are aware of the dangers in buying shares you should consider how worried you are by this and how that will affect the way you invest.

Your Risk Profile

As the above shows, the stock market is a risky place so in deciding how you wish to make money out of it you must understand your own risk profile. Only you can be the true judge of how much risk you feel safe with, but there are a few general points to be considered.

- Are you naturally a cautious person or do you like adventure? If you are cautious, it is no good going against your nature when investing and you should adopt a safer attitude to it perhaps buying big companies for the long term. If you are adventurous you may be prepared to indulge in speculative investing by backing riskier shares, such as smaller companies or technology stocks, on a short-term basis.

- Are you an optimist or a pessimist by nature? In stock market terms we talk of bulls, people who believe a share price or the whole market will rise, and bears, those who believe a share price or the market will fall, making them cheaper to buy later. No one is really sure about the origins of the terms, although some suggest animals are used because Wall Street used to be a farming area. Certainly the characteristics of the animals suit what they describe: bears hibernate while bulls charge.

- How old are you? The younger you are the more risk you may be prepared to accept for your money since you have plenty of time to earn returns and if the worst came to the worst and you lost your investment you could start again. Younger people typically invest for long-term capital gain, i.e. increasing the size of their investment lump sum. However, if you are nearing retirement or are retired you do not have time to make mistakes and you are likely to be less tolerant towards risk. Your emphasis will be on earning income from your investments; in the case of shares this would be from dividends.

- Regardless of age do you want income or capital gain? Traditionally income shares, those paying a relatively high dividend, tend to be seen as safer shares such as electricity and water companies. Shares most likely to deliver capital gains, because of the risk-and-reward relationship, tend to be more speculative, such as technology stocks.

By now you should be well aware of just how risky a place the stock market can be. Still want to buy shares? Good. Now it is time to decide what type of share investment you want to make. If you fancy playing the stock market but want to limit your risks you can do so through so-called collective investment, which enables you to buy several shares in one go and so spread your risk. If you are prepared to adopt a high-risk, but potentially high-reward strategy, then investing in individual company shares could be for you.

The next chapter will consider the first of these approaches.

CHAPTER **3**

Collective Investments – Unit Trusts and Investment Trusts

As we have seen, all shares carry a risk, but one way to minimise the downside is to put your money into collective investments, which is a financial strategy that reflects the old adage 'Don't put all your eggs in one basket'.

The idea of investors pooling their money in order to buy shares in a number of companies goes back several hundred years and as well as spreading the risk it is a way of investing small sums – perhaps as little as £20 a month – in the stock market that would not be worthwhile putting into a single share because dealing costs would eat into returns.

The vehicles that are used for collective investment are unit trusts, and investment trusts, and although broadly similar there are important differences.

Unit Trusts

Unit trusts are the easiest way to invest in the stock market and investors have shown a massive appetite for them. Before the stock market crash of October 1987 the unit trust industry managed funds worth about £50 billion; today that figure is more than £265 billion. The choice of unit trusts has also rocketed and there are now more than 2000 to choose from.

Unit trusts are managed by professional managers who use new money paid by investors to buy what they consider good investments for the fund. The fund is divided into units that investors buy and sell from the fund management group and the value of the units is determined by the value of the fund's investments, which are updated regularly, divided by the number of units in the fund. Therefore the value of the units fluctuates directly in line with the value of the underlying assets. Almost all unit trusts are priced on a forward basis, which means orders are taken from investors and the price they will pay for each unit is fixed at the next valuation, which for larger trusts occurs daily and normally at noon. Unit trust used to be priced on an historic basis taking the value of the underlying assets at the last valuation, which meant investors knew how much they would pay for their units. However, all but one or two management firms have abandoned historic valuations because they left them exposed to movement in underlying values and if share prices moved against them they made instant losses on the transaction.

When the fund managers buy an investment – for example, shares in a company – the shares are held on behalf of the unit holders by trustees, usually an insurance company or a bank.

Unit trusts are called open-ended funds because the more units investors want to buy the more are issued by the management company and the fund grows bigger. By the same token if investors sell units the fund has to sell some of its investments to pay them back and the size of the fund shrinks.

Unit trusts are set up under trust law, which means the assets of the unit trust – the shares it invests in – are legally separated from the fund management company and there is a trust deed that outlines the investment objectives of the fund and the maximum charges the management company can make. Investors are able to spread their risk because a trust is obliged to hold a mixed range of investments, so it is not overexposed in any particular area. Although there are thousands of funds, each has its own investment objective, making it easier for investors to spot which ones they feel most comfortable with.

There are three main types of unit trust:

Income funds invest in bonds – financial products issued mainly by governments and local authorities which pay a fixed amount of interest with a guarantee of returning the lump sum invested – or a mixture of bonds and shares. These funds tend to offer less chance of capital growth than other funds, but they are also less risky.

Capital growth funds include funds that mainly invest in shares and therefore are riskier than income funds.

Specialist funds are focused on a particular type of investment; for example, property, or geographical region, such as South America. The narrow focus means such funds are high-risk since there is an element of all your eggs being in one basket, but if the sector performs well the returns will not be diluted, as can happen with a spread of investments where some perform better than others. A lower-risk specialist fund would be a so-called tracker, which is designed to track a particular stock market index, such as the FTSE 100 index, by containing all 100 shares in the index. These fund are popular because they have a relatively low management charge (see below), often about 1 per cent, since they can be run by a computer program. Your investment will perform in line with the index it tracks although the return will be slightly lower since you must pay the management fee.

Charges levied by the management firm are one of the most important things investors should examine when considering buying a unit trust.

There is an initial or front end charge that tends to be about 5 per cent of the sum of money you are investing, although this can be less if you buy direct through one of the many discount brokers in the industry. Most people, however, buy through an Independent Financial Adviser and part of the initial fee is passed on to them as commission. The rest of the charge covers administration, regulation, compliance and advertising cost. After the initial charge there is an annual charge of between 0.75 per cent and 1.5 per cent to cover the costs of managing the investments. The annual charge is usually deducted from the income, such as dividends, of the fund, reducing the amount of income to be distributed back to investors. Some funds, however, take the charge out of the capital you invest, particularly those whose aim is generating income.

As a result of these charges it is important to remember, then, that even though you have invested, the price of your units may have to grow by at least 6 per cent just for you to break even. That is one of the reasons why unit trusts are seen as long-term investments. The value of units is determined by the value of the fund's investments, which are checked regularly, divided by the number of units in the fund. Therefore the value of the units fluctuates directly in line with the value of the underlying investments.

Currently unit trusts are priced on a forward or historic basis. The forward basis means orders are taken from investors and the price of each unit is decided at the next valuation. Whereas with an historic valuation basis the units are priced at the value of the underlying assets at the last valuation. All larger trusts have a valuation point each day, normally at noon.

Choosing a unit trust

When it comes to choosing a particular unit trust there are a number of factors investors should take into account. These include management, past performance and fund size.

Management

Using a unit trust as your stock market investment vehicle means that its day-to-day management is in the hands of expert fund managers. This can be a very good thing since many managers are extremely able although, as with any profession, some are better than others.

In recent years there has been much debate about the success of these so-called active managers measured against simply investing in a tracker fund, known as passive management. The debate is likely to continue raging since when the stock market generally is rising strongly – a bull market – it seems to be very difficult for managed funds to outpace it. However, when the market is falling – a bear market – managed funds with their expert share pickers are more likely to outperform.

Those who consistently beat the market – they are rare – and make bigger returns than their peers have earned reputations as star fund managers and can earn huge salaries. These people are highly prized by the industry and can be lured away from one fund management company to another with even bigger salaries. One star manager of recent years is Nicola Horlick who was dubbed super-woman for combining raising a family with heading a successful fund management team at City bank Deutsche Morgan Grenfell. Horlick was paid £1 million a year and sprang to prominence when Deutsche suspended her for having talks with a rival bank although she later resigned and joined Société Générale.

Because star fund managers can be lured away it is important to consider the all-round management strength of the team looking after your fund when you invest. This is one example of the need to keep an eye on all your investments even if you opt for a collective vehicle rather than buying shares in an individual company.

This is just one example of why, although you do not need the same degree of dedication as if investing in single shares, even with unit trusts you do need to keep an eye on your investment.

Past performance

Although the important phrase to remember when investing in shares is that past performance is no guarantee of future returns, it does offer something of a yardstick for investors in unit trusts.

Unit trusts will generally brag in their advertisements about their performance in the past, often measured against rivals or the general stock market. It is best to consider two aspects of a trust's performance: First over, say, a five-year period that gives some feel for performance over time and second on a year-to-year basis so you can identify how volatile a fund may be.

Size of fund

Although not a hard-and-fast rule, some experts believe that the larger a fund becomes the harder it is to manage. Smaller funds are easily monitored by managers and they can react quickly to changing situations, whereas action in larger funds can take longer hitting performance.

Buying a unit trust

Buying a unit trust is very straightforward. You simply contact the management company you have chosen by telephone or letter and ask for an application form or buy through your independent financial adviser. You can find these management companies and their funds, with addresses and phone numbers, in the Authorised Investment Funds section of the *Financial Times* newspaper, which also lists prices. Many also advertise in the financial press and industry trade body, the Association of Unit Trusts and Investment Funds (AUTIF) can provide a list of its member firms.

You can invest in a unit trust either through a lump sum or through a monthly savings plan. The minimum lump sum investment can be as low as £500, while a monthly contribution can be as little as £20. Whether you choose the lump sum or monthly method is up to you, although there can be an advantage in opting for the savings plan.

The lump sum simply buys the units at the price they currently trade, while a monthly investment means that if the stock market falls each pound of your investment would buy more units, although if it rises you would get fewer units. Since stock markets tend to fluctuate, drip-feeding your investment into the plan can help smooth out the bumps. Once the management firm has received your order, units will be purchased in the fund you have chosen.

Units trade at two prices: a bid price – the price at which the fund manager will buy the unit – and an offer price, which is the price at which the fund manager will sell the unit. The difference between the two prices – called the spread – varies from fund manager to fund manager but is generally about 6 per cent and covers costs and charges. Selling and buying prices for unit trusts are listed daily in the *Financial Times* and several other papers, while some management companies provide details of their prices on the Internet.

After the manager has bought the units you will receive a letter confirming you now own a certain number of units and a certificate for these units. As the shares in which the trust invests pay dividends, so these are passed on to the unit holders. Any income generated from the fund will be paid to you on set dates, but if you do not want this income to be paid to you in the form of cash, many funds offer the option for the cash to be reinvested by buying new units.

If you are more interested in growing your capital than receiving income some funds allow you to opt for so-called accumulation units. With these the income stays in the fund and although you do not receive extra units, the price of your existing units increases.

Keeping track of your investment

There are several ways you can do this.

- Manager's report: Every six months you will be sent a Manager's Report covering the progress of your unit trust. It will outline the performance of the fund, describe what has happened in the markets in which the fund invests and explain the manager's investment strategy. It will also assess the future prospects of the fund, list the shares held by the fund including changes since the last report and include the fund's financial accounts.

- Statements: Some fund mangers send out statements to investors showing how many units you hold, additional investments you may have made and the latest price of the units and their total value.

- Income payments: If the fund you invest in pays income it will do so on fixed dates each year including confirmation of the payments and a tax voucher. The income is paid either through a cheque or directly into your bank account.

- We have seen above that unit trust prices are quoted daily in some newspapers and on some Internet sites. To check the value of your holding look up the selling price for a unit in your fund and multiply it by the number of units you hold.

When keeping track of your unit trust investment, do not be too alarmed if that value moves up and down in the short term. Since the fund is invested in the stock market, where shares prices can go down as well as up, this is only to be expected. This is called volatility and the degree to which the fund will move will depend on what type of investments it has. If they are speculative, the fund is likely to be highly volatile, while if they are blue chip shares they are likely to fluctuate less.

If the stock market in general is rising but your fund is falling, it is worth checking its investment policy or whether there have been any changes, such as a different fund manager. Short-term falls of several months should be taken in stride since unit trust should be medium- or long-term investments of at least three to five years. And remember, no matter how much a fund falls in value you never lose money until you choose to cash it in.

Changing funds

People's reasons for investing change, as we have seen. When you are young you want to grow your capital but as you get older income is more attractive. You may also feel that a fund you have invested in, perhaps in a particular sector, is now fully valued, and would like to switch your investment into a sector you feel is undervalued.

You will normally have to pay an initial charge when you purchase a new fund, but if you switch to another fund run by your current fund manager you may be given a discount.

Cashing in

Selling your unit trust is a quick and easy process.

You do not have to sell your entire holding and can just cash in some units, but make sure it is enough to justify the charges for doing so and that you have sufficient left to meet the minimum investment requirements of the fund.

Your management company will give you information about how to sell your units when you first invest. This could be by simply completing a special withdrawal form on the back of your unit trust certificate, or you may be able to send a written instruction to the company detailing what you want to sell. Some companies allow dealing over the phone and you can also use an independent financial adviser to complete the transaction.

You will receive the selling price of the unit for your investment and once the request has been received a confirmation note detailing the terms of the sale will be sent to you. The whole process from selling to receiving the cheque normally takes less than a week.

Open-Ended Investment Companies

Unit trusts have remained unchanged in their format for many years, but recently a new type has emerged called Open-Ended Investment Companies (OEIC) – which is unfortunately pronounced 'oik'.

As far as investors are concerned there are few differences between unit trusts and OEICs, with both having the same range of investment targets and objectives. However, unlike the bid and offer prices of unit trusts, OEICs have a single buying and selling price, based on the value of the underlying investments, with the commission and management charges being shown separately.

While OEICs look very much like unit trusts they are technically companies and are therefore very similar to the types of investment vehicle common in continental Europe. OEICs allow so-called umbrella structures to be formed that allow a single OEIC to contain a number of sub-funds that can invest in different markets. Although relatively new and yet to take off in terms of popularity, some people believe OEICs will one day replace unit trusts.

More Information

The trade body for the unit trust industry is the Association of Unit Trusts and Investment Funds (AUTIF), founded in 1959. It has more than 139 unit trust and investment fund management companies as full members. Between them these members manage more than £260 billion and represent more than 99 per cent of the UK's open-ended fund management industry.

AUTIF's main objectives are to improve the regulatory, tax and legal environment for investment funds in Britain and overseas. The association publishes on its website and in hard copy form *Basic Guide (The Handbook)* and *Investment Guide*, which explain unit trusts and the upside and downside of investing in them. AUTIF's address is 65 Kingsway, London WC2B 6TD, telephone 020 7831 0898, website www.investmentfunds.org.uk.

Investment Trusts

The second main type of collective investment is an investment trust that has some similarities to a unit trust, but also crucial differences.

Investment trusts are closed-end funds because they are actually companies with a fixed number of shares in issue and quoted on the stock market. The business of investment trusts is investing in other companies' shares, so investors buying shares in an investment trust are spreading their risk by gaining exposure to a range of company shares in the same way they buy units in a unit trust.

Investment trusts have been around since 1868 and there are currently 350 quoted on the stock market with combined assets of about £60 billion. Because they are companies, investment trusts are subject to company law, unlike unit trusts that operate on trust law. As a result, investment trusts have slightly more freedom to invest than unit trusts and can invest more in unlisted or non-quoted companies. They can also borrow money to invest, which means they can make bigger investments than unit trusts by borrowing additional cash to fund purchases.

Gearing can be a good thing because, if the shares bought go up in value, shareholders in the investment trust benefit, but if they fall, shareholders lose out. Investment trusts have independent boards of directors and sometimes a team of salaried staff, although more often they contract the services of a specialist fund management company.

Price and net asset value

Because each investment trust has a fixed number of shares in issue the price of the shares reflects the supply and demand for the shares. If no one wants to buy them the price falls, but if the fund is popular and lots of people want to buy it the price rises. This means the price of an investment trust does not always reflect the underlying value of its assets, that is the fund's share investments. The value of these is relatively easy to calculate since they tend to be mainly stock market-listed shares. The total value of these investments is the trust's net asset value (NAV) which, divided by the number of trust shares, produces a net asset value per share figure.

Although net asset value provides a guide to the value of the investment trust share, its actual price will reflect the demand and supply of the shares from investors. As a result it might trade in line with the value of its assets or, if the fund is unpopular and investors are selling, at a lower value than the assets – which is termed trading at a discount. But if the fund is popular and there are lots of buyers they may drive the price above the asset value and it will trade at a premium.

Discounts and premiums are a useful tool for assessing the success of a fund and are calculated by dividing the difference between the share price and the NAV by the NAV and expressing it as a percentage.

Discounts

Most investment trusts tend to sell at a discount.

Back in the 1970s investment trusts were very unpopular with investors and often traded at substantial discounts – in some cases 40 per cent. However, they gained in popularity in the 1990s and discounts narrowed to 4 or 5 per cent. As a general rule discounts tend to narrow when stock markets are rising and widen when markets are falling.

Discounts can also relate to the skill and success of the fund managers behind the trust. The better they are deemed to be the narrower the discount and in some cases management is viewed as being so good and so successful at picking strong investments that the trust can trade at a premium to its net asset value.

In general, being able to buy a parcel of shares at a discount to their real price looks on the surface to be something of a bargain. The ability to pay 90p for assets worth 100p, if the trust trades at a

10 per cent discount, appears to provide an instant profit that could increase if the discount narrows. You are also getting more shares for your money and that means you will receive a higher income – dividends are paid twice a year. However, if the discount widens you could lose out since the share price is now lower than the figure you paid.

Some speculators have tried to make a profit from the discount at which most investment trusts trade by launching takeover bids. These so-called vulture funds have attempted to buy underperforming investment trusts with the aim of selling off their investments and reaping the profit, the difference between what they paid and what they realise for the assets.

Moves are being made in the investment trust industry to allow trusts greater freedom to buy back their own shares which would boost the underlying asset value for shareholders and reduce supply, which should also bolster demand.

Types of investment trust

As with unit trusts, investors should be able to find an investment trust to suit their personal risk profile. There are more than 350 UK listed investment trusts offering capital growth, income and specialist situations such as investment in a particular country or sector.

If you are uncertain as to what type to go for you could plump for a so-called generalist trust. These tend to be the older-established and larger trusts and invest in a broad spread of UK or international shares.

In the same way as there are unit trust trackers there are also investment trust trackers. A tracker investment trust simply matches its portfolio to the shares that make up a particular index, such as the FTSE 100, and is usually run using a computer program rather than by a fund manager.

Limited life: Some investment trusts have a limited lifespan, usually ten years. The idea is to give investors a date when the trust could sell all its assets and return the cash to shareholders. When the date arrives a vote of shareholders is taken to decide whether or not the trust should continue, modify its investment strategy or be wound up. Limited life trusts are a relatively recent development and not an option for older, established funds.

Split-Capital Investment Trusts: Known as splits, these were developed to help minimise the discount to which investment trusts are prey.

Split-capital, sometimes called split-level, investment trusts are designed to offer something for everyone. Basically they offer two categories of shares: one that has the right to all income from the trust and one that has the right to all capital growth. All splits have a wind-up date, usually seven to ten years from their launch.

During their life the income shareholders will receive all the income from the trust in the form of dividends with a fixed or nominal amount being paid at the time of the wind-up.

Capital shareholders will receive their payback at the end of the split's life when they receive the value of all the assets after the income shareholders have been repaid.

Both types of share can be bought and sold throughout the life of the trust. While capital and income shares are the main types of shares in splits there can be as many as five different classes of shares, each offering investors a specialised form of return.

The complicated nature of splits makes them a useful option, but one best considered by more experienced investors. At the time of writing splits were attracting criticism because of a so-called Magic Circle of fund mangers who had invested in each other's trusts increasing the volatility and risk in the sector.

Buying an investment trust

Unlike unit trusts whose managers are free to advertise to attract investors, investment trusts are not allowed to advertise. But buying investment trust shares is a straightforward process and there are two main ways to deal: either through a stockbroker or financial adviser just as you would for any stock market-listed share. This method does mean you will pay commission to the stockbroker, but you can avoid commission by choosing to invest through a savings scheme.

Unlike ordinary shares, many investment trust managers offer savings schemes that enable investors to put as little as about £30 a month into buying shares in the trust. The savings schemes benefit managers because they create demand for the shares, which helps narrow the discount and assists investors by smoothing out the rises and falls in the share price. When the price falls investors get more shares for their money that month.

If you set up a regular savings scheme with a direct debit you can stop with a month's notice and start as you like as long as you meet the scheme's required minimum amount in your account. You can also top it up with lump sums. To start a savings scheme find out the fund manager of the trust in which you are interested, contact him or her to receive a savings scheme form, complete it and either return it with a cheque or set up a direct debit.

There are charges that the management firm takes directly out of the trust rather than charging a separate management fee, but these are generally lower than with unit trusts. Keeping an eye on the money you have in your investment trust is easy since the shares are quoted on the stock market and can be checked through newspapers or the Internet.

More information

The trade organisation for the industry is the Association of Investment Trust Companies. Its stated policy is 'To work with member investment trust companies to add value for their shareholders over the longer term'. It does this by promoting the benefits of investing in investment trusts and ensuring they can operate in a favourable regulatory and taxation environment.

The AITC also publishes a monthly information service that highlights the performance of different trusts to provide a method of comparison to help investors choose a trust. The Association of Investment Trust Companies (AITC) address is Durrant House, 8–13 Chiswell Street, London EC1Y 4YY, telephone: 020 7282 5555, website: www.aitc.co.uk.

Unit Trust Versus Investment Trusts

Investors who want to put money in the stock market but have a low tolerance of risk may find pooled investment is the solution. It is an excellent method for regular savings and useful for financial planning such as retirement, buying a home or school fees. If pooled investing fits your risk profile you must then decide whether to plump for unit trusts or investment trusts. On the face of it there is little to choose between the two, but each has slight advantages and disadvantages over the other.

Investment trusts

1   Investments trusts tend to be cheaper than unit trusts because generally there is no direct management fee or annual charges. Buying an investment trust is also usually cheaper and slightly easier than a unit trust.
2   The structure of investment trusts means they can invest in a wider range of opportunities than unit trusts and they can also borrow to invest, gearing up their portfolio.
3   If an investment trust underperforms and sells at a substantial discount to its asset it faces being taken over, but unit trusts cannot be taken over.

Unit trusts

1   Unit trusts do not suffer in the same way as investment trusts from trading at a discount to assets. The unit trust always trades at a price directly related to its asset value, whereas investment trusts generally stand at a discount.

2 Unit trusts are slightly less sensitive to overall stock market movements than investment trusts and therefore tend to be less volatile.

INDIVIDUAL COMPANY SHARES

Although pooled investments are ideal for those inclined towards low risk, they can play an important role in any investment portfolio because, as we have said, not all your eggs should be in one basket. Some experts suggest that unless you have more than £100,000 to invest in the stock market pooled funds should be your only form of share investment.

One way to buy individual shares with the safety net of a pooled approach is to join an investment club.

A group of investors have more time to research shares than an individual and by clubbing together they may be able to invest more than you could afford on your own. The strength of these arguments is reflected in the rise of investment clubs in recent years. These allow groups of investors to act together in identifying shares worth buying and buying them using pooled funds. There are more than 9000 investment clubs in Britain alone with 37,000 in the United States and tens of thousands of others around the world.

In Britain clubs are formed by friends and work colleagues, and members come from all walks of life ranging from teachers to taxi drivers and housewives to farmers. According to ProShare, an organisation dedicated to promoting wider share ownership, hundreds of new clubs are being formed each month. The average club has 14 members, is most likely to meet in a pub, with each member putting in an initial lump sum of about £250 and then contributing £40 a month.

Although investing in a group has advantages over individual investing in terms of sharing out the burden of investigating companies and raising a larger amount of capital, research has shown that clubs also generate high returns, with women-only clubs producing the highest returns.

Investment clubs are clearly very popular, but they need to be carefully organised if they are to be effective. You should firstly look for a group of like-minded investors who share your risk-and-reward profile. If you are a fan of penny shares it is not a good idea to share a club with members who are only interested in blue chip shares. Your search may present you with an existing investment club that you can join, but if not you could consider setting up your own.

After finding a group of fellow investors you will need to decide what sort of investment approach you are going to take and how much money members should put into the club. Then you should appoint a chairman, a secretary and a treasurer in whose names the shares will be kept. You should also draw up a constitution that all members of the club must sign. This will ensure they all know exactly how the club operates and where they stand within it. The constitution should include such details as the investment strategy of the club, how often it meets – probably monthly – how many members can join the club and how members can join and leave.

One aspect of leaving the club will be that you will want to take out your money and hopefully any profits. To make this an easy process clubs operate a unit valuation system where each member is allocated units in the overall portfolio based on their contributions. Since the units have a value directly related to the investments, this makes it easy to pay out to members who choose to leave.

In deciding how many people should be in the club, three members is considered a minimum and the maximum is 20, since more than this could mean that your club will be considered a corporate entity and may be liable to corporation tax.

The club will then need to appoint a stockbroker, many of whom run investment club services. We will consider in a later chapter how to go about choosing a broker.

Obviously, making money is a major aim of an investment club, but even if you do not achieve huge profits the club is a very useful way of learning about share investment with a limited financial risk. The amount of cash you put in will be far less than you would need to invest to make individual share buying viable.

If you are interested in starting an investment club, ProShare produces a useful Investment Club Manual that is an ideal starting point.

Many people choose the investment club format to cut their teeth on stock market investment and then embark on investing in shares on their own account using the knowledge they have acquired at the club.

Whether you use it as a training ground or not, an investment club is an ideal way to dip a toe into stock market investment. However, while it is important to realise the value of pooled investments and their role for investors, the main purpose of this book is to guide investors who wish to invest in single shares. If you are prepared to embrace risk in the hope of making bigger rewards, investing in single shares may be for you. It takes discipline and determination, but for those willing to put in the effort the rewards can be high and what is more it can be fun.

For the remainder of this guide we will look at what individual shares are, what companies are and how they operate and can be understood. We will then look at how to analyse individual shares, how to develop investment strategies that work, how to build a portfolio, specialist investing and we will consider the tricks of the trade that can help turn ordinary returns into extraordinary ones.

4

Individual Company Shares

In the UK stocks include government bonds, which are called gilts and are used to raise money to cover shortfalls in public expenditure.

Another type of stock is a bond issued by companies and local authorities that offers a fixed amount of interest on the sum invested.

Generally these days, when we talk about an investment that offers part ownership in a company we use the term share. On the UK stock market there are shares issued by UK companies and also overseas companies' shares.

An umbrella term covering both stocks and shares is securities, which is the type of jargon you sometimes find in investment literature.

When you buy a share in a company you take a stake in the business and become part owner of that company. In the same way as when you buy a house the bit you own that is not mortgaged is known as equity, so shares are sometimes known as equities. As part owner you share in the success and failure of the company that is reflected in a rising or falling share price. If the company is very successful you should benefit from a growing share price that will increase the value of the capital you invested and the company may also return surplus profits in the form of dividends. However, if the company is less successful the share price could fall, valuing it at less than you paid, and in extreme cases if the business went bust as a co-owner you would lose your entire investment. As a shareholder in the business you may have certain rights connected with your ownership, but these and the returns you might expect on your investment depend on the type of share you hold.

There are several types of shares and they can have certain characteristics that are a useful guideline for deciding which is the best investment for you.

ORDINARY SHARES

Ordinary shares are the most common form of shares and because they carry the highest risk they also offer investors the greatest reward. These are what most people understand as shares when they refer to companies quoted on the stock market. Each has a nominal value that can be confusing for private investors. The nominal value is often just a few pence and, since shares can be worth many pounds, investors could be shocked to see their share said to be worth only pennies. In fact, nominal value is just a value given to the share when it is first issued and has little meaning once the price is set by the marketplace. If, for example, a company's issued share capital is worth £10 million and the shares have a nominal value of 25p, it has 40 million shares in issue. Shares in the UK are required to have a nominal value by law, unlike other countries where shares are deemed initially to have no value, called no par value.

As the owner of ordinary shares in a company you will have certain rights, although some of these will be at the discretion of the board of the company, which runs its day-to-day affairs.

Dividends

Ordinary shareholders have the right to receive any surplus profits distributed by the company in the form of a dividend, which is sometimes called a pay-out or a return. Traditionally, almost all companies paid dividends, but this is no longer the case. Many new or start-up businesses, particularly technology or biotech companies, have yet to make profits and therefore have none to return to shareholders. Even those that move into profit often prefer to plough their profits back into the business to finance further growth rather than return it to shareholders.

Of those companies that do pay dividends most tend to make two payments a year. There is a so-called interim dividend that is paid at the six-month stage or halfway through the company's financial year and a final dividend that is paid at the end of the year. Together the two payments represent the company's total dividend. It is up to each individual company how much they pay at the interim and full-year stages, but traditionally the final dividend tends to be larger.

The level of dividend is decided by the company's board of directors who take into account a number of factors including the profits of the company, the size of the previous year's dividend, how much money the company needs for investment and the prospects for the business. Companies are not obliged to pay dividends and there is no guarantee they will, even if they have in the past. Dividends can be cut, reduced from the previous year's level, or passed altogether if the company is in difficulties or considers the cash would be better used kept within the business. Generally, companies are reluctant to cut their dividends since it suggest they are in trouble and big increases in dividends are also rare because they may not be sustainable. This means that over time dividends paid by companies tend to be fairly stable, often rising by a similar percentage each year.

When thinking of investing in a share, particularly if you are after income, it is important to consider the timing of your purchase. Once a company has declared a dividend there is cut-off date for when the owner of the share is entitled to the dividend. If you buy before this date you will receive the dividend, but if you buy after this date the dividend is paid to the previous owner. In stock market jargon if a share is described as 'cum dividend' it indicates that if you buy the share you will receive the next dividend, but if you sell the share you will not receive the next pay-out. In contrast, if the share is described as 'ex dividend', if you buy the share you will not receive the next dividend pay-out, but if you sell the share you will receive the next dividend, although obviously not any subsequent ones.

Although dividends are generally paid twice a year there is nothing to stop a company from paying a one-off or special dividend. If a company has a large cash surplus, perhaps from selling a business, it might choose to return the cash to shareholders through a special dividend. This can sometimes accompany normal dividend payments or be completely separate them in timing. The move reduces a company's cash pile and therefore its assets, which often means the company's share price will fall.

For investors dividends can provide a useful income, but the main reason to invest in ordinary shares is the hope that the share's price will rise, producing a capital gain on your original investment.

Voting rights

As a part owner of a company through holding its shares you will be entitled to take part in some of the decisions affecting it. Although the day-to-day running of the business is in the hands of its board you will be able to exercise some control at certain times by using your vote as a shareholder. The most common time at which you will be able to use your vote is at the company's annual general meeting, which follows on from its presentation of its annual financial results, usually within a few months. You will be able to vote to approve the annual report and accounts, decide more general issues and appoint and reappoint directors to the board.

Sometimes you will be asked to vote on a move by the company outside the annual meeting, perhaps to approve a very large acquisition or disposal, or change the company name, and this will be through an extraordinary general meeting called for the purpose. Shareholders can vote in person at a meeting or by post. These meetings, particularly the AGM, also give shareholders an opportunity to comment and ask questions on the way the company is being run or quizzing directors about their actions. Depending on the size of the company these meetings can be huge affairs, with thousands of shareholders attending and they can last many hours, particularly if the issue being voted on is contentious. However, most attract only a handful of shareholders and last only a short time.

These meetings allow all shareholders to express their opinions and exercise their right to vote, and in theory they represent shareholder democracy at work. However, in reality, as many small investors know, the real power at these meetings rest with very large shareholders, such as pension funds and other big financial institutions. Because the weight of your vote is directly related to the number of shares you own and the large number of shares these organisations hold, it is normally the way they vote that determines the outcome of the meeting. Companies know this as well and are careful to sound out major investors ahead of such meetings to ensure they support the proposals of the board.

Although ordinary shares generally entitle shareholders to vote, there are some companies that have shares in issue which do not carry any, or only restricted, voting rights. While it is rare for a new company to issue shares that do not have voting rights, some existing companies have non-voting shares. These were often family-owned companies, which wanted to raise some money but did not wish to transfer control of the business to outside shareholders. If you are considering investing in such a company you should be aware of the limitations in the control you would be able to exercise as a shareholder.

Risk

While owning ordinary shares confers certain rights, it also carries significant risks, the biggest of which is that ordinary shareholders are at the tail end of the queue to get any money back if the company goes bust. This means you must be prepared to lose your entire investment if you choose to invest in ordinary shares. There is a pecking order of creditors – people owed money – if a company goes out of business and among those at the front of the queue are the taxman, banks and employees. Only if and when all these have been paid is any money left over distributed to ordinary shareholders. However, this is a worst-case scenario since as an ordinary shareholder your losses are limited to the amount you have invested and no matter what the level of the company's debts, you cannot be called upon to pay out more money. This is because all companies quoted on the stock exchange are limited, which means that your liability is limited to the amount you have invested. The only case in which you might be required to pay more is if the shares you own are only partly paid, that is you are paying for them in more than one instalment. Although this is unusual, it has been common practice among privatisation issues and in this case you can be required to pay up the outstanding amount.

Preference Shares

While ordinary shareholders are at the back of the queue when a company goes belly up, standing just in front of them are holders of so-called preference shares if they have been issued by the company. Some major companies, including HBOS and transport group P&O, sell preference shares in themselves to investors and in effect they are a form of borrowing. The shares pay a fixed dividend described as a percentage – for example, there is a HBOS 9.25 per cent preference share – and are therefore of interest to investors who want a regular income.

The dividend is generally quite high compared with the dividend on ordinary shares although, as with ordinary shares, it is not guaranteed and can be cut or not paid at all by a company.

Companies can issue more than one set of preference shares, but have to rank them in an order of preference. Most preference shares are known as cumulative, which means that if the dividend is passed or only partly paid the amount owed builds up and is carried forward. Until arrears have been paid the company cannot pay a dividend on any class of its shares.

Preference shares move up and down in value in the same way as ordinary shares, depending on demand for the company's shares, although they tend to be less volatile. This means investors can make a capital gain, a rise in the amount they initially invest, albeit less than with an ordinary share, as well as enjoying an income from the share. Because they pay a fixed dividend, preference shares tend also to move in value in relation to interest rates in the wider economy. As interest rates rise the price of preference shares will fall, so the fixed dividend represents a greater proportion of the share price. As interest rates fall, so share price tend to rise.

Preference shares get their name because they rank ahead of ordinary shares when dividends are paid and if the company goes bust, preference shareholders must be paid before ordinary shareholders.

Voting rights

As a general rule preference shares carry no voting rights, which means as a preference shareholder you cannot vote at annual meetings or extraordinary meetings. However, in rare circumstances preference shareholders are allowed to vote. These can include if the company needs approval to miss a dividend payment or wants to issue a further class of preference share.

Risks

The main risk associated with preference shares is that if the company goes bust, preference shareholders are among the last to receive any return of their capital. Although they rank before ordinary shareholders, they must still wait their turn after banks and other creditors.

There is also a risk, if you buy the shares for their dividend income, that the company cuts or passes the dividend.

Types of preference shares

There are several types of preference shares including convertible preference shares that allow you to exchange your preference shares for ordinary shares in the company at a fixed price at a future date. Convertibles enable investors to enjoy the regular income offered by a fixed-interest investment combined with the possibility for greater capital gain offered by ordinary shares. However, be careful when investing in convertibles since as the date for them to be converted into ordinary shares approaches their price moves in tandem with the more volatile ordinary share price.

Some preference shares offer no income and these are known as zero-dividend preference shares, which are issued by split-capital investment trusts that as we have seen, offer investors more than one type of share. Zero-dividend, or zeros as they are known, may not offer income but they offer capital growth and will rank ahead of ordinary shares in a split-capital trust.

OTHER CLASSES OF SHARES

For most investors ordinary shares will be their bread-and-butter investment, although preference shares will also sometimes make it into your portfolio.

However, there are other ways to invest in shares that we will briefly consider here before examining them in more detail in a later chapter. These are generally called derivatives, because their value is derived from some other underlying investments, and they are only suitable for more sophisticated investors.

Warrants

Warrants are a little like convertibles in that they offer the owner the right, but not the obligation, to buy a predetermined number of ordinary shares in a company at a predetermined price and date. They are traded on the stock market and the price of a warrant is determined by the difference between the ordinary share price and the conversion price of the warrant. Several large companies offer warrants, including Eurotunnel.

Options

Traditionally, these offer the right to buy or sell a certain number of shares in a company on a given date and at a pre-agreed price. They differ from warrants in that they cannot be bought and sold before the given date.

However, there are also traded options, which confer the right, but not the obligation, to buy or sell a certain number of shares at a set price on a given date, and which can be bought and sold before that date. Traded options are available in a much larger number of companies than offer warrants and, as we shall see later, can be a useful investment in their own right, as well as providing a form of insurance policy for your portfolio.

So there are many different types of shares, although the commonest are ordinary shares. Companies usually issue these to raise money and enjoy a higher profile by becoming a stock market-quoted business. However, there are other reasons to come to the stock market and other ways of issuing shares that we will now consider.

How and Why Companies Issue Shares

As we have previously seen, the main reason for a company to issue shares is to offer part ownership in itself in return for cash that it can use to develop its business. When a company joins the stock market it does so through what is known as a new issue, meaning an issue of shares. There are three main types of share issue as part of a flotation.

- An **initial public offering** in which some existing or new shares are offered to the public, although others may be kept by the original investors, offered to selected buyers such as friends or family, or earmarked for institutional investors.

- A **placing** in which some existing or new shares are sold directly to groups of institutional investors.

- An **introduction** where no new shares are offered since they may already be held between a large number of investors and no new money is raised. However, dealing in the share is made easier since they are now listed on the stock market.

There are other methods of coming to the stock market. These include demerger, where a company, that may already be quoted simply hands shares in one of its businesses to its existing investors. It is a form of introduction. There are also so-called reverse takeovers, where an unlisted company acquires a listed one and keeps its stock market quote. But IPOs, placings and introductions remain the most common methods.

- **IPO**s are favoured by companies that want to offer their shares to a large number of investors and often want to increase the company's profile and perhaps generate shareholder loyalty for its products. That is why many retailers choose an IPO when they come to the stock market. IPOs were also the method chosen for the privatisation issues of the 1980s and 1990s.

- **Placings** are a popular way of joining the stock market for both companies and institutional investors because they are fast and cheaper than an IPO. Companies still have to meet the listing requirements of the Stock Exchange, but the method by which they sell their shares is a lot simpler.

    The company produces a placing document that details its financial situation, explains its business plan and indicates what it will do with the money raised. Then, instead of offering shares to the general public, the company's advisers determine a price for the shares and sell them to interested financial institutions.

- **Introductions** do not raise new money for a company. However, they are an efficient way to achieve a stock market listing for a company whose shares are already widely owned by institutions. The company is subject to the rules and regulations of the Stock Exchange and its shares are listed on the market, allowing anyone to buy or sell them.

    Introductions are a common way in which overseas companies that have a stock market listing in their own country can achieve a listing in the UK. As we have seen above, it is also a method by which a company can demerge a subsidiary by simply handing shares in the new business to its existing shareholders.

Listing on the Stock Exchange

To achieve a listing, companies have to meet various requirements as laid down by the London Stock Exchange and must be sponsored by a stockbroker. Companies usually employ an investment bank to handle the issue.

In the past, companies have taken several years to come to the stock market, often indicating long in advance their intention to float. Some issue annual profit statements to make their business more transparent to potential investors well in advance of a listing. A trading history was once seen as essential for any company seeking to join the stock market but the growth in recent years of technology start-up companies that want to raise money to fund research and development means a trading record is not as important any more.

Pricing and underwriting

When the company has decided to list, part of the role of its investment bank and broker is deciding a value for its shares. Valuing companies is something we will consider in detail in later chapters, but generally they will look at similar quoted businesses, as well as the company's profits and trading record, to determine the price.

In recent years a method called book building has grown in popularity and is a way the market itself sets the price through gauging demand for the shares. Potential investors are asked to indicate how many shares they are prepared to buy at a certain price and the company's advisers use this to determine the price all investors will pay. To be sure the company receives all the money it is seeking its investment bank will often arrange for the shares to be underwritten. Underwriters, who tend to be other banks and financial institutions, buy at an agreed price any shares that remain unsold in the issue and receive a fee for their trouble. The company raises the cash it wants and the underwriters take the risk that not all the shares will be sold.

Until 1995, companies valued at more than £50 million that came to the market were obliged to offer at least some of their shares to the public. However, this condition was dropped and small investors can now have difficulty getting shares of first issues. Many companies now prefer to place the shares with institutional investors and small investors must wait for them to begin trading before being able to buy.

How to buy new issues

Some new issues have restricted access: the flotation of online bank Egg, for instance, which was available only to its customers.

If a new issue is open to the public small investors have several ways in which they can apply for shares. The first and most sensible is to get hold of a copy of the company's prospectus, which it is obliged to issue prior to its flotation. The prospectus will explain what the company does, give a breakdown of its financial figures and detail its management. It must also contain information about any special situations such as outstanding legal actions and detail risks associated with investing in the business. It will explain too, why the company is joining the stock market and what it intends to do with any money it raises. The prospectus will contain an application form to enable you to apply for shares and these are sometimes reproduced in adverts the company takes out in newspapers and specialist magazines. All you have to do is fill in the form and send it to the broker with a cheque for the amount of money you wish to invest.

Increasingly, the Internet is being used as a method of applying for shares and you can apply online for some issues. Indeed, for some Internet companies this has been the only way to buy the shares. If the issue has a set price you will know how many shares your cash will buy, but if the price is being set through a book-building exercise you will have to wait until the issue is priced before you know how many shares you will receive. This can mean that you simply send a cheque for, say, £1000 without knowing how many shares this will buy you and is therefore more risky, if demand is strong and the shares are highly priced, than knowing in advance the issue price. You can also apply for shares through the sponsoring broker or through your own stockbroker if you have one.

With privatisation issues the government created so-called share shops, often the broking arms of high street banks, which people needed to register with in order to apply for shares.

The advantage of new issues over buying shares at most other times is that there is no charge associated with the purchase.

Just because you have applied for shares in a new issue does not necessarily mean you will get them. If the number of people wanting shares exceeds the number of shares available the offer is said to be oversubscribed and the company's investment bank must decide how the shares are allocated. It has several choices.

- It may choose to **scale down** applications, which means you will only get a proportion of the total number of shares you applied for with the cash difference refunded.

- It might **ballot** applications, where applicants are picked at random and those chosen receive all or a proportion of the shares they applied for, while those not picked receive no shares and a full refund.

- It may **cut off** some applications. It might decide only to issue shares to investors who have asked for amounts below a certain level to ensure a large number receive shares. This means that small investors and institutions which applied for large numbers of shares will receive nothing.

Deciding allocations when an issue is oversubscribed is a tricky business and it is difficult to ensure everyone is happy. When Lastminute.com joined the stock market in 2000 applications were scaled back, so investors received just 35 shares each. After the shares initially fell in value the small allocation meant the cost of selling them would be a major proportion of their total value.

There is a rough timetable that a company follows when it comes to the stock market. It begins with an announcement about its intention to float with an approximate date given some months away: for example, the company might say it plans to join the stock market in the autumn.

Nearer to the float it is likely to confirm a date and issue an initial prospectus, known as a pathfinder. This is followed by the pricing of the company's shares, known as impact day. The offer is then open for few weeks during which time investors have the chance to return their application forms by the closing date for the offer.

The company will shortly afterwards announce how many applications for its shares it has received and whether the offer was oversubscribed or undersubscribed. If it was undersubscribed investors will get all the shares they asked for and the rest will be taken up by the underwriters, but if the offer was oversubscribed the company's advisers must decide on what basis the shares will be allotted.

Letters of acceptance are then sent to investors detailing the number of shares they have been able to buy, together with refund cheques if appropriate, and normally a day or two later dealings in the shares begin. At first these are so-called conditional dealings since share certificates, which are the physical proof that you own the shares, will not yet have been posted and your ability to trade shares is conditional on the certificate. It is normally possible to deal if you have received your letter of acceptance, but once the share certificates are sent out, dealing is said to be unconditional.

Existing quoted companies and shares

One of the main reasons companies join the stock market is to raise money and although most do this when they first list their shares, they can also raise cash at other times using their shares. Shares give a company a currency that has a value. This is whatever the company's share price is trading at.

Some companies actually use their shares to buy other companies, which may be private or may themselves be quoted on the stock market and we shall look at takeovers later in this chapter. However, if a company wants to buy another for cash or to fund its development, but does not want to increase its borrowings, it can raise additional funds through an issue of shares. Occasionally companies also raise money through share issues to reduce their borrowings.

There are strict rules governing what a stock market-quoted company can and cannot do regarding the issue of new shares. Every company when it sets up must have a memorandum of association, which sets out the authorised share capital of the company. Although it can be changed later, to do so the company needs the support of shareholders. Companies do not have to issue all their authorised share capital when they float, but it is against the law to issue more than the authorised share capital.

The interests of shareholders are protected by the London Stock Exchange whose rules oblige a company issuing new shares first to offer them to existing investors, unless it has the permission of shareholders not to.

A company has to bear these factors in mind when considering issuing shares for whatever reason. There are several ways a company can issue shares to raise cash, but it is usually done through a rights issue or a placing.

Rights issue

As the name suggests, a rights issue gives existing shareholders the right to buy new shares in the company in proportion to their existing shareholding.

For example, a company may offer shareholders the chance to buy one share for every five shares they own. This would be known as a one-for-five issue. There is no obligation on existing shareholders to buy the shares and they can choose not to. However, the upshot of a rights issue is that it will impact on the value of all the company's shares and therefore it is essential to understand it.

Shares offered in a rights issue are almost always priced at a discount on the existing stock market price. This is not only to encourage shareholders to take part, since they can buy shares cheaper than they can on the stock market, but also to create a buffer zone in case the stock market price falls between announcing the rights issue and getting in the money. If the share price were to fall below the rights issue price, companies would have difficulty convincing shareholders they should buy the rights shares when they could buy the shares cheaper on the stock market. Because of this possibility, rights issues are dangerous at times of stock market volatility and most companies prefer to use them when the market is rising or their own share price is enjoying strong demand.

Companies decide the level of discount based on the size of the rights issue, the attractiveness of the company and the underlying stock market conditions. If the issue is small, or in stock market jargon light such as a one-for-ten issue, the discount is likely to be small at perhaps 15 per cent below the current stock market price. However, if the issue is large, which is described as heavy such as one-for-three, the discount will be much larger, perhaps 20 or 25 per cent. Just as with a new issue, the company wants to guarantee it raises all the money it needs and therefore rights issues are underwritten by a group of financial institutions, like banks and insurance a companies, which agree to buy up any shares existing shareholders do not want. The underwriters charge a fee, usually a couple of per cent of the total amount being raised.

Occasionally a company offers its shares at a price well below the current stock market value of the shares. This is known as a deep-discounted rights issue. A deep-discounted issue could suggest that the company is unpopular and it is the only way it can get people to buy the shares. However, it can also be a way of guaranteeing all the shares are taken up without the need to pay out fees for underwriters.

When a rights issue is announced it usually pushes down the stock market price of a company's shares because it will dilute the value of the shares already on the market. This can make it difficult for small shareholders to know whether to take up their rights or not. One advantage for small investors with a rights issue is that they can buy more shares in their company without having to pay commission charges to a stockbroker, or tax. However, the issue of new shares may cause the existing shares to fall in price on the stock market since the value of the company will now be shared out among more shares, some of which have been discounted.

Although share prices can move for lots of reasons, in theory it is possible to calculate what should happen to a company's share price following a rights issue. Suppose a company has 10 million shares in issue and they trade at 100p a share, giving the company a stock market value of £10 million. If the company has a four-for-one rights issue at 80p a share it will raise 2.5 million multiplied by 80p, which equals £2 million. This means that following the rights issue the company should be valued at £10 million plus £2 million or £12 million. Since the number of shares in issue increases from 10 million to 12.5 million, the new share price should be £12 million divided by 12.5 million which equals 96p. Because someone buying the shares does not receive any entitlements to the rights issue shares, the 96p is called the ex-rights price. In theory it is the price someone taking up their rights at 80p a share could expect to sell the shares for.

If a company you invest in as an ordinary shareholder has a rights issue it will send you details through an offer document, explaining the details of the issue and what it wants to do with the money raised. You will then receive a provisional allotment letter detailing how many shares you are entitled to buy, with a deadline of a few weeks for taking action. You then face several choices as to what you should do.

- Take up your rights in full.

- Sell all your rights.

- Take up some of your rights and sell the remainder.

- Sit tight and do nothing.

Take up your rights

If you choose to take up your rights in full you will be deciding to buy more shares in the company. That means you should reconsider all the reasons that made you buy shares in the company in the first place. In addition you will have to consider what the company intends to do with the money it raises through the rights issue. If it is using the cash to buy another business you should assess whether the deal makes sense and whether it will generate value for the company. If the company is raising money to fund an expansion programme you must decide whether the plan is a good one or not.

On a personal level you must decide whether you can afford the extra investment necessary to take up your rights and whether the increased size of your shareholding makes sense in relation to the rest of your share portfolio. If you decide the investment case for the company remains strong and it intends to use the money for a good purpose, the discount offered by the rights issue might well represent a good buying opportunity. To take up all your entitlement you should simply return a cheque for the full amount with the form attached to the allotment letter.

Selling all your rights

If you decide not to take up any of your entitlement you have the option of selling your rights to the shares. Your provisional allotment letter will tell you your share entitlement and from the time the letter is issued to the time the rights lapse you can sell the entitlement on the stock market. Anyone buying the entitlement then has the right to buy the shares at the discounted rate and rights. In theory, the sale price should be the equivalent of the discount, the difference between the stock market price and the rights issue price, but since the quoted price moves, the actual price is likely to be different.

Buying and selling rights is called a geared investment, because a small percentage movement in the share price can lead to a big percentage movement in the rights price. For example, if the share price moved from 100p to 110p, a 10 per cent rise, then the rights price could also move by 10p but since this could be from 25p to 35p – in a four-for-one issue, it would translate as a 40 per cent rise. A movement the other way would result in big losses. Another downside with buying and selling rights is that you will be charged commission by a stockbroker, although there is no stamp duty tax to pay.

You could choose to sell only some of your rights, which could be a useful way of raising the cash to take up the remainder. In order to work out how many rights you have to sell to raise enough cash to take up the rest, multiply the rights price by the number of new shares you have been offered and divide by the ex-rights price.

Sit tight and do nothing

If you choose to sit tight and do nothing the company will sell the new shares that have not been taken up to the underwriters. It will then send you the cash for your share of the rights. However, this means you have no say in the price at which the rights were sold.

Placing

Rights issues have been the main method used by quoted companies to raise funds for many years. However, while rights issues are still used to raise very large sums of money, companies are increasingly turning to placings as a way of generating additional cash. As we have seen, placings are cheap, quick and easy to implement. They have not completely replaced rights issues yet, but some commentators believe the days of the rights issue are numbered.

Other actions companies can take on shares

There are several other actions companies can take to increase or decrease the number of shares they have in issue. Some make no real difference to your shareholding and some have important implications.

Splits and consolidations

Share prices, as cannot be repeated enough, can go down as well as up. If a share price keeps going up it can become worth many tens of pounds. In the US share prices are traditionally quoted in dollars and the value of individual shares appears high, but in the UK they tend to be quoted in pence and therefore share prices over £10 can become unwieldy. Although a share costing £50 is just as easy to buy and sell as one costing 50p, there is a psychological hurdle for investors to clear and UK investors seem to prefer prices in pence.

To get round this problem companies can split their shares. Remember that ordinary shares have a nominal value. Suppose a company has a share with a nominal value of £1 but it is trading on the stock market at £20. The company could split its nominal share into four, a four-for-one split. Each £1 share would be replaced by a 25p share and the effect would be to divide the quoted share price by four to 500p. As an investor you would have four times as many shares, but the total value of your shares would remain the same. Fans of share splits suggest that because there are more shares in issue it makes them easier to trade and improves liquidity in the share.

Just as a high share price can convince a company to split its shares, so a low price can encourage a company to consolidate its shares. This action is the flip side to a split. Its basis is the same investor psychology as a high share price. Investors view share prices of just a few pence as special situations, as we shall see below, and a consolidation can make them more attractive.

Suppose a company has shares with a nominal value of 5p and the share price is 10p. The company could launch a ten-for-one consolidation, which would see every ten 5p shares replaced with one new 50p share and the quoted share price rise to 10p multiplied by ten or 100p. As an investor you would hold fewer shares, but again the total value of your shares would be unchanged.

Scrip issues

Another way in which companies can increase the number of their shares in issue and investors can increase the number of shares they own without paying a penny is through a scrip issue – also known as a bonus issue or a capitalisation.

Although investors receive free shares, the total value of their holding does not rise because no new money has come into the company. The stock market price of the share will fall in proportion to the number of scrip shares issued, which is done on a proportional basis; for example, investors might receive one scrip share for every ten they own, which would be a one-for-ten issue. Scrip dividends are simply an accounting exercise. They create new shares from the company's financial reserves – which is all the money originally invested in the company plus its retained profits. The cost of the new shares is born by the financial reserve, but since it is used to create more shares within the company no money actually leaves the company.

The main motivation for a scrip issue is again a psychological one. It has the effect of reducing the stock market share price, which can in theory improve the share's liquidity. There is some evidence that share prices perform well straight after a scrip issue because the liquidity of the shares has been improved.

Buy-backs

In recent years share buy-backs have become increasingly popular with companies as a way to return surplus cash to shareholders and boost the share price.

A share buy-back is exactly what it suggests. A company that has a cash pile it does not need to use for anything else simply buys its own shares from investors. These shares are then cancelled, which means there are fewer shares in issue which, if everything else remains the same, should increase the value of the remaining shares. Shareholders benefit in two ways. First through the company buying shares from them and second from the rise in the value of their remaining shares.

Companies benefit because it improves their earnings-per-share, that is the amount of after-tax profit attributable to each share, since the same profit is shared between fewer shareholders. Companies have to ask shareholders for permission to buy back shares and generally they want the freedom to buy back up to about 10 per cent of the total number of shares in issue. Shareholders are usually asked to vote on the issue at the annual meeting and the permission lasts for a year.

The company is under no obligation to launch a share buy-back or to buy up to the limit of its permission. To a great extent the decision to do so will depend on the company's share price. If it is strong the company is unlikely to buy the shares, but if it is weak it might ask its adviser, normally an investment bank, to buy shares on its behalf in the stock market.

Although more and more companies are buying back their shares, the merits of the exercise are open to question. Companies which buy back their shares argue that it is an efficient use of their spare cash, especially at times of low interest rates. It can also be seen as a defensive move since companies with large cash balances can sometimes be seen as takeover targets. However, critics point out that the only shareholders who directly benefit are those who sell their shares since although in theory the share price should rise because there are fewer shares in issue, this is not always the case. Some have also suggested that a management which decides to buy back shares in its own company has run out of investment ideas for the cash.

Takeovers

Shares in a stock market-quoted company can be bought by anybody. That means all the shares could be bought by one party and the company can be taken over. The buyer could be an individual or a private company, a foreign company or another stock market-quoted company.

Takeovers are generally good for small investors since the price offered for the shares will be higher than that at which they were trading on the stock market. When the offer is in cash investors can easily weigh up the advantages of an offer for their shares against the market price. However, takeovers can be complicated if the company offering to buy all the shares is quoted itself and offers its own shares or some of its own shares and cash in exchange. If you are an investor in the company launching the takeover, in the short term your shares may well fall in value since the stock market tends to be nervous about such expansion moves. In the longer term takeovers have not always proved to be the most successful way to improve shareholder value.

All stock market-quoted companies can be taken over. It is a fact that often underpins a company's share price since if it falls low enough someone might bid for the company.

Takeovers occur for many reasons, which fall into positive or negative categories, some of which are mentioned below.

Negative

1 A company may have performed very poorly in terms of its financial results.
2 Its management may be seen as not up to the job.

3   The company's share price might be low due to the above or simply because few investors are interested in buying the shares perhaps because it is in a line of business which is rated lowly by the stock market.

Positive

1   The company may be performing very well and become attractive to predators.
2   The company may have grown as big as it can with its current product or customer base and it might make business sense for it to become part of a bigger company.
3   A combination of two companies might produce a stronger business and lead to cost savings.

In general, takeovers that occur for negative reasons tend not to be supported by the target's board of management and are termed hostile or contested bids, while those that happen for positive reasons are usually supported by management and are termed friendly, agreed or recommended.

Bids are a time when shareholders, including small investors, can exercise real power by either accepting or rejecting the offer. The first thing investors generally know about a friendly bid is when the two companies involved announce the deal to the stock market, usually after weeks of behind-the-scenes negotiations. Shareholders receive a formal offer for their shares from the company launching the takeover shortly afterwards. They also receive a letter from the board of their company recommending they accept the offer.

Both types of bid usually mean an immediate rise in the company's share price, but hostile bids can produce better returns and are certainly the most entertaining since they can get quite bloody, with one side attacking and the other trying to defend itself.

Since this is all done in public, it can make for knock-about stories in newspapers which enjoy the coverage they can generate. Newspapers encourage the warlike tone of hostile offers and refer to them as bid battles or takeover wars. Hostile bids are also popular in the City since they generate big fees for the advisers of both companies who have to work out strategies for their clients.

Hostile bids

When a company tries to take over another its primary aim is to win control of the voting shares in its target, which normally means buying more than 50 per cent of the company's ordinary shares. Once a company has a majority of the voting shares it can exercise a great deal of control over its target.

Although bidding for a company is generally open to anyone, there are strict rules drawn up by the City which govern the takeover process and the government can also have a say in the outcome of bids. In the City the Takeover Panel sets and administers the City Code of Takeovers and Mergers, which are the rules concerning takeovers. The Panel acts as a City watchdog and was set up in 1968 in response to concerns about unfair takeover practices. The Panel creates a level playing field for the bidder, the target and the shareholders. Although it has no official sanctions, the Panel is an example of City self-regulation and all companies abide by its rules.

The government takes a keen interest in friendly and hostile takeovers, particularly when they give rise to issues of market shares and threats to competition or the interests of consumers. It uses the Office of Fair Trading and the Competition Commission – both of which report to the Trade and Industry Secretary – to advise it whether a takeover would act against the public interest and has the power to block deals or impose conditions, such as the sale of some businesses, if it decides they do. If a bid is referred to the Competition Commission this alone can cause the offer to lapse since it can take six months for referrals to be investigated and for the government to make a decision based on the investigation.

The European Commission also has powers to block deals that it considers might hit competition in European markets, but the Takeover Panel's code is the main set of rules a company has to worry about in a hostile bid.

Often before a company launches a contested bid, it will build up a shareholding in its target company. This gives it a platform from which to launch its bid and means it is already some way towards securing more than 50 per cent of the shares. Companies can easily keep tabs on shareholders who have a significant stake in them because all shareholdings above 3 per cent have to be declared to the Stock Exchange. However, if a company wants to create a platform for a hostile bid it tries to do so quickly. Frequently, it will do so on the morning of the day it plans to announce its bid and this buying spree is called a dawn raid.

Under the Takeover Code the bidder can buy up to 15 per cent of its target's shares before it must pause. A week later it can acquire up to a total of 25 per cent of its target's shares, then it must pause again. Any shareholder buying more than 30 per cent of a company's shares is obliged by the Code to make an offer to buy the outstanding shares in the company. This is designed to stop a minority shareholder exercising too much influence over a company since a 30 per cent stake is a powerful voting base.

Once a bidder has announced its intention to launch an offer it usually posts a formal offer document to shareholders within a few weeks. The posting of that document sets the Takeover Code's bid clock ticking. The bidder then has 60 days to win control of the company and if its fails it must wait at least a year before it can bid again. At the start of a bid the offer is said to be conditional, since it depends on the bidder winning acceptances from shareholders owning more than 50 per cent of the shares. This means that even if you agree to accept the offer for your shares you can change your mind later.

In a hostile bid the offer document is the main document issued by the predator, while for its target this is the defence document, which can hit back at the rationale for the takeover and make forecasts about future prospects for profits, and produce a revaluation of its assets. Companies have many options for their defence, as well as indicating better times ahead. They include selling the business, changing senior management or sometimes as a last resort seeking a friendly takeover on better terms. A bidder that fulfils this function and often agrees to keep management in place and other sweeteners to gain board support is known as a white knight.

If another bidder does appear they also have 60 days to complete their bid and, to level the playing field, their deadline also applies to the first bidder. Under the Takeover Code a predator can raise its offer during a bid, but only before day 46 of the bid timetable, while the defence is not allowed to issue any important new financial information after day 39.

If the predator gains enough support from shareholders to give it more than 50 per cent of the votes in the target company the offer is said to be unconditional and shareholders who have not yet decided to reject or accept the offer must do so. The offer must stay open for at least another two weeks to allow other shareholders to accept. Most do at this stage rather than remain as minority shareholders in a company where one investor can call the shots. Once you accept an unconditional offer you cannot change your mind. If the predator secures more than 90 per cent of a company's shares it can compulsorily purchase the remaining shares.

If the bid does not succeed because the predator fails to win more than 50 per cent acceptances, shareholders who have accepted the offer will not have sold their shares. However, the predator may have built up a stake through buying shares in the market and can prove to be a thorn in the side of management, as well as retaining a platform, should it wish to bid again in a year's time.

Implications for shareholders: If you are a shareholder in a company that has received a hostile bid, knowing what to do is not easy. Whether you should sit tight and do nothing, accept the offer, reject it or simply sell your shares on the stock market will depend on the company, the circumstances of the bid and your risk profile.

You could choose not to do anything, but this is your company we are talking about and if you do not take action you will have to live with the decisions of others.

If you are happy with the management and performance of your company you might choose to reject the offer.

However, you might feel prepared to pass on the benefits of its future growth to another company if the predator is paying a big enough premium for ownership.

You must also consider whether the offer is in cash or shares. If it is cash the premium is easier to assess against the market price and potential price for the share in the medium and long term. However, if it is in shares you must make an assessment of the growth potential of the predator and whether you want to hold its shares. You should assess it on the basis that you would be buying shares in the company and therefore discover whether there is an investment case or not.

You could always choose to sell your shares on the stock market rather than await the outcome of the bid.

Tax, as we shall see in a later chapter, can be an important consideration in such a case. Selling in the market would crystallise cash and since the share price is likely to be at or even above the level of the bid it would appear you were getting your money quicker than if you waited for the bid to go through. But don't forget you will have to pay a dealing charge. Also, selling too early in the market could mean you miss out on the possibility of a higher bid or even a rival bidder appearing. However, it could be a smart move if you expect the bid to fail since the share price is likely to fall in this event.

If you are a shareholder in the predator you have less control over the outcome of a bid, although the company will need your permission at an extraordinary general meeting to launch the offer. Takeovers, particularly hostile ones, are uncertain affairs and the danger is always that a predator will overpay for its prey, which could undermine its share value and therefore hit your holding. Overpaying is easily done, particularly in a contested bid situation where there might be more than one bidder, and if a company pays too high a price it might have difficulty generating the cost savings necessary to justify the price. Shareholders in predators should keep a close eye on what is happening in a bid situation and the effect it has on their share price, and if you become nervous your company is overpaying perhaps you might sell your shares before the market devalues them. Knowing whether a takeover creates shareholder value in the end or not is very difficult to judge. Academic research suggests that half the time it does and half the time it doesn't, but deciding which will happen in the case of your company is impossible.

Reverse takeovers

Before concluding our look at takeovers it is worth quickly examining a special situation called a reverse takeover. This occurs when a stock market company makes an acquisition, but issues so many shares in relation to the size of its existing share capital that the owners of the company it is acquiring control the enlarged group. Reverse takeovers are most common when the quoted company has few if any businesses and is a way for a private company to achieve a stock market quotation through the company that is already listed. Often the listed companies owning few if any businesses may have cash raised from the sale of operations and they are termed shell companies because they are waiting for a business to move into them. Although the existing shareholders will have smaller percentage stakes in the new business – which is called being diluted – they will have shares in what is effectively a new business. Small investors should be alert for these shell companies. They are risky but can offer tremendous returns, depending on the type of business that reverses into them.

HOW ARE SHARES CATEGORISED?

We have considered the different types of ordinary shares, how and why companies issue shares and the fact that quoted companies can be bought through takeovers.

When considering investing in individual shares it is important to realise that each share has a different characteristic, which enables us to categorise them. We shall examine these categories in more detail in a later chapter when we will consider the relative investment merits of each type. For now a short roll-call will give you a flavour of the types of categories.

Blue chips

Named after the highest-value chip in a casino, blue chip shares are usually the largest, most respectable and reliable company shares.

Penny shares

At the other end of the spectrum, penny shares literally cost just a few pence and tend to be in companies that have fallen dramatically out of favour or are shell situations. They are inclined to be very popular with more speculative investors.

Recovery shares

Shares in a company whose share price has fallen, possibly due to poor trading, bad management or an acquisition that went wrong. The hope is that the setback is temporary and the share price will recover strongly.

Cyclical shares

These are shares in companies whose business follows a recognised economic cycle. For example, when chemical prices are high, chemical companies increase production to cash in by selling more product. However, the increased supply of product satisfies demand and leads to prices falling. Shares in chemical companies soar when product prices are high and slump when they are low.

Income shares

Shares in companies that pay a high dividend relative to their share price. The relation of the dividend to the share price is called the yield and with some shares you can enjoy a yield a lot higher, albeit more risky, than that achievable in a building society.

Growth shares

These are shares in companies that are likely to grow profits quickly. If they pay a dividend at all it is likely to be small but investors buy them for capital growth, that is the expectation that the share price will keep rising.

Defensive shares

An investment in a company whose shares will tend to hold their value even if the stock market is falling and the general economy is doing badly. Supermarkets, gas and electricity shares are in this category since people will always need to eat and use power.

There are clearly a large number of different types of company share that offer different risks and rewards for investors. We will consider investment strategies based on each of these types of share in a later chapter.

Before leaving individual shares we will look at a further way in which companies are categorised that is of great use to small investors.

The Stock Exchange puts each company listed on the market into a specific category, depending on its main type of business. Hence Lloyds TSB is listed under Banks and BT Group appears under Telecommunication Services. There are 38 categories, aside from investment companies, in which a company's shares may be listed. Since all the electricity companies will be listed together under Electricity and insurers under Insurance the categories provide a means for investors to compare the performance of rival companies.

However, some categories are very broad and comparisons of their constituents makes little sense. For example, companies in the Distributors category range from carpet wholesalers to car dealers. While the Leisure, Entertainment and Hotels sector includes football clubs, theme parks and computer games businesses.

As well as the individual business type categories there also exist broader measures of parts of the stock market as whole.

We considered the FTSE 100 index earlier and it is just one of several indices related to the London Stock Exchange. The FTSE 100, or Footsie, contains the 100 largest quoted UK companies by market value. Today the minimum qualification level is about £2 billion. The Footsie is calculated every minute of the trading day so changes in the valuations of its members are reflected instantly by the measure. Every three months the Footsie membership is recalculated, with companies that have increased in value replacing those that have fallen. Promotion or relegation from the index can have an effect on share prices since tracker funds buy shares in the index and sell them once they have dropped out. But there are also other factors connected with movements in and out of the Footsie that move share prices and in a later chapter we shall consider the importance of this for investors.

The Footsie has long been the standard measure for the financial health of the general stock market and is the index most often quoted in the media. In recent years, though, there has been a debate about how useful it is as a general measure of the market. The dominance of a few very big companies such as Vodafone and BP means that movement in their share prices has a disproportionate effect on the index. In fact, following the merger of SmithKline Beecham and Glaxo Wellcome, the drugs giant together with Vodafone and BP will account for 26 per cent of the Footsie and 20 per cent of the whole stock market.

Another concern is the rise of new technology companies, many of which have yet to make a profit but whose popularity among investors has driven their values high enough for them to enter the Footsie. The rise of risky technology shares together with the dominance in the index of just three shares means the FTSE 100's reliability as an indicator for the wider market is in question.

However, there are other FTSE indices, which give a wider picture of the market. The main ones are:

- **The FT Actuaries All-Share:** This covers about 900 quoted companies in total, which is about 98 per cent of the stock market in terms of value. It is an important benchmark for investment fund performance.

- **The FTSE 250:** As its name suggests this index covers the 250 largest companies after the FTSE 100.

- **FTSE Small Cap:** This covers 550 smaller companies. These are generally defined as companies with a stock market value of less than £200 million.

This chapter has clarified what shares are and the different types, how companies use them and how they are categorised. As we have seen, there is a lot to be said about shares, but always remember that behind every share is a company. Understanding companies and how they work is the key to working out which company's share is worth investing in.

In the next chapter we will look at companies, what they are, how they operate and how to find your way around their accounts.

CHAPTER **5**

Assessing and Understanding Companies

To assess the investment case for any share you must know how to understand the company behind it.

Investing in a piece of paper, a share certificate, is an abstract concept, but what you are really doing is taking part ownership of a business. Since the best investors should be able to decide when they buy and when they sell a share, understanding the company and how it works is essential for determining the timing of any action. A company is simply an organisation created to carry out business, with a separate legal identity from its owners. When considering companies as investments it is important to know what they do, how they are managed and, crucially, how to understand their financial figures.

What a company does

Companies quoted on the London Stock Exchange cover just about every type of business you could think of. They range from utilities such as water and electricity, to banks and pubs, steel companies and software businesses, tobacco groups and drugs companies. It is important to know what a company does because you can then compare it with similar companies that do the same thing and consider how it might be affected by changes in society such as fashions, eating habits and economic conditions.

What a company does will also have an effect on how strong demand for its shares might be. A biotech company working on a cure for a disease may experience that strong demand for its shares on expectations it will find the cure and generate massive profits. However, a water company will never have the potential suddenly to make huge profits, and investors know this and buy the shares for other reasons.

We have seen how stock market indices that categorise shares help explain to investors what the company does in very broad terms and also who its peers are. Many companies these days have informative websites that detail what they do. Knowing what a company does is one thing, but it is just as important to understand what a company does. This might appear fairly simple if it makes widgets for the engineering industry, but if it is involved in technology or medicine, grasping what it does might take longer to work out. But it can be worth the effort since, if you realise the potential of a company's products before other investors, you might get a chance to buy the shares at a lower price, before demand pushes them higher.

A company's history

Knowing about a company with an eye to its investment potential for the future includes knowing about its past. It is essential to know where a company has come from in order to gauge where it is in the present and where it may be in the future. If a company has fallen on hard times its shares may appear cheap at present. However, if its decline was due to it losing its market to a rival or its technology being superseded it is unlikely to rally in the short term. If a company has been around for a hundred years you are likely to look at it differently than if it is just a couple of years old. Likewise, if it has weathered recessions and stock market downturns you may consider it more resilient than newer businesses that have yet to experience wider economic cycles.

Management

Just as important as what a company does and where it comes from is who manages it. At the top of a quoted company there will be a board of directors. This normally comprises at least a chairman, a chief executive and a finance director.

The chief executive and finance director will be executive directors; that is full-time directors with day-to-day responsibility for running the company. Often other executive directors of the company will sit on the board and these tend to be the heads of its operating divisions.

These executive directors sit on the board with so-called non-executive directors and board meetings are generally held about once a month. The non-executives, of which the chairman is often one, are supposed to look after the interests of shareholders and are designed to be independent and act as a check and balance to the executive directors. They are part-time, generally working for the company for just a few days each month, for which they are paid salaries. The size of their pay varies according to the size of the company, but non-executives of a FTSE 100 could earn about £32,000 a year with a non-executive chairman paid about £175,000. The role of the non-executive includes deciding the pay of the executive directors through a body known as the remuneration committee, sitting on the company's audit committee, which is responsible for the validity of its financial figures, and playing a key role in the appointment of executive directors.

Occasionally non-executives can flex their muscles and are capable of ousting executive directors if they feel they are not doing their job. Non-executive directors played a crucial role when Sir Richard Greenbury was ousted as chairman of Marks & Spencer.

Indeed, the focus on non-executive directors is often greatest at times of crisis in a company. Non-executive directors come in many guises, but most provide experience and insights that are expected to add to the quality of the board. They can be former business people who have retired, high-profile executive directors of other companies and even people from the public sector.

The whole issue of directors and their roles came to prominence in the 1990s when so-called corporate governance, covering everything from directors' pay to business ethics, was one of the big issues for debate in the business world. Critics of non-executives claimed they were members of an old boys network, with many sitting on each other's boards and often reluctant to stand up against the executive directors when they feared something was going wrong. Although they were supposed to put shareholders first, many did not. Concerns about corporate governance in the City led to a series of committees chaired by leading business figures including Sir Adrian Cadbury, Sir Richard Greenbury and Sir Ronald Hampel during the 1990s. Many of the blueprints they developed for improving corporate governance have been adopted, but critics remain for the behaviour of some companies.

As a shareholder you must decide whether or not you are happy with the management of your company and, if you are not, you have an opportunity to register your complaint.

As well as speaking out at the annual meeting you can vote against the re-election of directors that is required on a regular basis.

The calibre of the management of a company is a crucial consideration for investors. It is probably most important in small companies whose growth is heavily dependent on the strength of management, but the wrong people at the helm of even the biggest company can be disastrous. Although individuals can be extremely capable, investors should be wary of companies that are seen as one-man bands. If anything were to happen to the individual or if he or she were to leave, the share price could fall because the person concerned was viewed as being closely linked to the fortunes of the company. By the same token if an individual who has been very successful at one company joins another, the shares of the new company could rise in the hope that he or she will bring success to that business too. Backing successful managers and management teams may not be the soundest of investment strategies, since it assumes they can repeat their success, but it is certainly a factor to bear in mind when buying shares.

Ideally, a company should have strength in depth in its management that means ready replacements if any of the top managers are lost. The City – which, as is the case with all investors, hates surprises – likes big companies to have a recognised succession in place. That way it is easier for investors to judge the merits of a group's management in going forward. When a chief executive leaves and a company takes a long time to find a replacement who, especially if from overseas, may be little known by investors, it can hit the company's share price. The new person may be very good at the job, but investors are likely to want to see proof of that fact before they buy the shares.

Understanding company accounts

While what a company does, its history and its management are important for providing a context in which to consider its shares as an investment, a bigger factor is the company's financial figures.

Stock Exchange rules insist that quoted companies produce at least two sets of financial figures each year, one at the interim stage, covering the first six months of the company's financial year, and preliminary results that cover the full year. A company's financial year is often the same as the calendar year and should not be confused with the tax year, which runs from 6 to 5 April. Some companies now report quarterly and this is particularly common among those with overseas interests or a following in the US, where companies report every three months.

However, the primary source for a company's financial information is its annual report and accounts, which companies are obliged by law to produce each year. The report and accounts usually follow within a few weeks of the company announcing its preliminary results to the Stock Exchange. Although it contains all the information in the preliminary announcement, it also offers additional information. Copies of the report and accounts are sent to shareholders a few weeks before the company's annual general meeting, and contain notice of the meeting, and any issues shareholders are asked to vote on.

The main parts of the report and accounts are the **profit and loss account**, the **balance sheet** and **cash flow statement**, the **auditor's report**, the **chairman's statement** and the **directors' report**. It will also give details of shareholdings in the group where investors own more than 3 per cent of the shares.

The raft of figures and jargon contained in a company's accounts is usually enough to put off all but the most disciplined and determined of investors, but you must persevere. Understanding a company's financial health is a key to unlocking its investment value. Much is contained in the annual report although investors need to learn what are the most important areas to consider.

The rest of this chapter is designed to help you cut through the trees so you can view the entire wood.

The annual report

While an annual report is a great source of financial information about a company, it is by no means definitive and should be approached with caution. Remember that it is an historical snapshot of what the company has achieved in the past and therefore is no guarantee of how it might perform in the future.

There are laws and regulations that control what and how information is presented in the accounts and because no two companies are the same each set of accounts should be considered carefully. There has been criticism that some companies use favourable accounting methods to show their figures in a better light. While some accounting practices may not be illegal, they do not necessarily reveal the full picture to shareholders and therefore caution should be your watchword.

That said, an annual report and accounts can offer some

pointers about prospects and is certainly the most comprehensive collection of a company's financial figures available. It is also easily available free to non-shareholders either through an annual reports service featured in some newspapers and websites, or simply by requesting a copy from the company secretary.

The profit and loss account

Also known as the p&l, a company's profit and loss account summarises last year's trading in figures. It shows what the company sold, what its costs were, how much profit it made, how much tax it paid, what was returned to shareholders in the form of dividends and how much was kept for reinvestment by the company. A p&l compares the last financial year with the previous one. Different companies lay out their accounts in different ways but the main facts are always conveyed. Losses, costs and taxes are also displayed and any numbers such as these that are to be deducted are traditionally shown in brackets. For example if after the line profit on ordinary activities before taxation was followed by £100 million this means the company made a profit of £100 million, but if the figure was displayed as (£100 million) it means the company made a loss of £100 million. Often a p&l number in isolation can be misleading and you will need to read the footnotes that accompany most accounts. These are normally indicated by a small number next to the figure that directs to the same number footnote. These will often break down the figure and explain it in more detail.

In order to understand just what information is contained in a profit and loss account and to bring it to life we will consider the real example of high street retailer Boots. Below is the Boots group profit and loss account for the year ended 31 March 2000.

THE BOOTS COMPANY PLC PRELIMINARY RESULTS

	Notes	Before Exceptional Items 2000 £m	Total 2000 £m	Before Exceptional Items 1999 £m	Total 1999 £m
Turnover:					
Turnover from continuing operations	1		5,189.4		4,912.4
Discontinued operation			–		132.2
Turnover: group and share of joint ventures	1		5,189.4		5,044.6
Less: share of joint ventures' turnover			(2.4)		–
Group turnover			5,187.0		5,044.6
Operating profit: Operating profit from continuing operations		573.3	551.3	561.4	485.1
Discontinued operation		–	–	2.7	2.7
Group operating profit		573.3	551.3	564.1	487.8
Share of operating loss of joint ventures		(8.4)	(8.4)	(1.7)	(1.7)
Total operating profit including joint ventures	2	564.9	542.9	562.4	486.1
Profit on disposal of fixed assets	3	–	12.9	–	4.9
Loss on disposal of business	3, 10	–	–	–	(318.9)
Profit on ordinary activities before interest		564.9	555.8	562.4	172.1
Net interest	4	5.9	5.9	(1.8)	(1.8)
Profit on ordinary activities before taxation		570.8	561.7	560.6	170.3
Tax on profit on ordinary activities	5	(168.8)	(162.5)	(169.9)	(146.3)
Profit on ordinary activities after taxation		402.0	399.2	390.7	24.0
Equity minority interests		(0.2)	(0.2)	(0.1)	(0.1)
Profit attributable to shareholders		401.8	399.0	390.6	23.9
Dividends	6		(221.7)		(214.5)
Profit/(loss) retained		–	177.3	–	(190.6)
Basic earnings-per-share	7	45.4p	45.0p	42.9p	2.6p
Diluted earnings-per-share	7	45.1p	44.8p	42.5p	2.6p
Dividends per share	6	–	25.2p	–	23.8p

1   **Turnover:** This refers to the company's sales. For a retailer like Boots this is fairly straightforward and is predominantly the money it has taken through its tills in its stores. However, the Note 1 figure points you to a table later in the accounts which breaks down the turnover from different parts of the group including the Boots The Chemists high street stores and the company's Halfords motor accessories business. The p&l separates turnover from Boots's continuing operations from turnover produced by discontinued activities – in this case DIY chain Do It All. Investors should be interested in the performance of the continuing operations, which would be expected to show an improved performance year on year. If Boots had bought a business during the year, its contribution to turnover would also be separately listed so you could see the performance of the existing business. The p&l shows that during the year group turnover from continuing operations was £5.1894 billion compared with £4.9124 billion in the previous year, a rise of 5.6 per cent. Although there is no interim breakdown in the p&l it is useful to get hold of the interim results so you can see how Boots did in the second half compared with the first half and whether it improved its performance. It is also important to check out Note 1 to see if all its operations improved turnover or if sales fell in some areas.

2   **Operating profit:** This is the money Boots has after it has paid suppliers, staff and other costs. Keep an eye on this cost line for if it is rising faster than turnover, profits could be threatened. Operating profit is the company's profit figure before interest payments or receipts, or sales of fixed assets or business disposals, and it gives a feel for the performance of the underlying businesses. Again, Boots breaks it down between continuing and discontinued businesses. It then includes losses – note the brackets – from joint ventures. Finally there is a figure for total operating profit including joint ventures. In fact, there are two figures: one before exceptional items and one after. Exceptional items are one-off costs or receipts that will

not be repeated. Although they can be very large and are therefore important to understand to get a feel for the performance of the underlying business, it is best to compare figures before exceptionals. In this case, as Note 2 reveals, there is a £22 million charge for the year to 31 March 2000 for reorganising Boots's head office in Nottingham. In the prior year exceptional items totalled £76.3 million and again Note 2 reveals this was made up of one-off restructuring and redundancy costs, and the cost of setting up an employee share ownership plan. Before exceptional items, operating profit including joint ventures is £564.9 million compared with £562.4 million in the previous year, higher than a year earlier but a rise of less than 1 per cent.

3   **Profit on ordinary activities before interest:** This line comes after operating profits, but before any interest payments or receipts. As we can see, again there are two figures in the Boots accounts: one before and one including exceptional items. In the last year the company made a profit on the disposal of a fixed asset of £12.9 million. Fixed assets are items such as property. Note 3 of the accounts details that Boots sold a property during the year for a profit of £12.9 million. The year before the company made a profit of £4.9 million by selling a property. Because selling property is not Boots's main business and because the figure can change from year to year and depends on what value the property is carried at in the company's balance sheet, Boots lists this as a separate item. There is also a £318.9 million exceptional loss recorded in 1999. This is detailed in Notes 3 and 10 to the accounts, which explain it was a loss on the sale of Do It All. These exceptional items mean Boots made a profit on ordinary activities before interest of £555.8 million in 2000 compared with £172.1 million in 1999. However, to understand the performance of the underlying business you should look at the profit before exceptionals.

4   **Profit on ordinary activities before tax:** This is the profit generally referred to in the media whenever a company reports

its results and tends to be shortened to pre-tax profits. It comes after the interest line that usually shows a charge, in brackets, because many companies have borrowings. However, it can also show a receipt, which indicates the company has cash on deposit that has generated interest for the company. In the case of Boots, in 2000 the company earned interest of £5.9 million, whereas in 1999 it paid an interest charge of £1.8 million. Note 4 to the accounts explains the make-up of Boots's interest payments and receipts for the two years under review. After considering the interest line we are left with profits on ordinary activities before taxation. Excluding exceptional items this was £570.8 million in 2000, compared with £560.6 million in 1999. However, for an investor considering the merits of Boots's profits growth it is important to bear in mind that £7.7 million of the £10.2 million increase was accounted for by the difference in the interest line between the two years.

5   **Tax:** Corporation tax can vary according to the size of a company and its profits, but the normal rate for a company the size of Boots is 30 per cent. Boots paid £168.8 million in total tax in 2000, which equates to about 29.5 per cent of its pre-tax profits. Note 5 to the accounts breaks this down into UK and overseas taxations, and also details some tax credits the company was entitled to. Some companies may enjoy large levels of what are termed tax losses because they have made considerable losses in the past. This means that should they move back into profit they do not have to pay tax for several years.

6   **Profit attributable to shareholders:** If companies do not have to pay tax it would leave them with more profit attributable to shareholders. This line comes after minority interest, which refers to a subsidiary business partly owned by someone else and is where their slice of the profits is deducted. The profit attributable to shareholders is the bottom line. It is the clear profit that the company has made. In the case of Boots this is £401.8 million compared with £390.6 million. This figure divided by the number of shares the company has in issue

produces the company's earnings-per-share figure, which we will examine in more detail below.

7   **Dividends:** The dividends line reveals the total cost of paying both the interim and final dividend. In this case £221.7 million in 2000 against £214.5 million in 1999. Note 6 to the accounts points out that the directors of Boots have proposed a final dividend of 17.7p a share which, added to the interim pay-out of 7.5p, takes the total to 25.2p compared with 23.8p a year earlier.

8   **Profit/(loss retained):** Whatever money is left after the dividend has been paid. For Boots in 2000 that was £177.3 million, whereas because of exceptional items in 1999 it was a loss of £190.6 million. This money, if it is a profit, is available to be reinvested in the business.

9   **Earnings-per-share:** This sits on two lines, one covering basic earnings-per-share before and after exceptionals, and one covering diluted earnings-per-share before and after exceptionals. Note 7 explains that the basic earnings-per-share figure is the profit attributable to shareholders divided by the number of shares in issue, which gives a figure of 45.4p before exceptionals. The diluted earnings-per-share figure includes outstanding share options which, if exercised, would increase the number of shares in issue and therefore reduce earnings-per-share, in this case to 45.1p before exceptionals. Most analysts believe the diluted figure is the most accurate one to use. When considering earnings-per-share it is important to realise the factors that can affect it either on the profits side or on the number of shares-in-issue side. If a company's pre-tax profit were the same from one year to another, but its tax charge rose or fell sharply and the number of shares in issue remained the same, the earnings-per-share would either drop or rise.

If a company issues more shares, perhaps for an acquisition, but profits and tax remain the same, earnings-per-share will fall since the profits are divided among a larger number of shares. This is what is meant when it is said that an acquisition is earnings dilutive. It means the new company has not produced sufficient profits to counterbalance the increased number of shares in issue. The flip side is if an acquired company does lift profits enough to boost earnings and therefore the deal is described as earnings enhancing.

10 **Dividends per share:** The final line of the profit and loss account echoes what we have seen above and is the total amount paid in dividends divided by the number of shares that will receive the dividend.

The balance sheet

This offers a snapshot of everything the company owns – its assets and what it owes: its liabilities – at the end of the financial year. The difference between assets and liabilities belongs to the shareholders and is called shareholders' funds. This is theoretically what would be left over for shareholders if the company realised all its asset by selling them and paid off all its debts. As well as telling you what the company's assets are, the balance sheet tells you how they are financed. If the p&l tells you how the company has performed during the year, the balance sheet reflects its fundamental financial health, although it only shows the position at the year end. The balance sheet tells you the value of the company's assets, but not the value of the company itself. That is determined by its share price. The figures are usually quoted in millions of pounds and, as with the p&l, negative figures are shown in brackets. The previous year's figures are also shown as a comparison, however potential investors should always look back several years to try to discern a trend.

Because stock market companies often own or control a number of subsidiary businesses they provide a balance sheet that includes these subsidiaries as well as the parent company. It is called a consolidated balance sheet.

Balance sheets tell you how much shareholders have got invested in a company and enable you to work out what sort of return the company makes from the capital invested in it. Although balance sheets can vary from company to company, the key measures are the same. As with the p&l, we will use Boots as a real example to work through.

Boots balance sheet 31 March 2000

	2000	1999
£m £m. Fixed assets		
Intangible assets	62.3	64.4
Tangible assets	1,799.0	1,788.6
Investment in joint ventures	8.0	6.2
Other investments	133.2	106.2
	2,002.5	1,965.4
Current assets		
Stocks	689.5	722.0
Debtors falling due within one year	404.5	388.1
Debtors falling due after more than one year	4.0	14.1
Current asset investments and deposits	379.2	105.8
Cash at bank and in hand	43.0	32.2
	1,520.2	1,262.2
Creditors: Amounts falling due within one year	(1,153.2)	(1,191.0)
Net current assets	367.0	71.2
Total assets less current liabilities	2,369.5	2,036.6
Creditors: Amounts falling due after more than one year	(489.2)	(230.7)
Provisions for liabilities and charges	(26.8)	(25.3)
Net assets	1,853.5	1,780.6
Capital and reserves		
Called up share capital	224.8	228.8
Share premium account	252.5	252.0
Revaluation reserve	266.9	276.2
Capital redemption reserve	40.8	36.8
Profit and loss account	1,066.6	986.4
Equity shareholders' funds	1,851.6	1,780.2
Equity minority interests	0.5	0.4
Non-equity minority interests	1.4	–
	1,853.5	1,780.6

1 **Assets and liabilities:** Assets are sub-divided into two categories: either fixed assets or current assets. Fixed assets can have a physical presence such as buildings, machinery, cars and are called tangible assets. Those assets of a company that do not have a physical presence, such as patents and brand names, are called intangible assets. Fixed assets are shown in accounts at

what is called their book value. This means how much the asset originally cost minus an amount each year to cover its depreciation. Assets are gradually written off over their lifetime, which can vary since a car is likely to depreciate a lot more quickly than a building. However, you should read carefully the notes concerning the company's depreciation policy. A slow depreciation charge can boost profits, while writing off assets immediately can hit one year but then make the next look a lot better. Arriving at a book value for intangible assets is a lot harder. A brand name like Halfords, which Boots acquired, is easier to value than Boots The Chemists, that is a brand it has developed itself.

2   **Fixed assets:** We can see from Boots's balance sheet that the company's intangible assets were £62.3 million at 31 March 2000, compared with £64.4 million a year earlier. The company's tangible assets were £1.799 billion at the end of its financial year versus £1.7886 billion at the start of the year.

The next two lines on the balance sheet refer to investment in joint ventures and other investments, which all refer to longer-term investments, e.g. in other companies. All these fixed assets combined to produce a total of £2.0025 billion, up from £1.9654 billion a year before.

3   **Current assets:** The next section of the balance sheet concerns current assets. These are cash and things that can readily be turned into cash. They include stocks that can be sold, debtors – people who owe the company money and are due to pay it back within a year or shortly afterwards – and short-term investments.

The Boots balance sheet shows the company's stocks at £689.5 million, down on the £722 million level of a year earlier. Debtors expected to pay back money within the year at £404.5 million and those expected to pay after more than a year at £4 million. Current investments were £379.2 million and cash in the bank and at hand was £43 million. Altogether, Boots's current assets were £1.5202 billion.

4   **Liabilities:** A company has current liabilities and long-term liabilities. Its current liabilities are usually debts which it must pay within a year. The people it owes the money to are its creditors. Hence the line in the Boots's balance sheet that covers creditors: amounts falling due within one year which amounted to £1.1532 billion. The difference between Boots's current assets and current liabilities produces a net current-asset figure of £367 million. Adding this figure to Boots's fixed assets produces a figure for total assets less current liabilities of £2.3695 billion. This is an indication of the short-term value of the company. From this figure must be deducted long-term liabilities, which include debts due after more than a year, and other provisions and liabilities that in Boots's case totalled £516 million. As a result Boots's net assets at the end of March 2000 were £1.8535 billion.

5   **Capital and reserves:** Shareholders' funds – which is what investors in Boots would in theory get if the company sold all its assets, repaid its creditors and divided what remained among investors – are the sum of the company's capital and reserves. Called-up share capital is the nominal face value of all Boots's issued shares which in this example is £224.8 million. If shares have been issued above their nominal value the proceeds go into the share premium account, which in this case is £252.5 million. The revaluation reserve is the amount by which assets – mainly property – have been revalued since they were bought in order to keep the values up to date. Other reserves may also feature here. Finally, in the capital and reserves section of the balance sheet is the profit and loss account, which reflects the profits earned by Boots during its public lifetime that have not been paid out in dividends.

6   **Shareholders' funds:** In Boots's case the shareholders' funds are £1.851.6 billion which together with minority interests comes out at £1.8535 billion, in balance with the net assets.

Cash flow

Concerns about accounting techniques have led investors to put less reliance on the balance sheet in recent years. So-called acquisition accounting, which covers the way in which companies that are taken over are accounted for, can blur the true picture of a company's financial position. While creative accounting may not be illegal, it is certainly a danger to potential investors who need to get the clearest picture of a company they can. Increasingly investors have turned to the company's cash flow statement as a more accurate reflection of its underlying financial health.

No matter what type of business they are in, companies deal in cash. It comes in to the business and flows out, and in order to thrive they must bring in more than they let go. Again, we will use Boots's cash flow statement as an example to work through.

GROUP CASH FLOW STATEMENTS FOR THE YEAR ENDED 31ST MARCH 2000

	Notes	2000	1999
£m £m. Cash inflow from operating activities	8	(753.7)	(601.9)
Returns on investment and servicing of finance		(9.8)	(24.9)
Taxation		(154.4)	(112.4)
Purchase of fixed assets		(265.7)	(372.1)
Disposal of fixed assets		92.5	73.7
Purchase of own shares		(57.9)	(160.1)
Disposal of own shares		10.1	–
Purchase of businesses	9	(0.3)	(9.0)
Disposal of businesses	10	(2.3)	64.2
Equity dividends paid		(216.3)	(207.1)
Cash inflow/(outflow) before use of liquid resources and financing		149.6	(145.8)
Management of liquid resources		(283.6)	122.8
Financing	8	172.8	28.2
Increase in cash		38.8	5.2

Cash is defined as cash in hand and deposits repayable on demand, less overdrafts repayable on demand.

1   **Cash inflow from operating activities:** This is the first line and includes cash received from customers through the company's tills, the amount Boots paid out to its suppliers for the goods it sold, salaries and wages paid to staff and any other cash

payments. In Boots's case this produced a cash inflow of £753.7 million, against £601.9 million a year earlier. Note 8 to the accounts breaks down the details of this item. This figure should be positive since it is fundamental that if a company is to stay in business it should be able to sell its good and services for more than they cost.

2   **Returns on investment and servicing of finance:** This represents the amount of interest earned and paid. The word 'servicing' refers to the reward the suppliers of the finance demand for providing the cash. In this case it totalled a payment of £9.8 million.

3   **Taxation:** Self-explanatory, although it does not match the p&l figures because of the timing of tax payments.

4   **Purchase and disposals:** The next set of items in the cash flow statement covers purchases and disposals. These include the purchase and sale of fixed assets during the period and purchases and sales of the company's own shares. It also includes acquisitions and disposals-related associate, joint-venture or subsidiary businesses.

5   **Equity dividends paid:** These are the dividends paid to Boots's ordinary shareholders during the period covered by the statement. Companies quite often declare a dividend that is shown in one year's p&l account but is not paid until the following year. Hence timing is an issue on this figure, which for Boots in this year was £216.3 million.

6   **Cash inflow/(outflow) before use of liquid resources and financing:** This is the crucial line in the cash flow statement and shows whether the company is producing cash or using it up. If there are large cash outflows from the business, as there were for Boots in 1999, investors should ask questions and demand to know why. However, in 2000 Boots showed a healthy cash inflow on this line of £149.6 million.

7   **Management of liquid resources:** This relates to payments and withdrawals of short-term deposits or other investments held as liquid resources (this means they are readily convertible into cash). It would cover such items as government bonds (known

as gilts) or shares in quoted companies. Boots shows a £283.6 million outflow on this line.

8   **Financing:** The next line is called financing and includes receipts and repayments of any form of external finance such as loans or shares. Note 8 to the accounts shows that during the year Boots issued a bond and raised £300 million. However, it also spent £95.4 million buying back some of its shares and together with other items, receipts and repayments the final figure was a cash inflow of £172.8 million.

9   **Increase in cash:** The £38.8 million figure represents the net increase – although, of course, it could also be a decrease – in cash over the period covered by the statement. Cash here means notes and coins, such as those in the tills, as well as deposits in places like banks where the money is accessible within 24 hours without incurring a penalty for premature withdrawal.

Analysing the figures

Investors can learn a lot about a company from a cursory glance at the p&l, the balance sheet and the cash flow statement. For example, if turnover in the p&l is lower year on year the company's sales are falling and the company will have to come up with an explanation. However some year-on-year comparisons can be misleading: if profits rose by 4 per cent over the previous year that might seem good, but if inflation was running at 4 per cent, profits stood still in real terms. Investors should always try to look beneath the bare figures to get a real feel for how the business is performing. One effective way of achieving this is to analyse the figures, which is most often done by examining the relationship of pairs of figures from the accounts. These figures could come from both the p&l and balance sheet, or one from each. These two figures in relation to each other are called ratios and while some can offer a little information on their own they really need to be used as comparison to makes sense. Comparing the ratio with the same ratio from an earlier period means you can determine whether there has been an improvement or a deterioration in performance. Comparing with management targets can tell you whether or not the company has underperformed, met or exceeded its plans. Finally, the company's ratios can be compared with those of rivals. They provide a useful measure for assessing a firms performance against its peers in a competitive market.

There are three forms of ratio:

1   A percentage – for example, when profit is described as a percentage of turnover.

2   A multiple – such as sales being a certain number of times capital employed.

3   A traditional ratio – when the ratio of current assets to current liabilities, is for example, 3:1.

These forms apply to the two types of analytical ratios: operating ratios and financial ratios.

Operating ratios provide a checklist for the company's latest annual results and allow comparison with earlier years and rivals. They combine figures from the p&l and balance sheet. Financial ratios provide a measure of the financial health of a company and monitor how much pressure it is under. These ratios are mostly calculated from the balance sheet. Here are a few useful examples of each:

Operating ratios

Profit margin: Operating profit as a percentage of turnover. Profit margins vary from company to company and industry to industry. They are therefore of most use in comparing the margins of one company with a rival. You should also check profit margins against the stated policy of a company. A business might be showing a low profit margins because it has decided to sacrifice profits in the short term in order to build market share that should pay off in the longer term.

Return on capital employed (ROCE): Operating profit as a percentage of capital employed. Here capital employed is defined as shareholders' funds plus borrowings. It also equates to the total assets less current liabilities line in the balance sheet. ROCE takes all the assets employed in running the business and measures the company's annual return on them. Again, ROCE varies but consider a ratio of about 20 per cent to be fair. If a company has a low ROCE it is using its resources inefficiently. The ROCE can determine whether or not a company should borrow money to invest in its operations. If the ROCE is lower than the cost of borrowing, increased debt will reduce shareholders' earnings. If the return on other investments is higher than the ROCE a company should not invest in its own operations.

Stockturn: Stocks can represent a significant investment for a business. In the case of a manufacturer, for example, stocks might be a substantial proportion of the total assets it holds. Knowing how quickly a company is able to shift its stocks is therefore an important consideration for a potential investor. This can be shown in two ways: either turnover divided by the year-end stocks, or stocks divided by sales and expressed as a percentage. In the first case the higher the figure the more efficient the company is at turning over its stock, in the second case the lower the figure the more efficient the company is. Again, you should consider the type of business the company is in, with manufacturers and retailers traditionally holding higher levels of stock than some other companies.

Debtors and creditors days: It is useful to know how efficient a company is at collecting money owed to it and how long it can keep its creditors waiting to be paid. If it is quick at collecting and slow at paying, this means it retains more cash in the business. Trade debtors divided by sales multiplied by 365 shows how long it takes for the company to get paid for what it sells. On the other side of the fence trade creditors divided by sales multiplied by 365 shows the period of credit taken from suppliers. The higher this figure the more free finance the company gets from its suppliers. However, companies have to weigh up the benefits of making their suppliers wait, taking into consideration the loss of goodwill, and in some cases damage, delayed payment can have on small suppliers.

Financial ratios

The ratios above examine how efficient a company is in controlling costs, the use of its assets and its profitability. However, to prosper companies must also keep an eye on their liquidity position, that is their ability to meet debts in the short and long term. Companies need short-term assets to pay short-term debts, such as payments due to employees or suppliers. They must also be able to repay longer-term debt.

In the short term there are two ratios to consider: the quick ratio, also called the acid test, and the current ratio.

Quick ratio: This is current assets minus stocks divided by current liabilities. It is a measure of liquidity derived from lines of the balance sheet of a company that shows whether the company has enough cash and assets that can easily meet short-term debts. It is known as the 'acid' test because it measures the ability of a company to repay its creditors instantly. That is why stocks are excluded since a company cannot easily turn its stocks into cash in one day. The quick ratio is crucial to the company's survival and in theory it should be at least 1. However, as we have noted, companies have their differences and some, such as supermarkets, survive on current ratios of less than 1.

Current ratio: This too is a measure of short-term liquidity, but not so extreme as the acid test. It is current assets divided by current liabilities. It includes stocks, which suggests there would be time at least to hold a fire sale to liquidate them to produce the cash to pay creditors. A ratio equal to 1 would mean that current assets just equal current liabilities. Ideally, the ratio should be well in excess of 1, probably about 1.5 to 2. However, if it is too high it suggests the company is keeping too many assets in cash rather than investing in its business to produce profits. Again, because all companies are different it is best to consider the current ratios of companies in the same sector to get a feel for how efficient a particular business is.

In the longer term there are several important ratios including gearing and interest cover.

Gearing: This is borrowings as a percentage of shareholders' funds or borrowings as percentage of capital employed, that is a ratio between what a company owes and what it owns. A high level of gearing can be both a boon and a danger. If a company's cost of borrowing is low and the uses it puts the borrowed money to creates higher returns, the additional earnings boost profits beyond what they would have been if the company had not borrowed any money. But if the return from using the borrowed money is below the cost of borrowing, the company's profits turn into losses. Generally, a highly geared company, perhaps 100 per cent or more, is more risky than one with low borrowings. Some companies – property businesses, for example – traditionally operate with high levels of gearing.

Interest cover: Until the last few years investors paid a great deal of attention to gearing. They viewed highly geared companies as risky and low levels of gearing as desirable. However, as was pointed out above, some companies can thrive on high levels of gearing. In order better to understand the comfort level of companies in terms of borrowings, interest cover has become an increasingly important measure. The interest cover ratio is the operating profit divided by the interest payable. The higher the ratio the lower the risk of borrowings. Even for companies with traditionally high gearing levels this can be comfortable at five times or more. What it means is that there would have to be a big fall in profits before the company's profits were unable to cover its interest payments. The lower the level of profits coverage the greater the risk that the company will be unable to meet its interest payments. One important factor to bear in mind with interest cover is that while profits may comfortably cover interest payments at the current rate of interest, if interest rates were to rise sharply cover could shrink rapidly. You should also pay attention to the quality of earnings. If profits are fairly steady, such as with a utility, a higher level of gearing and lower interest cover may be more acceptable than in the case of company whose profits are volatile.

Having considered the three most important elements of the annual report and accounts as far as investors are concerned, we will finish by looking at the other three sections mentioned earlier.

Auditor's report

One of the roles of shareholders is to elect an independent person, or more usually a firm, to act as auditor. The auditor's main function is to express an opinion as to whether the financial statements in the annual report and accounts show a true and fair view of the company's finances, and comply with the law and accounting standards. The auditor is a safety device for shareholders to ensure the directors are acting in a way they should and presenting accurate financial information on which investors can make decisions. Usually the auditor's report concludes with an opinion that the figures do give a fair and true view and have been properly prepared. It is when the auditors qualify their reports that alarm bells should start to ring in your head. This usually happens when auditors disagree with the way the management has prepared some aspect of the accounts. Auditors may say they have been unable to check certain information in the accounts and this prevents them from forming an opinion. They may disagree with the way some items in the accounts have been treated and raise this as an issue. Finally they might disagree so strongly with a particular accounting treatment that they say the accounts do not give a fair and true view. Should the auditors say the accounts have been prepared on the assumption that the company is a going concern, run for the hills because it is going bust.

Chairman's statement

The chairman's statement tends to be more interesting for what it doesn't say than what it does say. If the company has had a poor year it is likely to be full of excuses and if the company has had a good year it will contain fulsome praise of the company's staff and customers. Chairmen often have a dig at wider economic issues such as interest rates which have some effect on their business. The statement should also be carefully read for indications about current trading and it can also give a feel for trading in the year ahead.

Increasingly, companies include a chief executive's report after the chairman's statement, particularly when the chairman, as good corporate practice increasingly demands, is a non-executive. The chief executive offers a progress report on the company's business activities and financial health.

Directors' report

While the chairman's statement and now the chief executive's report are conventions, the directors' report is required by law. The company has to detail who its directors are or were during the year, their remuneration, including pay, share options, bonuses, benefits and pensions, and also their shareholdings in the company.

It includes an outline of the company's principal activities, the dividends proposed, details of any significant events that have occurred since the company's financial year end, any charitable and political donations made during the year, information on employees including health and safety, and policy towards disabled people.

CONCLUSION

You should now have a better feel for just what a stock market-quoted company is and what information it has to make available to investors, as well as understanding that financial information will give you a major advantage when it comes to choosing shares to invest in. You should be able to pick those companies in a sector whose financial health is better than their rivals'. You should also be able to discern the financial warning signs that tell you when to leave well alone or when to get out if you are already invested in a company's shares. Armed with this knowledge, it is now time to put it to use as we consider different ways of analysing individual company shares.

6

Analysis – Analysing Shares

If you have decided to invest at least some of your money in individual shares, your biggest problem will be to decide which ones to buy. There are thousands of shares to choose from and they will by definition underperform the market, perform in line with it or outperform it. The ones you obviously want are the ones that will outperform. But how do you find them? Is there a magic formula? Is it down to hard work? Or is it just luck?

Generally speaking, there are three schools of thought when it comes to trying to pick winners in the stock market race:

1   **Fundamental analysis:** This theory suggests that all you need to identify the winners is to know the numbers – the financial figures – associated with them and to be able to analyse them. It is used to determine a company's fundamental value and predicted changes in its expected earnings. The analysis of a company's value and its forecast earnings can then be compared with its share price to determine whether it is cheap or expensive, that is whether it is a buy or a sell. In its wider sense fundamental analysis involves analysing all aspects of a company from its management to its markets and also external

factors such as inflation and interest rates. We shall consider it further later in this next chapter.

2 **Technical Analysis:** Investors who follow this theory believe that by studying the movement of a company's share price in the past its future direction can be predicted. It is also called charting, because such analysis requires careful examination of share price graphs. Technical analysis is controversial and regarded by some as a black art with little merit. On a suck-it-and-see principle that investors should try out all theories to find if they are suited to them we shall also examine the basic principles of charting later in this chapter.

3 **Luck:** Everyone from professional investors to amateurs has a common aim and that is to beat the market. Some academics suggest it cannot be done and offer theories as to why if investors do beat the market it is more to do with luck than judgement. We shall consider below whether or not they have a point.

Being told that no amount of hard work or judgement will guarantee successful investment is something no investor will take. Yet this is what many academics who study the movement of share prices believe. They subscribe to the so-called **Random Walk** theory, which states that it is impossible to forecast movements in share prices either through fundamental or technical analysis. It is therefore impossible over the long term to make more money from fundamental or technical analysis than it is from picking a selection of shares at random, such as by throwing darts at the share prices page of a newspaper – indeed, it is sometimes called the **Dart Board** theory and appears to reduce investing on the stock market to placing a bet in a casino.

The academics more often call this a random walk because they suggest the movement of a share price is unpredictable in the short term, rather like someone taking a walk and flipping a coin at each road junction to decide whether to turn left or right. The implications of Random Walk are that past movements in share prices become irrelevant in predicting future patterns. Therefore technical analysis, which professes to do this, does not work. Likewise, since prices are random it is questionable whether fundamental analysis can work.

Some academics took the basic Random Walk principle and developed it into the grand-sounding Efficient Market Hypothesis. A basic definition of EMH would be that share prices quickly and accurately readjust to reflect all the relevant information that might affect them. However, EMH has three forms. Weak, semi-strong and strong.

1 **Weak:** This is the basic Random Walk idea: that past movements in share prices have no influence over future price movements. Therefore chartism cannot work.

2 **Semi-strong:** Here EMH outpaces the Random Walk. This version says that not only is the past no indication for the future, but that the current share price reflects all the published information about the company. When new information is published the share price instantly adjusts either upwards on good news or downwards on bad news. That means fundamental analysis that involves analysing all the published information, about a company such as accounts, in order to work out the real value of its shares, is a waste of time. An investor using fundamental analysis, as long as he or she can view the same published information as everyone else, has no advantage because the market has already assessed the information and the share price has responded.

3 **Strong:** In its strongest form EMH suggests share prices reflect all the information there is to know about a company, both published information and insider knowledge. According to this theory professional analysts have considered all the possibilities for the company and the share price has taken all these possibilities on board. One upshot is that even those who act on inside information cannot consistently turn it to their advantage. Strong EMH states that the only thing that has any real impact on the share price of a company is a truly random event or information which, since it cannot be known in

advance, offers no help to investors when they try to choose shares.

There are reasons to assume that markets are efficient. The stock market is very competitive and it is hard to outperform it because there are plenty of other investors out there trying to do the same thing. If making money were easy, more and more people would be attracted to investing and it would become even harder to beat the market. Random Walk and Efficient Market Hypothesis do not say that you should not buy shares, only that you cannot consistently choose shares that beat the overall performance of the stock market.

There is no dispute that over time most companies grow at least in line with inflation and therefore the value of their shares should increase in the long term. The idea that you are better off buying the market than trying to pick individual shares lies behind the growth of tracker funds which, as we have seen, follow a particular index such as the FTSE 100. If the Random Walk and Efficient Market Hypothesis theories are correct, the only way to beat the market is to accept above-average risk in your investments. However, the fact is there are flaws in them that suggest individual share selections can be made profitably.

Problems with Random Walk and Efficient Market Hypothesis

1   Even if we accept that stock markets are generally efficient they are clearly not totally so since they sometimes overlook things. Smaller companies are followed by few stock market analysts and are therefore under-researched, which means not all the information regarding their shares may be in the price. The share price of some companies trade at a discount on others in their sector, even though there may be no discernible reason why, except that they are cheaper. Companies can also issue

profits warnings, which by definition is information that cannot be in the share price and which usually drags the price lower.

2 Stock markets can also overreact which suggests they cannot be totally efficient. If there is a stock market crash, a big slump in prices across the market, all companies tend to suffer. However, there will clearly be many companies that remain good investments and yet their share prices will have been dragged lower by the market fall. Market crashes can also be overreactions anyway, since most losses tend to be regained in a relatively short time.

3 If it is not possible to beat the market why does the City have an entire industry in the shape of company analysts and fund managers trying to do so? Their existence suggests there are excess profits to be made from trying to beat the market or else it would not be economical for firms to employ them.

4 Some people do beat the market. As we shall see in a later chapter, investors such as Warren Buffett, the so-called Sage of Omaha and a legendary US investor, have managed to achieve greater returns than the market as a whole over long periods.

5 The stock market is not the same for all investors and not all investors are the same. Professional investors have access to more information than small investors, although thanks to the Internet small investors are catching up fast. So some can buy and sell in reaction to price-sensitive news faster than others, which means the market is not efficient for everyone. The dealing room of an investment bank will have banks of computer screens including a direct Stock Exchange feed that means dealers can respond instantly to an announcement. However, as the amount of information available on the Internet increases, the balance of power may shift to some extent. The advantage of being a small investor is that you can quickly sell or buy shares online or by telephone while the institutional investors can find it hard to increase or decrease at speed their large shareholdings.

All of these examples suggest that while the Random Walk and

Efficient Market theories may contain some truth, they do not exclude the possibility that excess returns can be made through stock picking. The rest of this chapter will consider methods of analysing individual shares to pick the winners.

FUNDAMENTAL ANALYSIS

There are various ways in which share prices can be valued using financial figures, but they all have the same ultimate aim. The idea is to find out the true value of a company and examine whether the share price accurately reflects this or not. If the share price is lower than the analysis suggests the value of the company to be, the shares are a buy. If the price is higher than the suggested value the shares are overvalued and may be expected eventually to fall in price.

For this to work we must accept two assumptions about fundamental analysis. The first is that it is indeed possible to work out a reasonably accurate value for a company's shares. The second is that the company's share price will tend to gravitate towards the underlying value of the company.

In answer to the first point we shall consider a number of financial ratios that do indeed offer a method of valuing a company. They rely on published reports and accounts, and link the company's financial figures to its share price. They include price /earnings ratio, dividend yield and dividend cover, net asset value and net current asset value and discounted cash flow. These measures certainly provide a financial health check for the company and produce a common yardstick to enable different companies to be compared.

However, valuing some companies on fundamentals is hard because they may not produce the figures that allow us to adopt traditional valuations. For example, a technology company may have yet to produce a profit and is unlikely to pay a dividend for many years, if at all. Nonetheless, it is possible to try to value these companies and we shall consider methods of doing so.

The assumption that over time a company's share price will

tend to move towards the company's underlying value can be harder to swallow than the assumption that it is possible to work out an accurate valuation for a company. It assumes that markets are reasonably efficient and that share prices react to new information about a company's financial health. Sometimes this is slow to happen and occasionally companies remain out of favour for a very long time, no matter how good their prospects. But eventually value will out. This is clearly demonstrated by what happens to a company whose share price fails to reflect its underlying value. The fact that takeovers by other companies or even management buyouts take place shows that if a share price fails to move towards a company's true value other agents who recognise that value will act.

Valuing a company's shares

While there is no single method of evaluating a company and its shares, a combination of some of the more commonly used methods should provide a fairly accurate assessment. In Chapter 5 we considered several ratios that allow us to compare a company's financial health with that of its peers. Below we shall consider some of the most widely used measures for evaluating a company's shares with an explanation of each and an illustration of how they can be used.

The price/earnings ratio

The price/earnings ratio is also known as the PE ratio. It takes the current share price of a company and relates it to the reported or forecast earnings-per-share of the company. You work it out by simply dividing the current share price by the earnings-per-share figure which, as we saw in Chapter 5 the company reports at its full-year results. As a reminder, a company's earnings-per-share figure is derived from its after-tax profit attributable to shareholders divided by the number of shares it has in issue.

How to Calculate the Price-Earnings Ratio

Suppose a company has 100 million shares in issue, they are currently trading at 200p each and last year the company's after-tax profits were £5 million. The company's earnings-per-share figure would be £5,000,000/100,000,000 = 5p and the PE ratio is 200p/5p = 40.

Another example would be a company with 150 million shares in issue, a share price of 80p and after-tax profits of £15 million. Its earnings-per-share would be £15 million divided by 150 million shares, which equals 10p. The PE ratio is eight – 80p divided by 10p.

The PE ratio therefore tells an investor how many times greater a share's current price is, relative to its last reported earnings-per-share. This is known as the historic PE because it is based on the company's last reported earnings-per-share figure. It is the figure you will see as part of a company's share price listing in a newspaper. Although the historic PE provides a snapshot of how the company stands relative to its most recent financial figures, most investors are more interested in the company's value looking forward. A forward-looking PE is known as a prospective PE and is based on estimates of the future profits and earnings-per-share of the company. These forecasts are most often worked out by financial analysts employed by large stockbrokers and investment banks, although occasionally companies do indicate their likely full-year earnings either through profits warnings or sometimes, if the market has got its estimates wrong, by indicating profits will be higher than expected. The PE ratio is used to judge the relative merits of the shares of different companies. Although it is only a general rule it is a fair assumption that the higher the PE ratio the greater the market's expectations that the company will show strong profits growth.

In very broad terms a PE ratio is considered high when it is above 20. Typically, a growth company, such as a technology business, would be expected to have a high PE. This reflects that investors believe the company's products or expertise mean it will rapidly increase sales and earnings. It suggests investors are willing to pay a high price for the share today because they expect to benefit from its growth in future. Often companies with high PE ratios do not pay dividends, preferring to keep money invested in the company, and shareholders are happy to forgo income in the expectation of capital growth. However, a high PE can also mean that a share is overvalued and could be ready to fall in value. The conflicting signals offered by a high PE ratio serve to underline to investors that there are risks associated with buying such a share. It also often follows that a high PE ratio means the share price will be volatile and is likely to rise and fall sharply over the short term. The stock market is often very unforgiving of companies with high PE ratios that fail to meet earnings expectations. If a company's profits fall short of expectations its share price is likely to slump.

A PE ratio may be considered low when it is below 10. Low PE ratios are traditionally associated with companies in mature industries that are unlikely to show startling growth. Hence food producers and engineering companies tend to trade on single multiples of their earnings. This is not necessarily a criticism of the company since many blue chip companies have single-figure PE ratios and merely reflects the low growth nature of the business areas they operate in. They tend to be reliable and steady performers, and often pay healthy dividends to investors who look on them to provide income rather than capital growth. However, in the same way as a high PE can indicate a company's shares are overvalued, a low PE can suggest a company's shares are under-valued. This may be because of a temporary situation affecting the company's markets that has meant investors have shunned the shares. It could also be that investors have not realised the potential for the business in terms of earnings and low demand for the shares means a low PE ratio. Such a situation, where a share price is detached from the earnings potential of the share, may be termed an anomaly. It can provide an excellent buying opportunity for investors. According to the Efficient Market theory, anomalies do not last long before the market wakes up to the fact that the share price does not reflect the earnings and the gap is closed through a rerating. Of course, a low PE ratio can also mean that the company is in trouble and may even be going bust. That is why investors need to investigate other factors about the company rather than use the PE ratio alone as a guide to the investment potential of a company.

Indeed, in isolation the PE ratio tells us very little. It is really only of use when it is used to make comparisons against the stock market generally, the sector in which a company sits and rival businesses. Even then, true comparisons can only really be made between two companies in the same sector.

Judging a company's PE ratio relative to the market or other shares tells us whether the company's share price is expensive or cheap compared with them. At its simplest level this implies that if two engineering companies are the same size, have very similar customers and the same prospects, if one trades on a PE of 9 and one on a PE of 6 the one trading on the lower PE is the best buy for investors. However, this can be fraught with difficulties since, for example, a high PE ratio relative to a rival does not tell us whether the company has better growth prospects, is a takeover target because it is good or bad, or whether analysts' forecasts for earnings are wrong.

You should also be sure that each company that is compared calculates its earnings-per-share figure in the same way. Some companies use different tax treatments that can distort their figures. It is true, too, that no two companies are exactly the same, often they have a slightly different mix of businesses even if they are in the same sector, and therefore comparing PE ratios can only ever be an approximate guide to their merits.

PE ratios are not very useful for companies in so-called cyclical sectors such as insurance or chemicals, which traditionally have a few years of good profits before overcapacity forces down prices and can lead to several lean years. Such erratic earnings can distort PE ratios. Neither is the PE ratio of much use in areas such as property where the value of a company's assets is a far more useful guide for investors.

An attempt to refine the PE ratio has produced a measure known as the PE relative or PER. This attempts to compare the PE of the company in relation to the stock market as a whole or the company's own sector. A sector's PE ratio is an average across all the PEs within it.

How to Calculate the PE Relative

PERs are normally expressed as a percentage. So if a company has a PE ratio of 10.7 and its sector has a PE ratio of 8.6, its PE relative would be 125. That is 10.75 divided by 8.6 multiplied by 100 equals 125.

If a company has a PE of 4.3 and its sector has a PE of 12.4, its PER would be 4.3 divided by 12.4 multiplied by 100, which equals 35.

Investors can use the PER to judge how the market has valued a share relative to its sector. If the PER is above 100 the company is valued higher than the sector and if it is less than 100 the company is valued at less than the sector. A company may justify its superior rating to the sector, but it may also be a warning sign that it is overvalued. While a rating below the sector could be justified because the company's performance is poor compared with its peers, it may also highlight an undervalued company that would present a buying opportunity.

Although useful, the PE ratio has its limitations and therefore we should also consider other methods of evaluating shares.

The PEG ratio

In looking for ways to supplement the evidence that a PE ratio can give us as to the attraction of a particular share it is worth at least a cursory glance at the price/earnings growth ratio or PEG.

The PEG shows a company's PE ratio in relation to the rate at which its earnings are growing. It is calculated by dividing the prospective PE ratio by the estimated future growth rate in earnings-per-share. These figures are usually derived from stockbrokers' estimates.

How to Calculate the PEG Ratio

A company with a prospective PE ratio of 10 divided by an estimated 25 per cent growth in earnings would have a PEG of 0.4.

A company with a forecast PE ratio of 18 divided by an estimated growth in earnings of 15 per cent would have a PEG of 1.2.

Investment expert Jim Slater developed the measure and his aim was to identify shares with a PEG of well under 1. He argued that, unlike PE ratios, PEGs compared like with like since a low PEG implied investors were paying comparatively little for the future growth of a company, while a high PEG meant they were paying more than they should. The idea is to find a share that offers strong growth in earnings that has yet to be reflected in its share price.

Slater does have several additional criteria that he views as important when using a PEG to assess an investment opportunity. These include that the PEG is only relevant for growth companies, which he defines as those showing at least four consecutive years of earnings growth, although this can be a mixture of historic and forecast earnings. He also warns that high PE ratios can be unreliable and suggests targeting companies with PEs. In addition he points out a low PEG factor alone is not a sufficient reason to buy a share. It should also be remembered that, as with investment decisions based on prospective earnings estimates, the success of the PEG depends on the reliability of stockbrokers' estimates and forecasts that are not an exact science. However, as you develop your own investment techniques to find the ones that best suit you personally it is certainly worth considering the PEG as one criterion to use.

Dividend yield and dividend cover

Another traditional method of valuing a company's share price is by examining what it pays out in the form of dividends relative to its share price.

The **dividend yield** is the total annual dividend paid out by the company, usually announced after tax at 10 per cent, divided by the price per share and expressed as a percentage.

How to Calculate the Dividend Yield

If a company pays out a dividend of 5p and its share price is 100p, the yield is 10 per cent, which is 5 divided by 100 multiplied by 100.

Another company pays a dividend of 8p and its share price is 400p, the yield is 2 per cent: eight divided by 400 multiplied by 100.

The yield should be viewed as the income offered by the share and can be used to compare it with other shares. It can also be used to compare with income rates from other sources such as building society deposit accounts. But it should be remembered that although a share may yield more than the interest rate on a deposit account, unlike with a building society, your capital, the lump sum you invested, is at risk since shares can fall in value.

An historic yield shows you what you would get at the current share price if the company paid out the same dividend as last time, while a prospective yield is based on forecasts of future dividends. Generally a company may be expected to raise its dividends in line with earnings but dividends can be cut or even passed altogether, which means dividend yield as a yardstick is not totally reliable.

Dividend yield can be a pointer to how the stock market rates a particular company. If, for example, there are two companies each paying the same dividend, their yields may differ according to the characteristics that underline their share price. If one company shows fast earnings-per-share growth it will tend to have a high share price and if the other has slower earnings-per-share growth its share price will tend to be lower. Although both companies may pay the same dividend, the first will have a lower dividend yield than the second.

A share may also show a high dividend yield because investors expect it to be cut and the share price has already fallen to reflect this belief. However, it could also be high yielding because investors have overlooked the share or simply because it has fallen out of favour and may be ripe for recovery. A low yield may mean the company has been reluctant to pay out too much of its earnings in dividends and sometimes companies step up the size of their pay-outs to rectify the situation.

In order to judge whether a yield is high or low it is worth comparing it with what the previous yield for that share has been, what rival company shares yield and even what the stock market as a whole yields. Traditionally, high dividend yields have been characteristic of mature companies, those operating in slow-growth industries such as food and regulated businesses such as power companies. Since these businesses do not have large investment needs relative to their often substantial earnings and because capital growth is likely to be slow they tend to return a large proportion of their earnings to shareholders in the form of dividends. These companies are often termed yield stocks.

By the same token, fast-growing companies tend to reinvest most of their profits in their businesses and pay little or no dividends. Investors are happy to accept this because they prefer the capital growth offered by the shares and if they want income they can sell some of their holding. Small dividend payments from growth shares mean the dividend yield will be low.

Dividend cover is worked out by taking a company's earnings-per-share and dividing it by its dividend per share.

How to Calculate Dividend Cover

A company has earnings-per-share of 12p and pays a dividend of 4p, so its dividend cover is 3, which is 12 divided by 4.

Another company has earnings-per-share of 4.5p and pays a dividend of 6p, so its dividend cover is 0.75.

Dividend cover is a measure as to what extent a company can afford to pay its dividend. If the dividend cover is 1 all the company's earnings are being returned to shareholders in the form of a dividend. If it is less than 1 the company is returning all its earnings plus it is dipping into reserves to make the pay-out. Both these situations should send out warning signs to investors since such action is unsustainable. It could be that the company has had one bad year and the management have shown their faith in the rapid recovery of the business by paying a low covered dividend. However, a low level of dividend cover together with a high dividend yield should generally set alarm bells ringing with investors. It is probably a signal that the dividend will have to be cut, although the worst-case scenario is that the company is heading for the wall. At best it could mean an undervalued share and represent a buying opportunity, but such situations should be approached with caution and thorough research into the company is advised. A dividend cover of more than 1 and preferably at least three or four times earnings means the company can easily afford the dividend and the cover is described as healthy. The exact comfort level will vary from company to company and once again investors should compare it with the previous level for the company, as well as the dividend cover of the company's peers.

One other way to value a company's shares based on dividends is to use a so-called **dividend discount model**. Since the owner of a share is entitled to any future dividends from that share the dividend discount model suggests that the value of the share should be equal to the present value of these future dividends. If you add up all the payments you expect to earn from the share you should ask whether the current price of the share is more or less than this figure. If it is more, the share can be described as expensive, but if it is less the share is cheap.

Of course, this model does not work where a company does not pay dividends or its pay-outs are deliberately low because it reinvests most of its earnings back into its business. However, for investors who want income from their investments the dividend discount model could be worth a spin.

When working it out it is important to remember that you cannot just add together all the dividends you expect to receive from a share. There is a time value associated with money, which means that £100 today is worth a lot more to you than £100 in a year's time, even forgetting about inflation. Hence a dividend paid today can be reinvested and produce more growth, while a dividend you have to wait for is worth less. Also, dividends in the future are more uncertain since a company may cut them or pass them altogether. Because of this it is necessary to discount the value of future dividends to reflect the fact that they are worth less to you. The discount rate is usually based on the returns you could expect from a safe investment, such as a government bond, together with a risk adjustment to take into account that investing in shares is less safe than investing in bonds and therefore the rewards need to be higher.

These figures should be incorporated in a formula that assumes an annual growth rate for the dividend and a risk discount. The formula looks like this:

> Present value of dividends = First Dividend + Second Dividend/(1 + discount) + Third Dividend/(1 + discount) + Fourth Dividend/(1 + discount) . . .

You can work out the dividend flow for as long into the future as you wish but five years should give you a realistic measure. If the solution equals the current share price you are paying what they are worth to you in terms of income. If it is less, the shares are expensive and if it is more they could be worth buying.

The problem with the dividend discount model is that it relies heavily on the assumptions you make about future dividend growth and the level of discount you set. If you make all the right assumptions it is a very accurate model for determining a share price. However, the margin for error is slim and if you are even slightly out with your projections the result is likely to be false. In addition, since future events are uncertain the further into the future you attempt to take the model the more inaccurate it is likely to be. Even if it were to work, the result would still give you a false impression of value since it would probably undervalue a share. That is because the dividend discount model assumes no capital growth, yet a company paying out a regular stream of improved dividends would do it on the back of good earnings growth, which should lead to an improvement in the share price.

However, even given all the limitations of the model it can be a useful discipline since it gives investors a foundation for assessing the value of a share when share prices are volatile. If a share price is swinging wildly investors can use the model to gain some idea, at least, of whether the share price is underestimating or over-estimating the future value of dividends from the company.

Net asset value and net current asset value

Although net asset value per share is not directly related to a company's earnings or its shares, it can provide a useful measure of whether or not to invest in a company.

As we saw earlier, it is a very useful guide when buying investment trusts, but it does still have some merits for assessing individual companies since it is what shareholders might expect to get if the company sold all its assets and settled all its liabilities, and the remaining sum were divided among investors.

It is calculated by taking the book value of the company's net assets – after deducting liabilities – and dividing by the number of shares in issue. The equation uses figures in the company's balance sheet, although often a company will produce a net asset value per share figure in its accounts.

How to Calculate Net Asset Value

Suppose a company has net assets – after liabilities – with a book value of £120 million and has 100 million shares in issue. Its net asset value would be 120 divided by 100, which equals 120p. If the company's share price were 100p it could be said to trade at a discount to net asset value. If the share price were 140p it would trade at a premium.

The measure offers shareholders a basic figure to use as a yardstick for value. Usually a share price will have no relation to a company's net asset value. This simply reflects the diversity of companies. Some service companies, such as advertising groups, have very few material assets since their employees are often their most important assets. However, manufacturing companies often have lots of assets such as plant and machinery and factories. The measure is also extremely useful in assessing property companies where property values are the main factor underpinning their share price.

Shares in most companies trade well above net asset value because investors expect them to use their assets to grow earnings and while the price includes the asset value it also includes the earnings. If a company's shares are trading at below asset value the shares may be a buy. It could show that the company is using its assets poorly or that they are simply undervalued by the market. It can also make the company vulnerable to a takeover bid since any new owner would in theory be able to break up the business, sell its assets and get back more than it cost to buy. In this regard asset values offer a floor to a company's share price if it has fallen because of poor trading by the business. However, there are downsides about using net asset values as a hard and fast measure of a company's true worth. There is a big difference between what the book value of a company's asset may be and the break-up value. A fire sale – that is a quick sale to the first buyer who comes along – is unlikely to achieve full value and any sale would be likely to give rise to a tax charge that would eat into the amount raised. The asset value in a company's balance sheet may also be open to question since it may not have revalued its assets for some time.

One slight refinement on net asset value that presents a slightly truer picture is **net current asset value**. This takes into account only the most liquid of a company's assets such as stocks, debtors, and investments and bank balances, which either are cash or can be tuned into cash quickly.

How to Calculate Net Current Asset Value

If a company has net current assets of £50 million and has 200 million shares in issue its net current asset value would be 50 divided by 200, which equals 25p a share.

If a company's share price drops below even this level the risk associated with buying the shares is greatly reduced. Since the figure is produced after liabilities, such as debts and contingent liabilities, it suggests that even if the company went bust it could sell assets and pay back shareholders.

Discounted cash flow

As we have seen, using earnings-per-share as a way of valuing companies is not always that reliable since it depends on how a company calculates the figure and how accurate analysts' forecast are. Likewise, discounting dividends relies on forecasts and applying the right level of discount.

A rival method to these measures and one used by professional investors is to focus on the company's cash flow. Using earnings-per-share to decide investment is a perfectly acceptable method. However, by its very nature it is only suitable for use with companies that actually produce earnings. In the same regard discounted dividends are only of use if the company actually pays a dividend. Many of the so-called 'new economy' companies have yet to produce profits and indeed, with dotcom and telecom businesses heavy upfront investment means many may not make profits for years to come. Any money they do make is ploughed straight back into the business, so there are no dividends for shareholders who invest in the hope of capital growth.

One method of analysis that can work for them, though, as well as for companies that produce earnings and pay dividends is **discounted cash flow**. The cash flow in question is that money which the company may use for debt or interest repayments, dividends or share buy-backs. The assumption is that this measure represents the ability of a company to meet its future liabilities. Because it can include debt repayments the amount of borrowings a company has needs to be taken into account when working out discounted cash flow.

A valuation for a company that includes its debt is known as its enterprise value. If a company has no debt its value is simply its share price multiplied by the number of shares in issue – this is known as its market capitalisation or equity value and is the price someone would pay if they bought all the company's shares, forgetting for the moment about the need to pay a takeover premium. However, if the company had debts a buyer would not only have to pay the market capitalisation but also take on the debts, which would increase the overall cost. Likewise, if the company had a cash pile the buyer would pay the market capitalisation, but would then also own the cash, hence the overall cost would fall. Enterprise value therefore takes into account the market capitalisation of a company plus its debts or minus its cash.

Using discounted cash flow to arrive at an enterprise value involves forecasting cash flows with an appropriate discount, just as with the dividend discount model. In this case the appropriate discount rate is the cost of borrowing. As with other techniques we have looked at, the difficulty of this method is predicting future cash flows. It is made slightly easier by taking a medium-term forecast of five to ten years. Secondly we need to predict a so-called terminal value for the business. That is the value that extends beyond the forecast period of discounted cash flows. Even taking a relatively short period, forecasting cash flows is no easy matter. The simplest starting point is to take past cash flows and project them into the future. Terminal values are also tricky but one method is to divide the expected operating cash flow, without using a discount, for the final year under consideration by the discount rate. The terminal value must then be discounted back to its present value.

We now have the elements for the calculation.

Taking the forecast cash flows and discounting them back to today gives a present value of cash flows, add to this a present value of terminal value, derived from the estimated terminal value discounted back, and it gives an enterprise value. From this enterprise value we need to subtract net debt and that should leave us with a fair value for the equity. Divide this by the number of shares in issue and that will be a fair price for the shares.

How to Calculate Discounted Cash Flow

Suppose a company with 200 million shares and net debt of £100 million is forecast to grow its cash by 20 per cent a year. In year one it has £12 million, so in year two it has £14.4 million and in year three £17.28 million.

These figures then need to be recalculated using a discounted rate – the cost of borrowing, of perhaps 5 per cent – so growth will be 15 per cent and the new figures are £11.5 million in year one, £13.23 million in year two and £15.2 million in year three.

A terminal value would be £15.2 million divided by 0.05, which equals £304 million, but this needs to be discounted back three years to produce a present value of £261 million.

Present value of cash flows is £10 million plus present value of terminal value (£261 million) equals enterprise value (£271 million).

£271 million minus net debt of £100 million leaves us with fair value of equity at £171 million which, divided by 200 million shares in issue, gives a fair price for the shares of 85.5p.

Such calculations and estimates are probably beyond most small investors. However, it is useful to get a feel for the concept. Discounted cash flow is used by professional analysts and investors, and is one of the most used methods of valuing new technology stocks. It is not without its critics who point to its failure in several high-profile flotations. It was used to suggest high valuations for Eurotunnel and the cable television companies, most of which have proved poor investments. But its champions point out that it was also used to justify values in the mobile telephone market where investment returns have been stunning. Overall, the jury is probably out on the efficacy of DCF in the UK, although it is regularly used in the US but at present there are few alternatives for valuing start-up companies.

Special situations

Some yardsticks for evaluating the investment merits of a share are peculiar to certain types of company or sector. They can be useful in these connections but have little or no use in a general context.

Price to book value

This is the share price divided by asset value or the market capitalisation divided by total net assets. The lower the figure the more undervalued is the share. It is a very basic and crude measure but can be useful when buying shares in merging markets.

Price to sales ratio

To work it out simply take the share price and divide it by sales per share or take the market capitalisation and divide by total sales. A low figure is considered a good indication of a recovery situation. However, any shares identified through this system should also show prospects for improving profit margins. Critics say that sales without profits are no use.

Price to research and development ratio

This measure can be useful in industries such as drugs where research and development is vital to keep ahead of the competition and develop new products. It offers a ratio for comparison between companies, although just because a company is spending heavily does not guarantee it will develop profitable products.

The fact that forecasting is an important element in fundamental analysis calculations means investors are trying to predict what the present share price should be from the future outlook for the company.

However, there is a method of analysis that uses the past to try to predict the future. It probably has far more critics than supporters and has been described as a black art and of no practical use. But in its simplest form it is a method that most investors at least pay lip service to. It is called technical analysis or charting.

TECHNICAL ANALYSIS

Few investment theories attract such diverse opinions as technical analysis or, as it is also known, charting. For some investors charting is a ridiculous concept with no merit. But many others are intrigued by its simplicity and attracted by the suggestion that with very little effort it could hold the key to easy profits.

Chartists or technical analysts believe that simply by studying patterns in graphs of historic share price movements they can predict how the share price will move in future. The theory ignores the fundamentals of a company because, although these will have some impact on a share price, chartists believe their influence is small. They point out that share prices move up and down even when there is no fundamental information about a share. The reason for the movement, they maintain, is the psychology of buyers and sellers that produces certain patterns of movement. Chartists suggest these patterns are repeated and therefore if you can understand them you can foresee the next movement.

Technical analysis makes price predictions based on earlier prices and to some extent trading volumes in a given period and these indicate whether a particular share is a buy or a sell. In theory it makes no difference as to what sort of company is behind the share price since pure chartists do not delve this far. Fundamental analysts – who painstakingly research companies in order to achieve a forecast of their future earnings – find this hard to swallow.

Timing is everything in investment and chartists reckon their methods are more efficient at determining the timing of investment decisions than fundamental analysis. The latter can identify under-valued shares but simply knowing that a share price should rise is not sufficient to ensure profits. The rerating may not happen for months or years. Although chartists do not claim to be able to identify the exact moment at which a share is set to rise or fall, they do maintain that they can appreciate a rising or falling trend. This means they can flag a share as a buy not at the bottom, but as it recovers, and a sell not at the peak but as it starts to fall.

The up and downs of charts are the bread and butter of chartists and some dedicated practitioners claim they see charts all around them, in mountain ranges, hedgerows and even curtain folds. Such claims underline the obsessive nature of chartists, which is another reason why most investors treat them and their theories with scorn. They are also attacked for producing poor results. Critics ask why, if charting is so easy, they are not all rich. It also seems that when things go wrong chartists are always able to reinterpret their charts to point to what did happen rather than what they expected to happen.

However, despite the low esteem in which they are held, many stockbroking firms do employ chartists and to some extent even fundamental analysts use charting techniques, particularly when referring to share price graphs. Fundamental analysts have also adopted some of the phraseology of the chartists, talking about buying opportunities and recovery plays. These factors alone justify an exploration of the theory and a brief outline of a few popular charting techniques in this chapter.

Buyers and sellers

For chartists share price movements are the product of a ceaseless struggle between buyers and sellers. As buyers pile into a share, so following the law of supply and demand, the price of the share rises. However, it will reach a point when no more buyers of the shares are to be found and sellers begin to enter the market, forcing the price lower. This is called a resistance level. It occurs because after enjoying a price rise shareholders want to take profits. In the same way the more sellers there are of a share the steeper the share price fall until, that is, buyers emerge and break the fall. This is called a support level. It is suggested that when the share price reaches this level buyers join the market or existing investors add to their shareholdings.

This battle between buyers and sellers gives rise to the traditional zigzag pattern of share prices. What chartists try to discern is a trend among the peaks and troughs. They plot this with a trendline and at its simplest it is done with a graph, a pencil and a ruler. The trendline gives rise to a series of patterns that are defined by such terms as head and shoulders, flags and double tops. These trends can be fairly simple to observe. However, some chartists also use mathematically produced lines such as moving averages and relative-strength indicators. The moving average takes the average price of the share over a given period and plots it against the current share price. The relative-strength indicator is used to compare the progress of the share price against a sector or index measure like the FTSE 100.

The trend is your friend

Chartists follow the trend like a road map. If it is rising and they own the shares they can sit tight and wait for it to fall. If it is falling they can wait for it to turn and present a buying opportunity. They adhere to the motto 'Let the trend be your friend'.

Many of the principles of modern charting were established by American Charles Dow who also co-founded the US business newspaper *Wall Street Journal* and launched the Dow Jones Industrial Average, an index that measures the share price performance of key US companies. He gave his name to Dow Theory. This suggests share price patterns move in recognisable trends. It argues that share price movements can appear erratic because there are three phases of trends occurring at the same time: long-term trends, medium-term trends and short-term trends.

Long-term trends last for months or years, medium-term trends for weeks or months and short-term trends usually last just a few days. Chartists today argue that with the advent of day trading, where people buy and sell shares over a few hours in companies whose stock is usually quite volatile, these trends can last hours or even minutes.

Dow suggested short-term trends were relatively unimportant and were difficult to follow accurately because of their volatility. His focus was on the long-term trend, for as long as this was going up one should be able to make money by investing in the share. Share prices tend to trade within a band of prices or what chartists call a channel. The price may rise or fall but its general direction will be either up or down.

But sooner or later the chartist has to call a turn in the road. According to Dow Theory there is a recognisable point which signals that the trend has changed or rather reversed. In order to accentuate the channel chartists draw lines either side of the zigzag. In a rising trend the line at the bottom of the zigzag is the trendline, while in a falling trend the line at the top of the zigzag is the trendline. One American advocate of charting remembers it by thinking of the trend as an escalator. On the way up you look at the bottoms of the people in front and on the way down you look at their heads.

As a trend rises, chartists want to make sure the share price does not slip below the trend, which is why they focus on the bottoms. On the way down they are looking to see if it moves above the trendline, hence the focus on the heads.

Although a trendline can be drawn between just two points, this is a little unreliable given the zigzag nature of share prices. Therefore chartists tend to use three points to confirm the trendline.

There are more sophisticated ways of drawing channels including a system called Bollinger bands. This is a pair of lines drawn above and below a moving average of the share price to define a channel. A moving average takes the average price of a share over a period of days and with each new date the earliest date drops out of the equation. Bollinger bands need to be generated by a computer and take into account volatility in a share price. When a share price is zigzagging wildly the channel is wide and when the

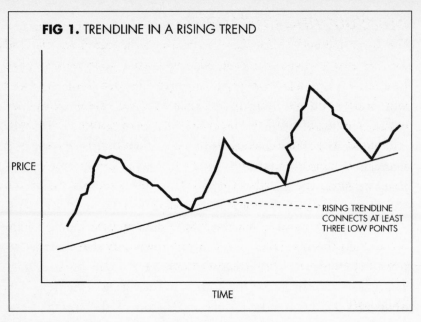

FIG 1. TRENDLINE IN A RISING TREND

PRICE

RISING TRENDLINE
CONNECTS AT LEAST
THREE LOW POINTS

TIME

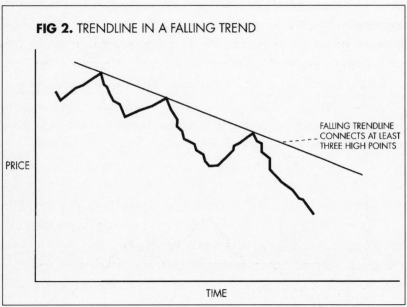

FIG 2. TRENDLINE IN A FALLING TREND

PRICE

FALLING TRENDLINE
CONNECTS AT LEAST
THREE HIGH POINTS

TIME

price has settled down the channel is narrow. The flexible nature of
the bands is designed to minimise the possibility of false signals.

Breakout and patterns

Whatever method a chartist uses to establish trendlines the end game is to discover a breakout. That is when a price breaks out of its channel. This could simply mean that the price has broken out temporarily and will quickly fall back into the channel, in which case it is nothing for the technical analyst to worry about. However, it could also be that the share price has broken out of its trend and begun to establish a new one. Chartists need to be sure that a new trend is being established but if it is, then this is the point at which chartists can make investment decisions.

In order to decide what is going to happen next chartists look for share price patterns. These are divided into two categories: reversal patterns and continuation patterns.

Reversals

As the name suggests, reversals indicate a change of trend. If they occur at a share price high they may indicate the price is likely to fall. If they happen at a share price low they may signal the price is likely to rise. The patterns for share price lows are the same as for share price highs, but except turned on their heads.

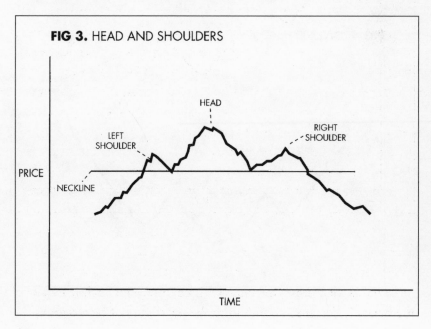

FIG 3. HEAD AND SHOULDERS

Examples of patterns

Head and shoulders: This is one of the most popular patterns among chartists. They rate it because it very often indicates a share price is about to fall and is therefore reliable. Also, it tends to occur frequently and is therefore a regular indicator of a likely share price fall. Its name is self-explanatory since it looks like a head between two shoulders with the base of each shoulder providing a so-called neckline.

As Figure 3 shows, the up trend falls back slightly as some investors take profits following the rise and forms the left shoulder. Then buyers return, although the volume is not usually enough to lift the price much higher before weakness sets in and the price slips until it finds support again at the neckline. Finally, there is a third rally, which can hardly sustain itself as sellers take the upper hand and the price falls below the neckline, completing the head and shoulders effect. Chartists reckon that this final fall will push the share price down at least as far as the distance between the top of the head and the neckline.

Figure 4 shows the inverse head and shoulders. It is a mirror

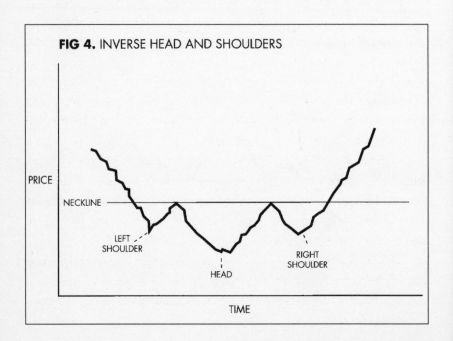

FIG 4. INVERSE HEAD AND SHOULDERS

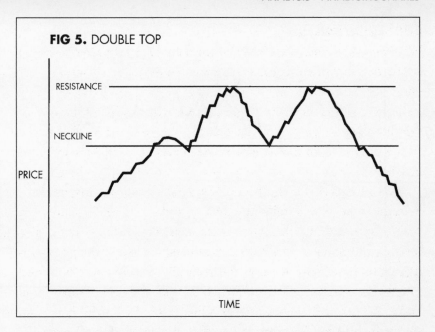

FIG 5. DOUBLE TOP

RESISTANCE

NECKLINE

PRICE

TIME

image of the normal head and shoulders, although this time the neckline represents a resistance level. Once this is overcome and buyers take control there is a breakout to a higher price.

Double top: As Figure 5 shows, this is similar to a head and shoulders but the buyers run out more quickly and sellers take command. The price rises to such a level that it meets resistance, fails to find buyers and people are persuaded to sell. It then slips back, encouraging a few buyers, but once the previous peak is reached the sellers have the upper hand and the price falls swiftly. Chartists believe the price will probably fall to the same distance below the neckline as it rose above it to the peak.

A reverse of this pattern is known as a double bottom, and occurs when a price falls to such a low level that it finds a support level and buyers emerge, lifting the price. It then slips back to the support level but attracts further buyers and the shares gather momentum and break out.

Other chart patterns closely aligned to these are the triple top and triple bottoms, which have three points of contact at resistance and support levels. These are considered extremely strong indictors of trend reversals.

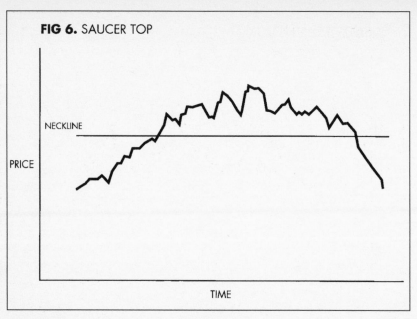

FIG 6. SAUCER TOP

NECKLINE

PRICE

TIME

Saucer top: A subtler pattern suggesting a reversal is the so-called saucer top and its mirror image the saucer bottom (see Figure 6). It is thus named because the peaks form an arc like a saucer shape. The saucer top shows a steadily rising series of peaks as buyers are attracted to the shares but at the highest point the share price encounters a resistance level and there is gradual selling on the way down. Also known as the rounded top, this chart is said to be a more consistent signal than the double top.

Continuations: Continuation patterns occur when a trend pauses and suggests once the share price starts moving again it will follow the already established trend. So if a share price had been rising it will continue to rise and if it had been falling it will continue to fall. Sometimes continuation patterns are seen as reversals that failed to break out. The main continuation patterns are rectangles and triangles, which tend to be longer-term formations. Shorter-term formations include pennants and flags.

Rectangles: Shares often spend a lot of their trading time in a rectangle (see Figure 7). The share price is bounded by horizontal resistance and support lines. Chartists look at the rectangle pattern, waiting for a breakout, and when this occurs they maintain the rise in the share price is likely to equal the height of the rectangle. Sometimes the share price may weaken as it breaks out and dips

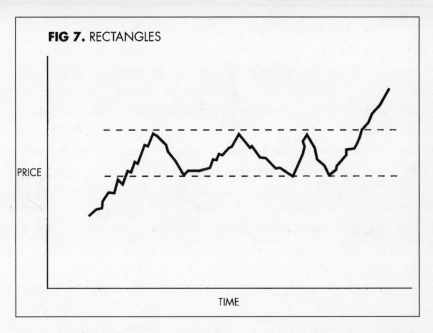

FIG 7. RECTANGLES

back inside the rectangle, but generally the breakout is swift and sustained.

Triangles: Ideally formed over four to ten weeks, triangles can occur in both up trends and down trends (see Figure 8). Although they

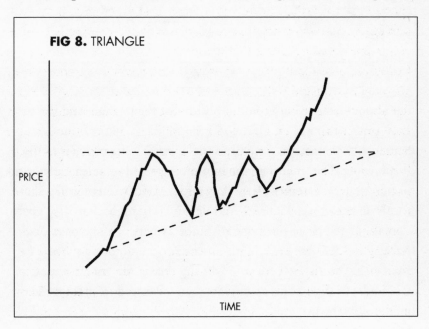

FIG 8. TRIANGLE

usually mark just a temporary pause in the trend, they can also signal its end. This reversal is marked by the price breaking out of the triangle in the opposite direction to the previous trend. If the share price zigzags right into the apex of the triangle the chances are higher that there will be a reversal. The most reliable sign is if a breakout occurs between halfway and three-quarters of the way towards the apex. If an upwards breakout occurs, chartists expect the share price to rise to the same distance as the base of the triangle,

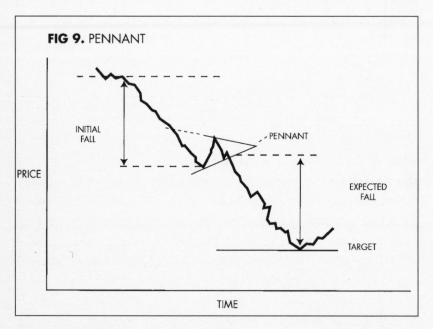

FIG 9. PENNANT

that is the distance between the bottom of the triangle and the first share price peak.

Pennants: A pennant is a small triangle, but it is formed over only a couple of weeks rather than the minimum period of at least a month for a triangle. It emerges after a fast and significant change in a share price's direction (see Figure 9). While with a triangle chartists expect a breakout to travel the same distance as between the base of the triangle and its first peak, with a pennant the target is expected to equal to be the distance travelled during the significant change to the base of the triangle. This distance is then measured from the pennant breakout to the target.

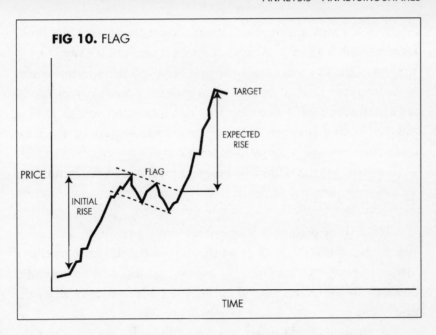

FIG 10. FLAG

TARGET

EXPECTED
RISE

FLAG

PRICE

INITIAL
RISE

TIME

Flags: Flags are very similar to pennants in that they form in a short period: days or weeks. They also amount to the same signal after a rapid and significant change in share price. However, they differ in that the defining lines do not form a triangle but rather run parallel to each other (see Figure 10). Flags occur because investors take some profits in a rising trend, selling shares that are then picked up by buyers. In a falling trend the share price reaches a low where it attracts buyers but these are not enough to compensate for the volume of sellers. Once the trend breaks out from the flag, chartists expect the share price to do the same distance it did before it entered the flag. Hence with a rising share price the breakout is expected to be as great as the initial significant rise to the top line of the flag.

Help with patterns

While technical analysts will spend hours poring over chart patterns, they accept that they cannot always be relied upon. Sometimes the pattern suggests a share price will break out, and rise, only for the share price to fall. At other times the chart may point to a price fall, yet the price then keeps rising. Even the most dedicated chartists recognise that supporting evidence is needed. For this they look to indicators such as volume, relative strength and momentum.

Volume: This is quite simply the number of shares in a particular company that change hands between sellers and buyers. If 20 million shares in ICI were traded yesterday, but only 2 million today, that could indicate underlying information about the market sentiment towards the shares.

Dow reckoned volume was a good indicator of the trend since it showed the amount of demand there is in the market on any given day for a share.

If the share price is in a long-term upward trend the volume of shares traded should be high on the days when the price rises and low on days when the share price slips or pauses. When the trend is downwards the shares should be heavily traded on days when the price falls.

A breakout could be signalled by a big price movement in the short term and could be confirmed by a large number of shares being traded. If there is a sharp movement in the share price, but the volume of shares traded is low, the signal is probably a false alarm.

Chartists use volume together with a chart of the share price. Volume is represented as a bar chart beneath the price graph, with high points indicating high volumes and low points low volumes. If the high points on the bar chart correspond with a reversal pattern such as a double top it will tend to confirm that the price movement is about to reverse.

Relative strength: A relative-strength chart tracks the movement of a share price in comparison with a particular sector such as, for example, transport, and the market as a whole. Such a chart is able to put a price movement in context. For instance, if a share price rises 10 per cent in one week it might be considered to have performed strongly, but if the company's stock market sector is up 15 per cent in the same week the share price may be said to have underperformed its sector.

To work out the relative strength of a particular company's share it is necessary to choose an index to compare it with, e.g. the company's sector or the whole stock market, and create a ratio between the two. This is done by dividing the share price on a certain day by the index, say, the All Share Index, and multiplying by 100. Repeating this at a future date will produce a second figure. The difference between the two ratio figures can then be compared with the difference in the share price between the two dates and the difference in the index over the same period.

The ratio is plotted as a continuous line over time alongside the share price. The share's relative strength indicator will explain how much of a share price's rise or fall is due to the strength of the company and how much it was buoyed or dragged down by the market. When following a particular share it is useful to know whether its good performance is due to its own merits or simply because all shares in the market were higher.

Changes in the relative-strength ratio should help to confirm a pattern in the share price. For example, if a reversal pattern indicates a share could be worth buying, an increase in the relative-strength ratio would underline the case for buying.

Momentum: Some chartists believe a good early indication of a large movement in a share price can be derived from the speed at which a share price moves up and down. They suggest that the up and down movement in a share price tends to slow down just before its trend reverses.

Momentum measures the degree of movement in a share price over a predetermined amount of time that can be 5 days or 20 days, or any period deemed appropriate for a particular share. One way of deciding what time period to choose for a particular share would be to look at historical share price data for the share and decide which time period would have produced the most reliable signals.

Taking a five-day example, the answer can be positive – the share price may have risen from where it was five days ago – or negative – it may have fallen. It is said to oscillate around zero, that is no change, and this measure is known as a momentum oscillator. When a share whose oscillator has moved towards the top of its normal range – again something which will need to be determined by looking at historical prices – it is said to be overbought. When it has moved towards the bottom of its normal range then it can be said to be oversold. Some followers of momentum argue that a share should not be bought when it is overbought or sold when it is oversold.

There is more

Charting is a huge subject and we have only scratched the surface here. Further study would reveal chartists who believe in patterns within patterns, the effectiveness of different types of graphs beyond simply line graphs and more exotically named secondary signals. But the above should suffice to give a basic grounding in the theory and there are plenty of publications available that explore it in more detail. If you want to have a go at using some of these techniques the simplest way to begin is with a sheet of graph paper, a pencil and some historical share price information, perhaps from a stack of daily newspapers. Although laborious, this will give you some idea whether or not you find the theory attractive.

If you believe it has merit, then for more serious study and certainly in order to save time you should consider one of the many computer software packages available, which offer charting or look at the Internet where many web pages dealing with share prices offer basic charting techniques. In addition there are various chart services to which you can subscribe.

No quick fix

While charting has its practitioners and supporters, it also has its critics. Those who claim it has no merit suggest that while the psychological behaviour of investors plays a role in share prices it is not, as chartists assume, the most important determinant of share prices. There is also a major hurdle to overcome when interpreting patterns. Critics suggest that patterns may not repeat themselves with any meaning and argue that chartists often interpret them liberally in order to achieve the conclusion they want.

Critics also suggest that a practical flaw in the chartists' theory is that since investors use the patterns to predict future price movements the earlier they recognise those patterns the bigger the rewards. However, since more and more people will try to anticipate the pattern and buy or sell early, their action will itself distort the pattern and make the whole system unreliable.

Technical analysis does undoubtedly have its weaknesses and no sensible investor should ever consider using it in isolation. Its fundamental appeal is that it reduces buy and sell decisions to points on a graph, which saves the laborious effort of researching companies that fundamental analysis relies upon.

However, there are no quick fixes in investing. There is no harm in using some well-researched aspects of technical analysis to help with timing decisions, but it should always be used in collaboration with fundamental analysis.

CHAPTER 7

Investment Strategies

Developing the skills to analyse a company and its share price is important, but without a method for implementing what you know it is unlikely to deliver rewards. It is vital to develop an investment strategy to underpin your stock market investments. Analysing data can produce a shortlist of potential winners, but it is important that these shares fit with your overall investment strategy. There are almost as many investment strategies as there are companies to invest in and each has its own good and bad points. The important thing to remember is that no single strategy will work all the time or be suitable for your own risk-and-reward profile. As ever, it pays to experiment and find those ideas that work best for you and those that can outperform at times when the general stock market is in turmoil.

In this chapter we will consider an array of investment styles that have won fans and have some track record of success. As a very general pointer the strategies are divided into defensive investing techniques and aggressive investing techniques. And under each heading we will consider ways of identifying and managing opportunities.

Although, as we have already seen, all investment in individual shares is inherently risky the defensive strategies are designed to try to minimise that risk. We will look at methods of spotting shares, how to construct a portfolio of shares to reduce risk and how to manage them once they are in a portfolio. Defensive investing should be viewed as a medium- to long-term strategy.

The aggressive strategies are high-risk, but they can also deliver high rewards. Shares identified for aggressive investing may make it into your portfolio, but they will tend to be short-term investments.

DEFENSIVE INVESTING

Identifying shares

Top down and bottom up

For a general introduction to choosing which shares to invest in it is worth looking at the top-down and bottom-up techniques.

Top-down investors consider the general economic picture, and social and political trends, and they then look at the sectors that are likely to benefit as a result of the conditions, and only then at individual companies within those sectors.

In contrast, bottom-up investors come from the opposite direction and analyse individual companies, their accounts, management and prospects, believing focus can deliver answers. This is fundamental analysis, a subject we examined in Chapter 7.

Top-down investing is an attractive strategy because it appears simple to follow and easy to execute. If a top-down investor believes the oil price is set to rise, perhaps because of conflict in the Middle East or very cold weather in a major economy such as the US, they may buy shares in oil companies. They would argue that the macroeconomic changes behind the higher oil price means that all oil companies are set to benefit and they do not need to research which oil company will benefit most. Their motto could be that a rising tide lifts all boats.

For the bottom-up investor a higher oil price may well be a factor to consider when examining oil companies, but they will look at the fundamental financials behind each company and if these are not right, regardless of macroeconomic factors, they will not invest.

Top-down investing also appeals to common sense. Trends are constantly developing in society and while you may need some economic savvy to understand the implications of falling interest rates, other trends can be easier to spot and understand. Investors who follow the top-down approach point to developments such as the growth of the post-war Japanese economy, ageing populations in the West and increased spending on leisure as the type of trends that can lead investors to buying opportunities.

If, a few years ago, you had recognised the potential for mobile phones and decided to invest in a fledgling stock market-quoted mobile phone company called Vodafone you could have seen enormous returns on your initial investment. Not that calling the mobile phone market would have been that easy. Now that about half the population has a mobile phone it is easy to forget the scepticism of the later 1980s when with phones the size of house-bricks many did not believe they would ever take off. Vodafone is a good example of a company that could only really have been spotted through a top-down investment strategy. Because it was a start-up company and regularly made heavy losses as it rolled out its mobile network, ordinary bottom-up techniques, such as examining earnings figures, would have failed to pinpoint it as a potential investment. The same is true for a lot of high technology companies in telecommunications, electronics, computing and biotechnology, many of which are not expected to make profits for many years. A top-down approach, looking at developments in communications or health concerns, could lead on to identifying companies that are best placed to benefit and which could therefore be a good investment.

Of course, the bottom-up investor would argue that although trends may suggest a company might benefit from them, until it does there is no way of truly assessing its prospects. Thus a rising tide may raise all boats but who is to say whether you have put your money into one that is holed below the waterline? You should also keep an eye on the stock market as a whole, since a rising market could accentuate the gains of any particular sector. A further note of caution on top-down investing is that if everyone recognises the trend and decides to invest in a particular sector it could create a bubble that will sooner or later burst when investors begin taking their profits.

Top-down investing is certainly a tempting strategy for small investors to follow, but you will need to keep your wits about you. It is hard to say it is superior to bottom up or vice versa. Probably the best technique to pursue is a combination of both top-down and bottom-up investing.

Value investing

Closely allied to fundamental analysis is value investing. This is a method that requires great patience – do not expect shares picked through value investing to double in price overnight – but over time the shares identified should offer good returns. At its simplest, value investing involves discovering a company whose shares trade at a discount to the assets of the business. It can also apply to a company whose share rating is below those of comparable companies in the same sector. Value investors seek to buy these shares when they are cheap and sell them when the market has woken up to their underlying value and their share rating more closely matches their asset value.

For many investors value investing appears boring. It takes dedication and single-mindedness to identify undervalued companies and although you may have the belief that the market will eventually rerate the shares, there is no guarantee as to when this will happen. It is truly a philosophical approach to investment and utilises four assumptions.

First, that the value of a company's shares can be directly related to a true value for the company. This value can be calculated by examining its financial figures using the fundamental analysis techniques we looked at earlier.

Second, that shares are priced in the stock market as a result of supply and demand, which can be based on trends or irrational factors such as fear and greed.

Third, because of the way in which the stock market values shares, it is often the case that the share price fails to reflect the value of the company that can be calculated by fundamental analysis.

Fourth, the discrepancy between the company's underlying value and its share price will eventually be recognised by investors and the share price will move towards the former.

Of course, crucial to the concept of value investing is that a true value can be arrived at for a company and we saw when we considered fundamental analysis the various methods of valuing a company. If you feel confident about accurately calculating a company's true value and are prepared to trawl through many hundreds of businesses to find those whose share prices fail to recognise this value then value investing could be for you. But it is important to realise that there are difficulties with the technique.

One of the major problems is that the more investors there are who follow the principles of value investing the fewer undervalued share opportunities there will be. Putting the principles into action has also become a lot easier with the arrival of cheap computer software that can quickly analyse shares, making the information more accessible to a larger number of investors and therefore harder for individuals to find undervalued situations.

Value investing also appears to work best in a falling or bear stock market where valuations are generally low. When the stock market is riding high and all share prices are buoyant it is harder to spot undervalued businesses. Since it predominantly relies for its information about company values from past financial information, the accuracy of future financial forecasts is also a factor to consider. Identifying and purchasing a share can be a long drawn-out process for the value investor and there is no doubt they must be prepared to be in for the long haul once they have made their investment. This makes it an unsuitable strategy for anyone who may want to trade in their shares at short notice to raise cash.

Despite all the problems, though, the strategy does have a good track record of success.

Investing on yield

One comfort for value investors is that while they patiently wait for the market to wake up to the value of their shares and produce a profit for them they are likely to be enjoying an income from a dividend paid by the shares. The amount that a share pays in dividend relative to the price of the share is called the yield and this can often be a healthy sum compared with perhaps the savings rate available in a building society.

Companies may return a high percentage of their profits in the form of a dividend because of the type of business they are. For example, utility companies such as electricity and water businesses often generate a lot of cash and because they do not need to reinvest great sums and their earnings growth is slow but steady, they tend to pay large dividends relative to their share prices.

A company may appear to offer investors a good yield, but since yield is an historic measure based on the last total dividend paid, a high yield could indicate that the market expects the company to cut its dividend. But some companies provide a high yield simply because their share price has fallen, possibly because the company is out of favour with investors, and as a result the historic and forecast dividends are higher in relation to the share price. As long as the forecast dividend is likely to be comfortably smaller than the company's earnings, from which it makes the pay-out, such companies can be attractive to investors. It could be that the share price is temporarily weak and buying the shares makes sense on value-investing grounds. If this is the case, then while you patiently wait for the market to rerate the shares you can enjoy the income from them.

One investment expert has gone further and attempted to identify likely investment winners purely on the basis of their high yield. US investment manager Michael O'Higgins, in his book *Beating the Dow* published in 1991, developed a strategy called Dogs of the Dow based on the US Dow Jones Industrial Average Index of 30 leading US shares. His basic technique involved investing the same amount of money in the ten highest-yielding shares in the index and holding them for a year. Because the DJIA is made up of just 30 blue chip shares the theory suggests that these shares are the highest yielders because they have fallen out of favour and are therefore the dogs of the index – hence the name.

After a year the theory indicates that you should recalculate the ten highest-yielding stocks in the portfolio and sell any of your original ten shares that are no longer in the list, reinvesting the proceeds in the shares that are now in the list. O'Higgins suggested the technique would have delivered greater returns than investing in the index as a whole. He refined it further and added to its risk factor by suggesting investment in just the five highest-yielding shares and then buying just the highest-yielding share of the ten with the second-lowest share price. Both of these, he claimed, offered superior returns, although narrowing the size of your investment obviously creates increased risk.

Although O'Higgins focused on the Dow, his system could equally hold good in the UK, with investors choosing the ten highest-yielding shares in the FTSE 100 index, for example. Since the theory uses only blue chip shares, which are unlikely to go bust it is a relatively risk-free system. Although, as with value investing, there is no guarantee about when the market will wake up and rerate the shares, at least you should enjoy a healthy income while you wait.

Studies have shown that taking the dividend into account along with, hopefully, any rise in the share price of such investments produces a good return. But there are dangers. While it has been proven to work in the UK, companies here are less reluctant to cut dividends than in the US and therefore you should make sure that the companies you choose show no sign of doing so.

The yield figure can also be distorted by share buy-backs, which have become an increasingly popular way of returning cash to shareholders instead of lifting dividends. The theory also only holds true for companies that pay dividends and therefore it ignores many of the so-called new technology and telecom companies that tend to reinvest all their earnings back into their businesses. Some forecasters have suggested that paying dividends will become the preserve of so-called 'old economy' stocks whose low earnings growth will offer at best a slowly increasing share price. If this does happen, a high yield will not necessarily be the signal that a share price has fallen too far and is set to bounce back.

A final problem for the theory is the same danger that faces all investment techniques: they become universally popular. If every investor chose to invest in the ten highest-yielding shares, then simply because of supply and demand the share prices would rise. And if every investor held to the theory and sold in a year's time the share prices would crash. Therefore timing the entry and exit would be more crucial in maximising returns than picking the high-yielding shares in the first place.

Regardless of the pros and cons of the Dogs of the Dow theory, there is a very good reason to invest in high-yielding shares which is if you want your shares to provide an income as much as capital growth. If you are retired, dividends offer a useful and regular income for you and could be more important than capital growth in your shares that could take several years to achieve. Income stocks were sometimes referred to as widows and orphans shares because of the size and reliability of the dividends they paid. But nothing should ever be taken for granted as far as dividends are concerned and the pay-out should be just one factor you consider when making your investment.

Cyclical investing

Shares that have fallen out of favour can provide candidates for the Dogs of the Dow and one reason why they may not attract investor interest is because they are cyclical shares. By these we mean companies whose profits have a tendency to peaks and troughs. As a result, shares in these companies tend to follow the same pattern and rise just ahead and during the good times, and fall just ahead of the periods of lower earnings.

Classic cyclical stocks include construction, property and chemicals companies. These businesses tend to have a serious of tough years followed by a serious of good years. For example, in the chemical industry when demand is strong and prices for its products high, chemical companies expand their capacity. But as more production comes on stream the supply of products meets and then overtakes demand, leading to lower prices and in turn lower profits. Capacity is then shut down and prices begin to recover until additional capacity is added and the cycle is completed.

Some sectors such as chemicals and insurance create their own cycles through capacity or pricing policies, while other such as construction and capital goods – businesses making machinery that is then used to make other things – are more in tune with the general economic cycle, doing well in boom times and suffering in recessions.

Making money from a cyclical stock appears easy: buy just before the upturn in the cycle and sell just before the downturn. This is, of course, easier said than done, but if you can get the timing right you can make big profits.

Specialist knowledge or insight is helpful in predicting when cycles are turning for the better or the worse. It is slightly easier and less risky to call the upturn since buying into a recovery should leave the potential for further gains, whereas calling a downturn relies upon not being duped by short-term weakness in the share price as well as acting quickly enough to get out above the level at which you bought into the share.

The issues of timing involved in cyclical stocks are equally valid for all shares. Knowing when to get in and when to get out is crucial. Wise heads among investors have suggested always leaving something for the next investor, that is sell before you think the share price top may have been reached. Certainly you should never get greedy. Buy shares when they fit your investment strategy and sell before they no longer fit it. With cyclical shares your aim is to buy and sell within a window of opportunity. Buy when you consider the cyclical company you have spotted, which fits your various investment tests, is about to benefit from its sector bouncing back. You should sell when there is much comment in newspapers and elsewhere about the company's recovery, which probably means most investors have spotted it as a cyclical play. Other sale triggers would be the first sign of any weakness in its business, concerns about increased competition or wider issues that might signal a downturn in its sector or the economy at large.

Cyclical shares are not long-term investments; they are what might be termed trading buys. You buy the shares in the expectation that they will rise within a short- to medium-term period and deliver profits that you can then realise by selling the shares.

Recovery plays

Just as investing in cyclical stocks relies on good timing to make profits, so does buying into turnaround or recovery situations.

These are risky investments, but we will look at them under defensive investing since if chosen properly and if they meet certain criteria of value investing and yield considerations they should eventually deliver profits. We are not taking recovery stock to mean any company with a bombed-out share price well below previous highs. The problem with too many recovery situations is that they never recover.

Recovery stocks are once solid companies that have fallen on hard times. It could be because the business has been badly managed or has suffered a big contract loss, or even issued a one-off profits warning. As a result of any of these things investors may have neglected the company's shares, leaving them undervalued in relation to the underlying value of the business and probably trading at just a fraction of their previous highs. Sometimes the problems are insurmountable and the company may not survive, and it is important, although not always easy, to make the distinction between such shares and recovery shares. Companies unlikely to survive are those whose market has dried up, perhaps because of technological changes, or whose competitors have better and cheaper products.

The type of recovery situations you want to find are companies that have a fundamentally sound basic business both in terms of marketplace and products, as well as solid financial figures such as good sales, profits and dividends. There should be an identifiable reason as to why investors have ignored the shares. This may be because previous management took poor decisions or an acquisition went awry. Whatever the reason, it is important that it is no longer a factor and perhaps a new management is in place or the troublesome acquisition is now under control. In fact, changes such as the appointment of new management could provide a signal to buy the shares.

Signals for selling the shares are self-explanatory. Since it was bought for recovery, once this has occurred you should sell. Recovery may be measured by a return to profitable growth, but do not be afraid to take your lead from the share price if it recovers strongly in anticipation that the turnaround has worked.

Contrarian investing

To pursue both recovery situations and cyclical shares, investors must be prepared to buy at or near the bottom of a share price fall. Since a languishing share price indicates that there is no demand from investors for the stock such action involves bucking sentiment or rather the lack of it in the share. Going against the herd, which is stampeding to sell the share, takes bravery but this so-called contrarian investing can be a path to profits.

It seems almost perverse to buy shares that no one else wants, but since share prices are fixed by supply and demand, low demand and plentiful supply due to sellers could offer the opportunity to pick up shares on the cheap. The strategy of swimming against the tide does not pretend it is a good thing to buy a share simply because everyone else is selling or to fly in the face of logic and buy shares in a bad company. You should still decide whether or not a particular share is worth buying because of your own investment rules derived from some of the tests we have suggested. But if the company passes muster, buying its shares because no one else is should boost profits.

Many people buy shares because company sectors are fashionable or trumpeted as the next big thing. With money plunged into shares in these businesses there is less to invest in unfashionable sectors and so prices in these areas can fall. As a result, bargains are to be had. As well as lack of demand, share prices can drop due to bad sentiment and companies can fall out of favour due to factors such as adverse publicity which, although important, may not affect the company's financial health.

Contrarian investing is sometimes also known as bottom fishing since it involves trawling among sunken share prices to find a prize catch abandoned by others.

Blue chips

Although bargain basements are a good place to search for shares worth buying, many risk-averse investors prefer to hunt among the big fish.

Big and consistently strongly performing and well-established companies are called blue chips after the highest-value chip in a casino. Such companies are the constituents of the FTSE 100 index in the UK or the Dow Jones Industrial Average in the US. Blue chip companies may not appear to offer big profits, but you may be surprised at the rewards to be had considering the limited risks involved.

Certainly there are risks associated even with blue chip shares, as investors in engineer Rolls-Royce, which had to be rescued by the government in 1971, and conglomerate Polly Peck, which went bust in the early 1990s, will remember, but larger companies are generally thought of as safer than small companies for private investors. There are two reasons for this.

First, big companies tend to be well established. With a history of profits and dividend payments, they have substantial assets and can weather short-term problems and macroeconomic events such as recessions. They are dependable and generally their share prices tend to rise or fall in line with the stock market.

Second, their shareholders are mainly major institutional investors who keep a close eye on the business and would probably help out by backing a fund-raising if it got into trouble. Also, big companies have long-standing relationships with banks and stockbrokers who again could aid the business in times of trouble. Although these relationships and the reputations of advisers cannot always be relied on, they offer small investors some sense of security when buying shares in blue chips.

While blue chips are reliable and safe investments, and some can offer very good profits growth, they are at the less exciting end of the profits spectrum, although they almost all offer income through dividends. Because big institutional investors often have to buy them under the investment rules of their funds, they are very well researched. That means there is less opportunity for lack of knowledge about the business to create investment opportunities for value investors. This is not to say that the market always gets it right and blue chips can be cyclical and recovery. They are also a relatively safe place to begin if you are starting to invest for the first time.

Defensive shares

Just as blue chips offer a relatively low-risk way into investing, so do defensive stocks.

Shares in companies such as supermarket groups are considered defensive since, the argument goes, whatever is happening in the economy or to the stock market people still need to eat. The same argument can be used for electricity, gas, water and drugs companies. Demand for their products is relatively stable and therefore, regardless of general market conditions and factors such as recessions, they should make it through comparatively unscathed.

Because of the reliability of their earnings these types of companies are unlikely to see their shares shoot up in value, but they often pay a solid dividend and over the medium term their shares tend to perform steadily. Although insulated to some extent against the vagaries of the stock market, defensive shares will inevitably be influenced by its general direction. But because defensive stocks underperform the market, they will fall by less than the market as it tumbles, although their gains will be less when it rises.

As stated above, classic defensive stocks are food retailers and utilities, but some investors also favour sectors such as mortgage banks and brewers. While these do show defensive qualities such as stable demand for their products and low costs, they can be vulnerable depending on the nature of the recession. If an economic downturn is caused by high interest rates the mortgage banks may suffer from a lack of new business, while beer sales may fall because it is seen as a discretionary spend by consumers. These examples show that although certain companies and sectors can be tagged with the defensive label, investors should be careful to understand what they are trying to defend against before buying them indiscriminately.

Follow successful managements

One investment strategy that pays little attention to particular companies is that of following successful management teams. Such a technique does not involve painstaking research into individual businesses or concerns for wider economic issues before plumping for your choice. It simply demands that you find a management team with a proven success rate and hang on to its coat-tails. You might identify the management team from a company you have previously invested in, where they did a good job of creating shareholder value. Or it might be a management team that has shown a good track record of turning businesses round; or perhaps an entrepreneur who has moved into companies and consistently boosted their share ratings through his actions.

We are not talking about good managers who rise up through a company's ranks, hold top jobs and run companies well. The management of a company is one of many factors you should consider when you are weighing the merits of investing in a particular share. You should ask questions about the competence of the management and their commitment to the business. Are they there to serve shareholders' interests by working hard and taking tough decisions, or their own, by taking fat salaries and doing a poor job?

Here we are considering a strategy that involves backing management teams that have a history of creating value in several companies. Often managers or management teams will gain a reputation for delivering results. It could be that they are good at rescuing companies and often banks and institutional shareholders will put them into a troubled company in the hope that they can turn it round. Some managers earn the title of company doctors for their ability to nurse sick businesses back to health. The mere announcement that such managers have been installed can be enough to help revive a struggling company's share price as investors believe their investment has a future.

Other managers who could be worth following are those who have built up a small business into a medium-sized one that has then been taken over. If they decide not to stay with the business they might emerge at another smaller company. It might be worth investing in this business with the expectation that they might do the same again. But this is both the biggest advantage and disadvantage of this strategy. If management can repeat their ability to create value, investors will win, but there is never any guarantee that they can.

Following managers assumes they will lead investors to the same sort of returns as they have delivered before, but this may not be the case. A manager may turn out to be a one-trick pony and may be unable to repeat the success elsewhere. This may be because they were lucky or market conditions helped them first time round, or perhaps they have bitten off more than they can chew or their ability or judgement has weakened. Hanging on to the coat-tails of exceptional managers can be an exciting ride, but it may not always have a satisfactory ending.

Directors' dealings

If following management is a strategy that appeals to you, you should also keep a close eye on their investment in the business. All directors should own shares in their business and often through share options they form a crucial part of management pay packages. Although options and the often low prices at which they can be exercised have attracted a great deal of controversy, they are one way of linking directors' rewards to the success of the company.

An even greater link between directors and the company's fortunes is achieved if management buy shares in the company outside any options or bonus plans. What they do with these shares, adding to them or selling them, can provide useful clues for outside investors considering buying into the company. Private investors set great store by directors' dealings and many newspapers, investment magazines and websites carry details of the latest purchases and sales.

The logic for using directors' dealings as a signal for investors is simple. If directors who run the company think the shares are worth buying they should know and likewise, if directors are selling, they clearly think the share price is high enough. Directors are obliged by law to report any transactions in their own company's shares to the Stock Exchange within five days. Interpreting the action depends on how many shares were involved, whether they were bought or sold, when the transaction took place and which directors were involved. If it was only a small number of shares, whether they were bought or sold is probably of little consequence. Investors should be looking for large numbers of shares worth a material amount of money relative to what the directors earn or a sizeable percentage, say perhaps at least 10 per cent, of their existing holding.

Generally, sales are less of a signal to investors than buys, although they are often taken as a sign to follow suit and take profits. Sales can be for any number of reasons including that the director simply needs to raise some cash, perhaps from cashing in options. However, buys signal a clear belief that the director expects the shares to rise. The timing of any move is also important since directors are forbidden to deal during so-called closed periods, when they have price-sensitive information about the company. As this includes information about its interim and full-year results, there are many months in the course of a year when directors are unable to buy or sell shares. For example, they cannot deal for two months ahead of results. Because of this the timing of any move is not a particularly reliable indicator. But if, for example, a director bought after the share price weakened following results or perhaps a profits warning, investors might view the move as the director showing his or her faith in the company and a belief that the price had fallen too far. You should be careful, however, to make sure the number of shares bought in such circumstances is large. If the purchase is of just a few token shares it could be a device to prop up the share price with a show of confidence.

The number and position of directors who buy or sell shares in their own company can also offer pointers to investors. If only one non-executive director buys shares it is a weak signal, but if the entire board buy shares it is a very strong indication that directors feel the shares are undervalued.

Some investors believe that buying or selling by a company's finance director is a particularly strong signal, arguing that the finance director best understands the company's financial outlook. But it is also worth tracking any director who appears to have a good record of making timely decisions to buy and sell.

Directors' dealings are an interesting signal to watch, although private investors probably rate their importance too highly in determining which shares are worth buying. Use them as one indicator that might underpin your own investment research.

While company insiders do these deals they are not to be confused with insider dealing, which is a criminal offence. Insider dealing occurs when someone in possession of price-sensitive information, which could be anything such as knowledge about an impending bid or that a company's results are going to be worse than expected, either buys or sells shares on the basis of the information or passes it on to someone else to deal. If caught, insider dealers face heavy fines and even imprisonment, but despite the authorities clamping down on the practice in recent years, such cases are notoriously hard to prove. It is of little comfort that insider dealing is probably not as rife as some small investors believe.

One consequence of stricter rules to clamp down on insider trading is that a more level playing field has been created between private investors and the City. It used to be common for companies to tell stockbroking analysts who followed them a great deal about the business. These briefings would often include information that analysts could then distil and make available through their research notes to institutional investor clients. Such briefings are more rare now and often when they do occur the company makes a general statement to the Stock Exchange detailing what was discussed. In this way information, the lifeblood of investment decisions, is made available to all investors at the same time.

Follow the rainmakers

If, as with directors' dealings, you want to put your faith and money into people rather than primarily considering the merits of a company, you could always try following the investing superstars. These rainmakers, so called after the highly prized members of Native American tribes that were said to be able to bring the rain, include investment gurus and highly successful fund mangers.

There are two ways to follow them. Either adopt their theories or follow their leads. Among the legendary investors of the last hundred years are Benjamin Graham, Warren Buffett, George Soros and T. Rowe Price. We shall consider them and their theories in a later chapter, but the argument goes that if their investing techniques worked for them, maybe they will work for you.

A simpler method is to follow the lead of professional investors whom you admire or who have a successful track record. These could be fund managers or high-profile private investors, some of whom write newspaper columns. The simplicity of this technique is that if they buy shares in a company, all you have to do is follow suit and sit tight. The major advantage of this method over others is that it requires very little work except in reacting quickly to news that your chosen investment star has made his or her move. Following rainmakers may look simple enough, but getting results as a private investor is no easy matter.

We shall deal with the investment theorists in Chapter 11, but for now it is enough to say that while the theories are of interest and well worth trying, some were creatures of their time. By all means consider and experiment with them but the theory you need to develop is your own, which is suited to your particular risk-and-reward profile.

As far as following professional investors is concerned there are plenty of pitfalls to avoid. Professional investors may have more time and resources than you to devote to checking out the investment merits of companies, but that does not always mean they get them right. You will do well if you follow one of their successful share selections, but follow one of their duds and you will do badly.

Any share picked by a fund manager will also be just one out of as many as 100 shares that they manage in their fund, so if it falls in value it may well be counterbalanced by another share that has risen in value. It is wise for you to follow this portfolio approach and it is outlined below, but picking just one share because the fund manager has chosen it is a risky business. The weight you should put on fund managers' selections is also dependent on what type of fund they run. Among the most productive to follow are those who specialise in taking stakes in undervalued companies and then agitating for change at those companies. This might involve replacing management and changing strategy or even finding a buyer for the business. Companies whose share register includes these so-called shareholder activists are worth watching.

The importance of a balanced portfolio

Whatever techniques you find work best for you in choosing shares, you then face the decision of how many shares you want to buy and in how many companies.

One of the soundest pieces of investment advice is that you should never put all your eggs in one basket. In terms of investing in individual shares this means you should build up a portfolio of shares. This should give you safety in numbers. While it is unlikely that all shares in the portfolio will increase in value at the same rate, it is also unlikely all will fall in value. Spreading your investment across a number of companies and sectors should bring some defensive qualities to your investment strategy.

For example, you could have a mixture of lower-risk blue chip shares across a range of sectors such as retail, utilities and banks, combined with a spread of higher-risk smaller-company or technology shares.

It is very important to decide how many shares you want to invest in and the amount you want to invest – the weighting of an individual share in the portfolio – in each share. This is very much a personal decision and depends on your risk-and-reward profile.

It also depends on how much money you have to invest. While you can start buying individual shares with as little as a few hundred pounds, to generate meaningful returns and take into account the initial impact of dealing charges and other costs you should consider a minimum investment of £500 to £1000 in a share. The amount you have to invest is also an important factor in deciding how many shares there are in your portfolio.

In addition, remember that investing in individual shares demands that you keep a close eye on your investments. Obviously, the more shares there are in your portfolio the harder it is to follow each company. Depending on the amount of time you have to devote to investing, you should perhaps consider developing a portfolio of at least half a dozen shares, but a maximum of no more than 20. Many experts believe the optimum size for a portfolio is 10 to 12 shares. You do not have to buy them all at once, but aiming for a portfolio of a dozen stocks is a useful target. It is a manageable number of shares in terms of being able to keep an eye on your investments and it should offer enough opportunities to diversify your holdings between higher-risk and lower-risk shares, and across a range of sectors. At worst it means that if a company you invest in goes bust you will not be too badly hit overall because you have other shares.

The ability to construct portfolios containing just a handful of shares gives private investors considerable advantages over professional fund managers. These people who run investments for pensions funds and other institutions often have hundreds of investments. Not only are they harder to keep track of, but since your first investment is likely to be your strongest buy, the more shares you invest in the weaker becomes the case for buying. This is an obvious fact, since when you search for a share to buy and research numerous companies against your investment criteria some will match it more closely than others. Buying shares in the closest match is easily justified, but as you buy shares in the next-closest match your investment case is weakening. The main justification for doing so is because of the security of spreading your risk.

As well as deciding the overall amount you have to spend and the number of shares you wish to contain in your portfolio you should decide the weighting of individual shares within the selection. It could be that you decide to invest the same amount in every share or invest more in your top choice. But however you decide to slice your investment cake it is probably a good idea, in order to maintain the defensive balance of the portfolio, not to have any single share accounting for more than 15 per cent of the total value of the portfolio. It is possible a very successful share could grow in value to become a dominant one, but that is a different matter and becomes something to be considered in the management of your portfolio.

Having decided how much you have to invest and in how many shares, you should consider how your portfolio should be structured. Academics have come up with what they term 'Modern Portfolio Theory' to cover the concept of risk and return when investing in shares. Risk and return can be judged against putting your money in other places such as a bank deposit, as well as individual shares being measured against the stock market as a whole or a particular index.

We looked at the concept of risk and reward in an earlier chapter and it is at the heart of all investment decisions. Modern Portfolio Theory accepts the benefits of spreading risk and seeks to evaluate the risk profile of individual shares and then calculate how they move against each other in order to produce the best possible combination. This is defined as a portfolio that gives an investor the highest possible return for an accepted level of risk.

The key to MPT is efficient diversification. It argues that to hold, say, six retail shares is far riskier than holding half a dozen shares from six different sectors. This is clearly true, since if high street spending were to fall sharply and your portfolio contained only retailers they could all be expected to fall in value. However, if you had just one retail share in your portfolio the drop in that share would be less damaging.

Clearly, the larger the number of shares in your portfolio the wider the risk of any one share underperforming is spread, but as we have seen, there are practical limitations on the number of shares you can and should own.

Careful choice of shares can help alleviate risk and produce balance. A classic example is buying shares in a company that makes sunglasses and one that makes raincoats. In simplistic terms, when it is sunny shares in the sunglasses company should do well and those in the raincoat company should fall, but when the weather is wet the performance should be reversed. Obviously these shares will not both do well at the same time, but neither will they both do badly.

But no matter how carefully you choose shares they will be affected by movements in the stock market as a whole. Portfolio theory does, however, offer a solution to minimise the risk. It uses a system known as beta that measures how much a single share follows the performance of the stock market as a whole. A company's beta is derived as a result of painstaking research into how its share price has performed against the stock market over time. Fortunately, the figure is available in some publications and on some Internet sites, because it would be too time-consuming for small investors to work out. The beta measures the return on a particular share versus the return on the stock market, which is said to have a beta of one. If the stock market moves by X per cent, a share can be expected to move by X per cent multiplied by its beta. If the stock market as whole rises by 10 per cent a share with a beta of 2 should rise by 20 per cent and if the stock market falls by 10 per cent the share should fall by 20 per cent.

But if a share has a beta of less than 1, say 0.7 per cent, then although if the market rises by 10 per cent the share will only rise by 7 per cent, if the market were to fall by 10 per cent the share should only drop 7 per cent. Clearly a portfolio made up of high beta shares would be aggressive, enjoying stronger rises than the market when shares in general were up, but bigger falls when they were down.

On the other hand a portfolio made up of low betas would be defensive, since although it would not rise as high as the market generally in an upturn, nor would it fall as far if shares went into reverse. High beta shares tend to be high-growth companies, while low beta shares are slow-growing businesses.

Of course, beta is not an absolutely foolproof method since if it were investing would simply be a question of deciding how much risk you wanted to take on board together with a view of the general direction of the market. Lots of other factors are responsible for moving a share price, so do not rely entirely on betas when assembling your portfolio, but they are certainly one factor you should take into account.

Managing your shares

Having established your portfolio of shares, you must then know how to manage it to maximise returns and minimise losses. It is no good simply setting up your portfolio and expecting the profits to start rolling in. You need to decide a number of important things such as when you will sell, buy or add to existing holdings. How long you want to invest for and what you want to do with any income, such as dividends, generated by the portfolio.

Stop-loss systems

Whether or not you choose to operate a portfolio or simply invest in a single share, one of the most important lessons to learn is to run with your profits and cut your losses. It is very hard to invest without sentiment. No matter how dispassionately you try to invest, the common failing of small investors is that they allow their hearts to rule their heads. Hence, if a share rises in value, they want to sell and take profits, but if it falls in value they believe it is a temporary dip that will be corrected and indeed could represent a buying opportunity.

Sometimes their reaction can be correct. If a share rises sharply in value it can be worth taking profits and sometimes when a share price falls it is a short-term weakness and adding to a holding can be a wise move. But it can also be the wrong thing to do. As you buy shares with the expectation that they will rise, why sell after they have risen since the price might be rising higher still? And why buy more shares when those you own have fallen in value? Just because a share looks cheap does not mean it cannot get cheaper. Catching a falling knife is dangerous.

One method of taking the sentiment out of such investment decisions is to operate a stop-loss system that seeks to lock in profits and cut losses. A stop-loss is a limit that you place on the amount you are prepared to lose on a share as a percentage of its purchase price. If the share price falls below this level you sell the share and if the share price rises the stop-loss limit rises with it.

The amount of the stop-loss depends on your own risk profile and also the risk profile of the share. If you are a cautious investor you are likely to want tight stop-loss limits and if you have a higher risk threshold you will accept a looser limit. If you are investing in a traditionally stable blue chip share you might consider a tight stop-loss limit, but if the investment is in a volatile smaller-company or technology stock a wider limit might be acceptable.

There is no hard-and-fast rule as to what a stop-loss limit should be but perhaps 25 per cent is a good starting point for most investors. This means that if you buy a share that costs 100p and its value falls to 75p you should sell it. If its value keeps rising, the stop-loss limit should be raised along with the increase, so if the price reached 150p you should sell if it then fell 25 per cent to 112.5p. In this way you have at least locked in some of your gains.

The logic for the stop-loss system is that if a share has weakened by as much as 25 per cent there is serious downward pressure on the share price and it might fall further. By selling the share once it has dropped 25 per cent you are crystallising a loss, but you might be saving yourself from greater losses. While a 25 per cent loss is painful, it is a lot easier to stomach than a 50 per cent to greater loss. To make money out of shares you do have at least to stay in the game with some capital to invest.

Although the stop-loss limit should be viewed as an automatic trigger you should always try to understand why the share has fallen and turned what was a share worth buying into one it is necessary to sell. In some cases, perhaps with a profits warning from a company which is often severely punished by the stock market in the form of a savage cut in the share price, the fall may be so swift that you have no time to sell at a 25 per cent loss as the share price quickly drops further, but in these cases you should get out as quickly as you can.

Share prices seldom recover overnight from a profits warning, although sometimes there is short-term buying in the belief the fall has gone too far. This slight and often temporary rally is known as a dead-cat bounce. There will be examples when the price drop has been overdone and even though the price is below your stop-loss you may feel the share is worth holding on to. But these occasions should be rare.

If you choose to operate a stop-loss system, while you do not have to be a slave to it you should try to force yourself to follow it. The limits you set will not always be right, but the times when are should more than compensate for the times when they are not.

The stop-loss system enables investors to cut losses and run with profits. This is a key to successful investing, but too often human nature is to take profits and stick with falling shares because losses are painful. Stop-losses can save investors from their own worst enemy, themselves.

In the US most stockbrokers offer an automatic stop-loss system for shares that you hold in an account with them. This means that the moment the share price drops below your predetermined stop-loss limit it is sold. The automatic facility means sales can be achieved far more quickly than through manual monitoring of the share price and this gives an added level of security. Such systems are rare among UK brokers, although there is increasing demand for them from retail investors.

Reinvest dividends

While stop-loss systems are one way to maximise your returns, another method with proven efficiency is to reinvest dividend income. Some investors will choose shares for the dividends they offer and use the cash pay-outs simply as income, but if you want your portfolio to grow in value one of the most efficient ways to achieve this is to reinvest dividends.

The Barclays *Equity-Gilt Study* illustrates the importance of dividend reinvestment. It shows that £100 invested in equities in 1899 would have grown to just £260 once adjusted for inflation over the course of the next 100 years. But had the dividend income been reinvested the fund would have grown to £24,962, some 96 times larger. Ignoring the impact of inflation, £100 invested in 1899 without reinvesting income would be worth £13,396 and with income reinvested it would be worth £1,285,872.

Clearly, reinvested income accounts for a major proportion of the total return from a share. One reason for this is that company dividends tend to rise over time so the amount increases as a proportion of the original purchase price of the share. Further returns may also be generated because the additional shares bought through the reinvested dividends can also increase in value and produce dividends.

The concept behind the possible big increases in value when dividend income is reinvested is the theory of compounding. Albert Einstein once described compound interest as 'the greatest invention of all time'. And compounding is certainly regarded as a wonder by many investors.

At its heart is a simple concept. If you have £10,000 and increase it by 10 per cent in a year it will be worth £11,000, a rise of £1000. If you then grow the enlarged sum by 10 per cent in the next year the total is £12,100, an increase of £1100. After 10 years of annual growth of 10 per cent your initial £10,000 would be worth a shade under £26,000.

The benefits of compounding are clear and there are several ways in which you can reinvest dividend income. The most general way of doing so is to take your dividend from a company and use it to buy more shares in that company. A simpler method is if the company you invest in offers shareholders a dividend reinvestment plan whereby the company uses the cash dividend to buy shares in the market and allot them to shareholders. Although there will be a small charge for shareholders, it will be less than if investors had bought the shares themselves. An even more efficient way of reinvesting dividends is to take the pay-out in the form of a scrip dividend. This is when the company issues new shares instead of paying a dividend. Although in the past there have been tax advantages for companies in paying scrip dividends, recent changes in the tax laws has made such payments less attractive. You could always use cash dividends from one company to buy shares in another. This can be an efficient way to produce new capital to grow your portfolio rather than inject additional cash from your own pocket into it.

Buy and hold

Reinvesting dividend income assumes you hold the share long enough to earn the dividend and the full benefits of the strategy are only realised by holding the share and earning the dividends for several years.

The strategy of buy and hold is an important one to follow when constructing a portfolio and the most obvious benefit is in allowing reinvested dividends to compound returns. But it also has several other advantages including making portfolios easy to manage and minimises the timing risk of investments. Although even with a buy-and-hold strategy you should keep an eye on share prices to see whether they fall below your stop-loss limit, you do not need to watch the share price in the same hawkish way you would if trying to make a quick return on the share. Indeed, your stop-loss limit on a buy-and-hold share may well be much greater than on other shares in your portfolio. This makes a buy-and-hold share a low-maintenance share for investors to own.

Candidates for a buy-and-hold strategy can be more diverse than may be thought. Blue chip companies with a history of good management, reliable earnings growth and steady dividends make ideal buy-and-hold shares. The shares should offer capital growth and with reinvested dividends total returns can be very strong. But some more speculative shares may be worth buying and holding, particularly if it is a company such as a biotech business where a new drug may take many years to prove its importance. The share price may be very volatile in the short term, but in the long run the company will either prove itself or fail. Such investments are risky, since you must be prepared to lose everything, but only by holding for a long period will you stand a chance of owning the shares at the point when they may eventually deliver value. Growth shares, that is companies that deliver earnings growth rising faster than the market, should also be bought and held, although their potential for falling rapidly if it emerges that their growth is slowing makes them an aggressive rather than a defensive investment and they are outlined below.

Quite how long you should hold any share after you buy depends, as ever, on your individual circumstances and also the company. A typical investment horizon for a buy and hold is three to five years, a period of time that should avoid short-term volatility in the share price, as well as undue influence from the wider stock market, which could hold back the share if it is in the doldrums. A lesser time period and the share is more of a trading buy – a strategy detailed below – since few dividends will be earned and you will have to contend with general market conditions. But a buy-and-hold share can also be owned for many, many years and obviously the longer it is held – as long as dividend and capital growth are consistent – the greater the compound reward.

Perhaps one of the most efficient aspects of a buy-and-hold strategy is that you do not have to worry unduly about the timing of your investment strategy in terms of buying or selling the share. While timing is of crucial importance in maximising returns, the chances of correctly calling the bottom of the share price, in order to buy at the lowest level, or the top of the share price, in order to sell, is remote. By investing in a share you believe that its value will increase over time and even though the increase is unlikely to be a smooth, straight line, as long as the overall trend is upwards it does not matter when you join that trend. Over time the point at which you bought should prove to be lower on the line than a future point at which you can sell. But by trying to choose when to buy, on dips, and when to sell, on peaks, you could lose heavily if you get your timing wrong.

The ability of buy and hold to ignore the peaks and troughs of the market is best illustrated by considering an investment in the stock market as whole. While in the last 100 years the stock market has risen steadily, there have been times such as the market crash in 1929, the bear market in the early 1970s and the slump in 1987 when share prices have fallen. By moving in and out of the market your timing could have meant you bought before one of these slumps and your returns would have been hit, but by holding through them all your returns would definitely have increased. In fact, £100 invested in shares in 1918 would now be worth £1 million, ignoring the impact of inflation and assuming all dividends reinvested. But if you were out of the market for the 10 worst downturns during the period the fund would be worth £6.5 million. However, if you were out of the market for the 10 best months during the period the fund would only be worth £160,000.

Therefore a buy-and-hold strategy would have meant you missed the maximum return, but it would also have rewarded you a lot more than if your timing had been poor.

Pound-cost averaging

One investment strategy that can complement buy and hold is pound-cost averaging. If used properly it is a way of reducing risk, but it can be a dangerous and expensive technique if used wrongly.

Pound-cost averaging is a long-term strategy whereby you invest the same amount of money in a share at regular intervals such as every three months or every six months. It does not matter what the price of the share is when you buy, just as long as you invest the same amount of money at regular intervals.

The technique means that when the share price is low the fixed sum you invest buys more shares and you get more for your money. And when the share price is high your fixed investment buys fewer shares, so you get fewer shares for your money. But over the long term you will find that the cost of each share is lower than the average price per share during the investment period provided the value of the share has increased overall. Pound-cost averaging works best when pursued over a long period. Some experts suggest buying should be continued for between 7½ to 10 years since over the last century stock market corrections have occurred on average every 2½ years. Investing over 10 years or possibly three of these downturns should maximise rewards.

Although pound-cost averaging, which is simply a UK version of the dollar-cost averaging system developed in the US, works best for collective investments such as unit trusts where your regular investment buys more units when prices are low and fewer when prices are high, it can be adapted easily for individual shares. Its advantages are that you do not have to have a large lump sum to begin investing and it limits risk by drip-feeding money into shares, which should help overcome the problem of mistiming your investment.

But as an investment strategy it is not without its problems. The technique could prove prohibitively expensive to adopt by small investors because each time you buy a new parcel of shares you will incur dealing costs. The system also limits profits in a share that shows a sharply rising price trend with only small reversals since your average purchase price will be higher than if you had invested an initial lump sum.

The other major disadvantage with the technique is that it is too often used by investors to try to recoup losses. An investor may buy 1000 shares in a company at 100p each because they believe the share price will rise since the company is good business. If the share price falls to 75p, rather than follow their stop-loss limit and sell, they may decide if the share was cheap at 100p it must be cheaper still at 75p and buy 1000 more shares. Their argument is that although they have now spent £1750 on shares in the company the average price they have paid is £1750 divided by 2000, which equals 87.5p a share. Therefore all the share price needs to do is rise above 87.5p for them to be back in profit. The logic appears sound until you realise there may be nothing to stop the share price falling even further, in which case they may have wasted a further £750 instead of limiting their loss to just £250. Of course, you must judge every investment situation on its merits and there may be rare exceptions to the rule and times when following such a strategy is justified, but generally throwing good money after bad is a poor way to invest.

Trading buys

While there are considerable advantages for small investors in having buy-and-hold shares in their portfolio there should also be room for more speculative shares that may be termed trading buys.

Trading buys are broadly those shares that you believe will rise in value in the short term. This could be for many reasons such as bid rumours, undervalued companies that are ripe for a rerating or momentum investing where a stock or sector, such as Internet companies, suddenly becomes fashionable and investors pile into the share.

Although these are aggressive investments and are examined in more detail below, a well-balanced portfolio should allow space for some high-risk shares that add a bit of fun and excitement to share investing. While when it comes to a trading buy the short term could be anything from a day to six months or more, such shares can still be put into a portfolio. They will inevitably increase the overall risk profile of the portfolio but the presence of other more defensive shares to balance the purchase should mean that you will not have risked everything on the punt. Also, a trading buy is a short-term position, so if the rerating does not happen and the share price remains flat you could find the share in your portfolio for some time. Stop-losses on a trading buy should be tight, since you have bought the share in the belief that it will rise in the short term. If it falls, you will want to admit your mistake and exit quickly with minimal losses.

Aggressive Investing

You should have realised by now that investing is all about balancing risk with reward and the higher the level of risk you are prepared to embrace the greater the potential reward. All investment in single shares is inherently risky although following a number of the defensive investment strategies detailed above will help to reduce the risk. But some of you will want to take on risk in the expectation of earning the high rewards that can accompany it. For you the following aggressive investment techniques are worth examining.

Growth investing

This philosophy is at the heart of aggressive investing and growth investments contrast sharply with value investments. While value investors patiently trawl through fundamental analysis to detect undervalued companies in steady reliable sectors offering good dividends and consistent earnings, growth investors rush for what they judge will be the next big thing. Value investors look for shares that are cheap compared with the assets of the company, while growth investors look for shares with strong earnings growth.

In its purest form, growth investing is about uncovering exceptional companies whose profits and therefore share price will outperform the market over a long period. The idea is to pick an acorn such as a Microsoft or Glaxo and watch it grow into a mighty oak. But that definition of patient growth investing has waned and now the concept is more readily understood as meaning any investment that can deliver a fast return almost regardless of the fundamentals of the companies targeted for investment. Often this means a company whose shares can deliver capital growth rather than income.

Spotting these types of shares contrasts with the way in which value investments are identified. Value investments are found using quantitative techniques, where investors examine the numbers such as cash flow and asset values. Growth investing relies on qualitative techniques where investors make value judgements about a company based on an appraisal of its products, management and markets. The need to examine and judge these criteria for growth stocks is often because such companies have yet to make a profit and therefore there are no earnings figures to examine. Such businesses may be telecom companies that have yet to make a profit because they have invested heavily in building a network which, once up and running, should deliver earnings.

Great growth shares appear to emerge in two distinct ways. Either they are linked to technological changes or they become dominant players in their sector.

New technologies ranging from the railways in the nineteenth century to computers at the end of the twentieth have always produced companies that have made huge profits. Hanging on to the coat-tails of one of these growth companies is a route to riches, but the investment needs to be closely watched. Computer company IBM dominated the mainframe market, but its leading position in the computer industry was lost with the rise of personal computers and the importance of software over hardware. Canny growth investors would have switched out of IBM and into Microsoft at the first sign of IBM's growth rate weakening. But growth industries are by no means certain to throw up growth companies. Sometimes competition is so intense and barriers to entry so low that companies find it difficult to grow profits strongly, however exciting the growth of their industry.

Dominating a particular business sector, which in itself does not need to be a dramatic growth area, can also create the conditions for a growth company to emerge. Coca-Cola, for example, dominates the global soft drinks industry and has expanded internationally for many years. The use of strong distribution networks or a franchise system appears crucial if a company is to achieve a dominant position in a niche sector.

The strategies of great growth investors such as American fund manager Peter Lynch and Britain's Jim Slater will be considered in a later chapter, but it is useful to outline here signals for buying and selling growth shares.

Identifying a growth stock requires the same sort of dedication to research as does value investing. You need to find a company with a strong earnings record that is forecast to continue growing on the back of increasing prices for its products or increasing sales volumes. It needs to be well managed and resourced with good products and a position in its market that gives it an edge over competitors.

Choosing when to buy a growth stock depends on when you identify it, but the trick is to buy it as early as possible since this will multiply any gains. Clearly, if you buy a growth stock at 10p a share and it rises to 100p you have made ten times your original investment, but if you buy it at 20p a share then at 100p your investment has only grown five times. The ultimate growth stock would be one that keeps growing and therefore all you need do is buy it, sit tight and watch your investment increase in value. But this is an unrealistic prospect, so it is important to consider when to sell such a share.

As with any share, it is important to run with profits and cut losses, so again a stop-loss system would be useful as a way of limiting losses. But growth stocks are particularly vulnerable to certain triggers, which can cause them to fall so sharply that unless you are watching very carefully the price may quickly drop below the stop-loss limit. The lesson here is that such companies do need to be watched closely for any evidence that their growth story is coming to an end.

At one extreme this could be a profits warning, but it could also be a downbeat trading or annual meeting statement. It could be the emergence of competition that threatens to take sales away from the company or perhaps the resignation of a key director, such as a founder of the company. Since growth investing depends heavily on sentiment, anything that might count against the company is a potential trigger for the shares to fall in value.

That said, growth investing is a test of nerve and you should be sure that a situation has changed fundamentally before selling. Just as holding on to a growth stock when its growth starts slowing is a bad move, so can be selling too early. Sometimes a growth stock may have shown tremendous gains over a few years convincing the investor to sell, but unless the outlook for the share or sentiment in the company has changed for the worse you could be missing out on even more profits.

Small companies

A fertile hunting ground for growth investors is among so-called small-cap stocks, those with a tiny stock market value. Research in both the British and American markets has shown that companies with small stock market capitalisations produce better returns than bigger companies. By small we mean companies with a stock market value, derived from their share price multiplied by the number of shares in issue, of at most £250 million and probably a lot less. These companies may be listed on the Alternative Investment Market or the main stock market when they will be included in the FTSE SmallCap Index.

There are clear reasons why they should outperform their larger cousins. Smaller companies tend to be those that are just starting out and therefore have the potential to grow from a small base, multiplying any gains. They are also often under-researched by financial experts and may have only a limited number of institutional investors, if any at all. Because not many people know about the company the stock market is not very good at accurately placing a value on it. This can mean it is cheap, but it also means that private investors often get to spot these shares first.

As we have seen above, blue chip shares rarely increase rapidly in value – elephants do not gallop – but smaller companies can move up in value very quickly. Of course, they can also go in the other direction and being small are more vulnerable to market downturns and changes in investor sentiment, which is why they are an aggressive investment strategy.

Potential problems faced by smaller companies include access to capital, since it often costs these businesses more than larger concerns to borrow money to finance their plans. They may also have untried management teams who may not be able to cope as the company expands. They may have a problem raising their profile, so they do not appear on the investment radar of potential buyers and there is little demand to drive the share price. Also, small companies have a lower level of corporate activity than a larger business so the news flow, the lifeblood of any share but particularly for a smaller company, is limited. Sometimes it is restricted to just half-year and final results, with the occasional trading statement and deal. Shares in small companies can also be tightly held by just a few investors, perhaps including founders or their families. With only a small number of shares available for other investors, known as a small free float of shares, the share price and volume of shares traded can be volatile. At worst this can even mean that you may have trouble finding a buyer for your shares if you try to sell. Shares in smaller companies can also have what is know as a large spread, that is a big difference between the buying and selling price of the share.

Make no mistake, investing in smaller companies is risky. While they may perform better than larger ones over time, there is no guarantee that the particular smaller company share you choose will do so. But if you do get it right the rewards can be great.

Penny stocks and shell companies

If the smaller companies sector excites you, you might want to explore the even riskier side that comprises penny shares and shell companies.

A penny share is one that trades below a certain price which could be as high as 50p but tends to be below 20p and even just a couple of pence. The companies themselves can be quite large, perhaps worth as much as £100 million, but because they have a large number of shares in issue the value of each is low and the spread between the buying and selling price will be 10 per cent or more. They are often companies that have fallen on hard times and need fundamental changes in their business, such as new management, to start motoring again. In this regard they may be looked upon as recovery plays.

Penny shares tend to react to company-specific information,

rising on good news or prospects and falling on negative information or lack of news, rather than being influenced by the general
direction of the stock market. Their main appeal for small investors
is psychological and that is what makes them risky. It appears to be
common sense that a share valued at 5p could easily double to 10p
and therefore you would double your investments. But it seems less
likely that a major company with a share price of 400p would see it
double to 800p.

This is a dangerous assumption and many small investors fall
into the trap. The share price alone means nothing. It is entirely
possible that a company with a 5p share price might see it rise to
10p, but it could also fall to 2.5p, halving your investment. In
isolation a company's share price tells you nothing. You need to
consider the business behind it and its potential for recovery before
deciding a penny share is a risk worth buying. Shares can easily be
expensive at 5p and cheap at 400p.

Sometimes penny shares have fallen so far in value and their
business has shrunk to such a degree that among their most valuable
assets is their stock market listing. In these cases the companies can
be described as **shell companies**. They are more or less empty vessels
waiting for new management and new businesses to be injected into
them. If there is an existing business it is normally sold and the ideal
is to have a clean shell, that is a company that has no debt and no
businesses. The new management is able to use the stock market
listing to issue new shares to raise cash or as a currency to buy
businesses that are often privately held. These businesses will
normally be worth more than the quoted shell acquiring them and
such deals are known as reverse takeovers. Often the businesses
belong to the new entrepreneurial management, but perhaps
because they do not have a long enough trading record are unable to
get a stock market listing through the traditional route. The
injection of new blood and businesses is often enough to drive the
shell's share price higher, increasing its value as a currency and
enabling it to pull off more deals.

The success rate of shell companies is patchy, but those that do succeed can offer very high returns to investors who bought early enough. The classic example of a successful shell involves advertising guru Martin Sorrell who turned shopping trolley maker WPP into the world's biggest advertising group. More recently the involvement of a group of highly regarded retailers, including former Asda supermarket boss Archie Norman, sent shares in shell company Knutsford soaring, although the share price later fell when the shell did not prove to be the retail acquisition vehicle many had hoped for.

The earlier investors can get involved with a shell company the greater the potential rewards, but as with the downside on all share investing there will also be a greater risk. High-risk investors may want to jump the gun by trying to identify potential shells and getting in at the basement rather than even the ground level.

Potential shell companies have certain characteristics that you should look for. They will tend to be small market cap companies with a value of perhaps just a couple of million pounds. They will be drifting in business terms, with operations that are not large enough to grow the company and they will not have much, if any, debt.

Trying to spot a shell company is fraught with danger since even if one fits the criteria there is no certainty it will be adopted as a shell and you might sit on your investment for a very long time as you wait. If it never becomes a shell you could well lose everything.

Slightly more cautious investors will wait until a shell company has been identified and management moved in. Some investors have developed a reputation for finding shell companies, which they then market to potential management teams or employ to generate fees if the companies are used in reverse takeovers. The term 'shellmeister' has been coined for these people and their presence on a company's share register is a useful signal to private investors that the company may become a shell.

After the shell has been identified and management moved in, the next stages in reducing the risk in what will always be a risky strategy will be speculation about a deal, then the deal itself and finally investing once the deal has been completed and the company and the management have had several months of trading behind them.

Making money out of shell companies is not easy, but if it is a strategy that appeals to you then one way to reduce your risk is to invest in several potential shells, increasing the chances that one will be transformed into a winner.

Special situations

Investing in a shell is an example of a special situation that you may be able to take advantage of for gain. Other special situations might include bid targets or bid situations and corporate changes such as demergers, new management or strategic reviews.

Bids

When a stock market-listed company is taken over the acquirer nearly always pays a premium to the share price of its target. The premium is a form of compensation to the shareholders in the company being bought for them giving up future dividends and capital growth in the company for an immediate lump sum.

If it is a friendly takeover, that is it is supported by the board of the company being bought, the premium may not be that high. Indeed, if the currency used is shares the agreed deal is basically a merger of the two businesses and in recent years so-called nil-premium mergers have proved popular. With these deals no premium is deemed necessary since both sets of shareholders will continue to share in the dividends and potential capital growth of the enlarged group. That said, investors should not be afraid to take at least some profits following a merger since research has shown that integrating two business cultures into one new company is not easy and often leads to weakness in the new group's share price.

But not all takeovers are friendly and hostile bids, particularly when more than one bidder emerges, can force up the share price of the company being targeted quite sharply and often the winning bidder is forced to pay a considerable premium. Spotting potential bid targets is therefore an aggressive investment tactic and several types of company can be readily identified as takeover targets.

The most obvious candidate for a takeover is an undervalued company. Value investing should show if a company's stock market valuation is below that of its peers or the stock market generally. If it is and investors fail to recognise this and buy its shares, the share price will remain subdued. In that case it will appeal to a bidder who may be able to get a bargain even if it pays a premium for the shares. Such companies can fall to rivals, financial buyers or even their own managements.

Poorly performing companies can also be takeover targets provided the reason for their poor showing is a short-term one, such as temporary weakness in their markets, or bad management. A bidder may be attracted to the company because it believes it can resolve the problems. Companies that have survived a hostile take-over attempt, but where the predator still retains a sizeable stake, also have a high chance of facing another bid once the year-long freeze on such a move, which is required under Takeover Panel rules, expires. As with shell companies, even if a company fits all the criteria of being a bid target there is no certainty it will receive an offer and you could be stuck with a shareholding in a lowly valued or underperforming company. So this is a risky strategy.

But if you have successfully identified a takeover target and the company does receive a cash bid you must then decide whether to sell the shares in the market or wait for the outcome of the bid and, if it is successful, take the cash from the bidder.

Selling the shares in the market will incur dealing charges and the share price is likely to be at least a couple of pence below the offer price, reflecting the risk premium of waiting for the deal to be completed. But by selling you will benefit from the higher share price in the face of the bid and you will be able to bank some money. Although it is unusual for an agreed bid to fail it can happen, and hostile bids can be seen off and are usually followed by a fall in the share price of the targeted company.

By waiting for the outcome of a successful bid you will receive the full offer price for the shares, which will include the takeover premium and will not incur any dealing costs. In a hostile-bid situation where there is more than one bidder, timing can be crucial if you are not prepared to wait for the final outcome, but want to sell in the market. If, for example, there is one bid already on the table and another higher offer emerges you must decide whether you believe it is a knock-out blow, or whether the first bidder will return with a still higher offer. If it does increase the value of its bid the question is whether the second bidder will be prepared to increase its offer.

Bids that develop into auctions are very good news for shareholders in the target company, although not always for investors in the company that eventually wins, since it may have overpaid as a result of the battle.

Demergers

Another special situation that aggressive investors can profit from is if they can identify companies that are likely to demerge businesses. This occurs when a company decides to hive off one of its operations and often does so by offering free shares to existing shareholders that are then listed on the stock market. This can give an investor two shareholdings for the price of one and the history of demergers shows they are quite efficient at creating value. Companies such as Racal, ICI and British Gas have all delivered considerable shareholder value through demergers.

Companies worth looking at for demerger potential are conglomerates, which are groups with diverse business operations that have become deeply unpopular in the age of business, and utilities such as electricity companies that often have other businesses such as service operations or telecom arms which might be spun off.

If focus is a route to shareholder value, demergers may deliver healthy rewards, although one downside can be that investors are left with very small and uneconomic shareholdings in the demerged businesses.

Demergers are not a cast-iron certainty to deliver value,

although their record is good and companies that might demerge operations are certainly worth a look.

New management

When new management moves into a company there are likely to be changes that could create value for investors. News flow, particularly in smaller companies, moves share prices and new management is one of the most important changes a company can make. New management might be appointed because existing managers are retiring or it could signal a change of the old guard, or it could follow a boardroom coup where former directors are ousted. But whatever the reason for the new management the odds are that it signals change. A company with new management may enjoy an initial jump in its share price as investors decide to buy on the expectation that the changes will be for the good. The share price may then drift as it waits for the new management to outline its strategy. The third stage is the pronouncement of the strategy and the verdict of the stock market, which could see the shares rise even higher or fall if the path ahead outlined by management disappoints.

Strategic reviews: One of the first things a new management team is likely to do when it takes over at a company is to launch a strategic review. Such reviews tend to look at all aspects of the business, what is working and what is not, and as a result formulate a plan to take the business forward. Since change is the main thing investors are looking for in a poorly performing company, news of a strategic review is generally a good thing for the share price. But the effect of the conclusion of the review can be a lot harder to judge. Normally investors will have a knee-jerk reaction to the conclusion for better or worse, resulting in a sharp rise or fall in the share price in the short term.

FTSE joiners and leavers

As we have seen, stock market-listed companies are often placed into an FTSE index. This can be for the sector in which they operate, but it can also depend on their stock market valuation. Hence the 100 largest companies will be listed in the FTSE 100 index.

The behaviour of a company's share price as it joins or leaves the FTSE 100 index can provide a short-term trading play for aggressive investors.

In recent years so-called tracking funds have increased in popularity. These funds operate with relatively low charges since they are basically computer programs that buy the constituents of an index and your investment in these funds will broadly track the performance of the index. In the case of the FTSE 100 index trackers buy the 100 largest companies on the stock market. Since these companies are generally blue chip investments they are also targeted by many managed funds. Because all these funds need to buy shares in companies once they are listed in the FTSE 100 the weight of money they put into the shares tends to make them rise, which can mean that a private investor who buys the share before it enters the FTSE 100 index may profit. This is an example of a situation where the small investor can move more quickly than the professionals who have to wait for the share to enter the index.

Targeting potential FTSE 100 constituents is not too difficult since there is always a reserve list of companies, in case an FTSE 100 company drops out of the index after perhaps it has been taken over at any time other than at the quarterly revue of the index. Checking the market capitalisation of companies in this reserve list, perhaps numbers 101 to 105, together with the lowest-valued companies in the index, perhaps numbers 95 to 100, will provide guidance as to the companies likely to fall out of the index and be promoted into it.

Although this investment strategy is most easily pursued using the FTSE 100 index, in theory it also works for the FTSE 250 and FTSE 350 indices. Beware, though, because it is an inexact strategy. In theory, companies entering the FTSE 100 should rise in value but this is not always the case. While there will be more buyers of the shares, the share price will also be vulnerable to overall stock market movement and the higher profile of the share will mean company announcements are examined more rigorously.

Momentum investing

One reason why the share price of a company that joins the FTSE 100 index is likely to rise is because of the weight of investment fund money that piles into the share once it joins the index. Since every company only has a finite number of shares in issue the more investors who want to buy those shares the higher the price of the share is likely to go. This gives rise to the theory of momentum investing.

At its basic level momentum investing involves buying a share simply because everybody else is buying. It is like riding a wave. You invest in a company whose share price has begun to move higher on the back of sustained buying and you keep buying until the volume of buying begins to peak. Once you are on the crest of the wave you sell before it comes crashing down. In this regard momentum investing has nothing to do with the fundamental value of a share or even its growth potential, but everything to do with exploiting a short-term situation.

Although momentum investing can be seen in individual shares, it is more commonly experienced in the context of sector trend or investment fad. In these cases investors act with a herd mentality, piling into certain so-called hot investment sectors and dumping less attractive situations. Their actions become a self-fulfilling prophecy since the more investors put money into a share or shares in a sector the higher values will rise. And the more investors who choose to abandon a particular share or sector the lower prices will fall.

Such actions, taken with no regard for fundamental values or growth potential, are irrational and, as we examined earlier, give rise to such situations as the South Sea Bubble and Tulipmania. The psychology at work is the belief that a rising tide lifts all boats. More recently, at the end of the twentieth century investors blindly put money in technology and telecom shares, particularly those linked to the Internet. While most knew that not every company could be a winner they invested anyway since, with others following their example, share prices continued to rise.

The expectation that other investors will continue to invest after you have bought shares lies behind momentum investing, but it is also its greatest weakness. Investment sages have always cautioned that you should leave something for the next guy. The moral here is not to get too greedy and always take a profit even if you think there could be bigger rewards to come. The problem with momentum investing is that there may not be a next guy. If there are no more buyers after you have bought, or at least not enough to sustain the momentum of the share price, the fall is likely to be quick and brutal.

As some sectors come into fashion quickly, so they can fall out of favour just as quickly. It can then take a long time for the market to rate them again and if you are left holding the shares it could take some time to regain value. Timing is crucial with momentum investing, but since this is often a case of luck rather than judgement it remains a highly speculative strategy.

New issues and stagging

Another aggressive investment technique that to some extent relies upon momentum investing is buying new issues, particularly when you intend selling almost immediately.

As we saw in Chapter 4, companies can join the stock market through an initial public offering of their shares to investors. Generally the shares on offer are priced at a slight discount to the value the company and its advisers believe they are really worth. This is designed to create an after market for the shares so that once they are listed they will still attract buyers who can detect value. It may also help to avoid the embarrassment and the hit that the company's credibility would suffer if the shares started trading and fell below their offer price.

With private companies that come to market the estimated discount may be small, but with privatisations the discount tends to be large. Governments that privatise businesses want to attract as many members of the public as possible to invest in them and cannot afford for their credibility to suffer as a result of a failed privatisation and therefore deliberately price shares below their estimated value.

Privatisation issues are very different from normal company flotations since they can include hefty discounts, guaranteed allotments of shares and very often sweeteners such as bonus share issues if you hold your shares for a certain period of time.

But both privatisations and normal shares will have a built-in premium designed to ensure the share price rises once it is on the stock market. Such a share may be described as being 'priced to go' and can offer investors the opportunity of making big short-term gains. Buying shares in a new issue with the aim of selling them at the first available opportunity is known as stagging. An investor who follows this speculative strategy is known as a stag. A stag has no interest in the company behind the share and it does not matter what business the company is in, who its management is or what its prospects are. The aim is merely to make a quick return on investment.

This can often be achieved through the outlay of a small amount of money, perhaps as little as a couple of hundred pounds, and the great thing for small investors is that there are no buying costs other than a few days' lost interest on your money. Usually even the application address is a freepost one.

More serious stags actually borrow money in order to stag a new issue. The reasoning is that the borrowed money can be repaid as soon as the shares are sold. Since the money borrowed covered the outlay for the shares, almost all the difference between the cost of the shares and what is realised for them will be profit.

Stagging sounds like an easy strategy, but it has several downsides. One is being able to buy sufficient shares to ensure a profit after taking dealing costs into account. If the issue looks likely to get away and open at a premium, demand for the share is likely to be high. That means the offer could be oversubscribed several times. This is when investors want to buy several times the total number of shares on offer. The usual method for dealing with over-subscriptions is either a ballot or a scaling back of applications. With a ballot potential investors are put into a draw and those picked are allowed to buy the shares, while those not chosen will have their cheques returned. When applications are scaled back investors will receive merely a fraction of the total number of shares they applied for.

In both cases the company is likely to have cashed your cheque and therefore you will have lost interest on the money, albeit only for a couple of weeks. But with a scaling back you could be left with an impractical number of shares. When Internet retailer Lastminute.com floated, demand was so high that the company scaled back applications so that every investor was given just 35 shares. Such a small number of shares is often uneconomic for small investors to hold since dealing charges would eat into any profits they might make.

Another factor working against stags is that, increasingly, companies are tending to price their shares through so-called book-building exercises, where the amount big institutional shareholders are prepared to pay for the shares dictates the price small investors have to pay. This means small investors will not know the price of the shares when they apply for them. Instead, they send off a cheque for the total amount they are willing to invest and only know how many shares they will receive once the price is decided.

While getting into a new issue can be difficult for a stag, so can getting out. With most new issues, including privatisations, letters of allotment that confirm the number of shares the investor has bought are not issued until after dealing in the shares begins. Even if you are able to deal straight away you will not be sure how many shares you have been allocated. If you sell what you think you will get, then find you have received fewer shares, you will have to buy more shares in the market to meet the number you have sold, which could be costly.

The other danger with stagging is that new issues do occasionally flop. Most at risk are blue sky investments such as technology companies that are raising money to develop their business, have yet to make a profit and are therefore hard to value. If the market takes an instant dislike to the share and there are no buyers, those who bought at flotation face watching the value of their investment plummet. But even seemingly blue chip companies can come unstuck, particularly if the stock market should fall as they make their debut and drag them down with it. If you have stagged these issues it could prove to be a very expensive strategy, especially if you have borrowed heavily to buy the shares.

While stagging is inherently dangerous, so too can be buying new issues as a straightforward investor. As we noted above, sometimes new issues flop and that means the shares are cheaper to buy at a later date.

Even if the shares of a newly floated company have a relatively good start in life on the stock market they may not perform well over time. Most companies tend to join the stock market when both their trading record and wider stock market conditions are good. Even allowing for the fact that the shares have been priced to allow for a premium on flotation they will have floated at a good price. Since conditions – the trading record and the state of the market – may not be as favourable again for some time, the flotation price may prove high, at least in the short term. Although buying new issues is easy, with many offered through newspaper advertisements or even the Internet, and cheap in terms of the absence of dealing costs, it should be approached with caution. Stagging can backfire expensively and even if you are buying with a long-term investment horizon you could be better off judging the value of the share once it has floated and there is a share price history.

You may decide new issues are too much of an aggressive investment for you but it is certainly still worth registering an interest in them. This will mean the company at least sends you its prospectus, which will contain useful information for you to keep on file should you consider buying the shares at a later date.

Borrowing to purchase shares

When stagging a new issue many investors apply for more shares than they can really afford to hold for the long term. They are able to do so because they borrow the money in the expectation that they will be able to repay it quickly and still make a profit.

The advantage of borrowing money in order to invest is that you do not risk your own capital and so long as the profits you make are greater than the interest charges it is a way of leveraging your investment. By this we mean you are able to invest far more than you would otherwise be able to afford. The bigger the investment the bigger the profits if it pays off. If you borrow half of what you invest your profits are doubled. If you have an account with some stockbrokers they will allow you to have an overdraft limit built in to your account. This enables you to buy using so-called margin trading, which means you need only put down a deposit for the shares you buy and pay the remaining cost later. It is a very common method of investing in the US and is becoming more widespread in the UK.

Of course, the downside of increasing your exposure through borrowing or margin buying is if the shares fall in value. If you borrow half of what you invest, you lose twice as fast as you would if you had not leveraged your position. As we have seen when considering the issue of stagging, you can come badly unstuck with such a strategy. It can also be costly if you choose to borrow money to invest in longer-term plays. You will still have to meet repayments and unless the share price is increasing sufficiently to enable you to sell a few shares each time a repayment is due to meet the demand, you could still be faced with large costs once all the shares are sold.

The dangers of borrowing to buy shares is illustrated by the Wall Street Crash of 1929 when the US stock market collapsed. Many investors had bought shares on margin and, as share prices fell, stockbrokers and banks called in their loans and investors found they could not repay the money through share sales.

While the attractions of borrowing cash are strong, particularly when interest rates are low, you should be clear about the type of returns you will need to generate from your investments to meet the demands of the loan. The fact that investors in ordinary shares can lose all their money encourages discipline when investing. To lose money that is not even yours but belongs to the bank and is a sum you will still have to pay back is not a sensible position for an investor to be in. The moral has to be to trade only with what you can afford to lose.

Short selling

Borrowing to buy shares can be dangerous because share prices can fall in value. While the main thrust of this book is about identifying shares that will rise in value, there are ways for experienced investors to make money when share prices fall. One is to sell shares short, a dangerous strategy with a low success rate.

It involves selling shares you do not own in the hope that their price will fall, enabling you to buy them back more cheaply later and make a profit on the difference between the price at which you bought and that at which you sold.

Selling short can be used as a way of making money in a falling stock market. Since shares are generally falling in such conditions, the shares you have chosen to short would have to move against the market in order for you to lose out.

You should stick to shares where there is plenty of liquidity – that is they are popular and there are plenty of the shares in issue that are regularly bought and sold. Shares in the FTSE 100 would fit the bill.

As with investing generally, timing is crucial if you are pursuing a short-selling strategy and there are several signals that you should look out for when picking a share. Bad news will almost always send a share price lower, although anticipating when this will come is not easy. Profits warnings in particular can send a share price sharply lower because by their very nature they tend to come out of the blue. Unless you have a very close understanding of the company, its business and its markets, which would enable you to conclude that a certain set of factors would hit the company's profits, you are unlikely to be able to foresee such a warning.

A more accessible method of determining a company is overvalued is to consider its fundamental financial situation. Just as fundamental analysis can throw up undervalued companies, so the same techniques can pinpoint companies trading on excessively high price/earnings ratios, which points to a potential fall in share price.

As we discussed earlier, fans of technical analysis also suggest that share price graph patterns can indicate when a share is likely to fall in value. Taking the classic head and shoulders pattern, chartists maintain that the base of the two shoulders represents a support level for the share price. If it falls through this it will keep falling. So in theory such a move below the support level would be a signal for selling a share short. Selling short is certainly an aggressive strategy because it is risky and complicated. If the share price rises rather than falls, in theory there is an unlimited cost to you of buying the shares at a higher price than you agreed to sell them. Only experienced investors should ever think of using it as a strategy and even then they should approach it with caution.

Day trading

Buying shares is a long-term investment strategy. You should generally buy shares with the intention of holding them for at least three to five years, since this period of time is usually enough to smooth out any volatility in the general stock market that might impact on your individual share. It is also a sufficiently long time for other investors to realise the true value of a share if you have bought one that you consider is fundamentally undervalued.

But as we discussed earlier, there are legitimate circumstances for taking a short-term view on shares and such trading-buy investments can offer quick returns, albeit for higher initial risk than with a buy-and-hold strategy. Taking a trading buy to its ultimate conclusions the short-term view can be a matter of minutes and it is here that we enter the world of the day trader. These people take a view that a share price will move in a short time – as little as a few minutes and at most a few hours – and deliver a very quick profit. Although day trading has always been available to professional investors, the rise of the Internet, which offers instant trading and a mine of information, has put it within reach of private investors.

Day traders attempt to make profits on relatively small share price movements through buying and selling large numbers of shares throughout the day. Although amateur day traders have only emerged in the last few years, they appear to fall into two camps. First, those who that hold a portfolio of shares, but deal frequently and possibly as much as every day. Second, those who do deal every day and start each day with cash, deal during the day and end the day selling all their shares so they have cash again.

The first type of day trader is akin to a normal investor. They will have a continuous portfolio of shares, but they will buy and sell a lot more frequently than the average investor. Sometimes they will sell all the shares they own in a particular company, but more often they will sell just some or even add to their holding. Although they may buy and sell frequently, a lot of their profits or losses may not have been realised since they will still hold shares, some of which will have increased in value while others will have fallen, at the end of each day. This means they will carry winning or losing positions into each new day.

In contrast, the second type of day trader does not want to have to reassess their exposure to profit and loss at the end of each day by holding shares. Instead, they will start the day with cash, buy and sell during the day and close all their positions towards the end of the day, leaving them with cash to invest again the next day.

Both types of day trader are looking for liquid shares that attract high volumes of buying and selling each day and are therefore expected to move, although perhaps by only a few percentage points. Although small shares are tempting, the danger is that low volumes mean the price may hardly move and therefore the opportunity for returns is limited. Share price movements do not have to be great, since day traders tend to buy large numbers of shares and risk substantial sums of money.

With such big investments, which given the short time period are little more than bets, the dangers of day trading are obvious. Your capital can quickly shrink if you make a series of loss-making investments. Even if your investments move into profit you must be careful that these are not eaten away by the costs of dealing and running an Internet connection that enables you to monitor prices and deal during the day. There is also the practical problem that you will have to spend many hours each day glued to a personal computer screen, which can be exhausting.

If these reasons are not enough to deter you from day trading, bear in mind the difficulties of identifying buy and sell situations over such a short time-frame. Spotting that a share is fundamentally undervalued is one thing, but to make a profit you need other investors to notice the same thing and buy, so pushing up the price. There is no guarantee they will do this over weeks or months, let alone a single day. Even calling the market response to news events is hard to quantify. Often, for example, shares will fall sharply on a profits warning, but the drop can be overdone and buying by bargain hunters can lift the price the next day. But this recovery may not come and if it does it may only be a temporary respite before another fall. Getting the timing right is very, very difficult. The psychology of day trading is that returns can be achieved quickly, but the flip side is that so can losses.

Tips

Share prices move because investors choose to buy or sell shares. If more buy than sell the share price is likely to rise and if more sell than buy the price is likely to fall. While individuals may decide to buy or sell shares in a company for many reasons, such as their own fundamental research into a share, large-scale buying or selling is unlikely to occur without some sort of news flow around the company.

This news flow may come from the company itself in the form of interim and preliminary results announcements, annual meeting and trading statements, notices of board appointments or profits warnings. Such news is likely to move a company's share price, but for most companies these announcements happen infrequently.

Share prices, though, move all the time so there are clearly other factors at work that encourage or discourage investments in particular companies. One of these is information about a company that does not come from the company itself. Information is a valuable commodity for an investor and newspapers, investment magazines, brokers' circular and investment websites on the Internet are all sources of information. Some of these sources of information offer little more than rumours and speculation, and carry a major health warning.

This is particularly so in the case of Internet bulletin boards, where anybody can post a message about any company. These forums are open to abuse and unscrupulous investors can use them to spread rumours designed to drag down or buoy a company's share price. They occasionally succeed because they appear to provide the tips, rumours and inside information that many investors crave. All investors want to know that a certain company's shares are about to jump in value, but just because you want to believe it, that is no excuse for doing so.

Tempting though it is to act on a tip that someone has given you down the pub, you should never do it. It is just not sound investment strategy and at worst can be illegal. Acting on inside information, for example, is a serious criminal offence under Section V of the Criminal Justice Act 1993. This is when you profit from so-called price-sensitive information that is not available to shareholders as a whole. If you are told by someone working for a company that they know it is about to be taken over and you then buy shares in that company in anticipation of profiting from a rising share price you are acting illegally and as a result you could be sent to prison.

While such tips should play no part in your investment strategy, there are some sources of information that are worth more serious consideration. Information and suggestions from professionals such as stockbroking analysts and financial newspapers and magazines should never be slavishly followed, but they can provide a useful insight into companies. In turn, you can use this insight as one argument when you assess the investment potential of a company.

You can at least check the track record of an analyst or newspaper commentator and they have to spell out their arguments for suggesting a company's shares are worth buying or selling. If the argument is weak or based purely on anecdotal evidence or emotion, it should rightly be dismissed. But if it points out, for instance, that a company is trading on a low price-to-earnings ratio and has a healthy dividend yield then it might provide a reason for you at least to look more closely at the company as a potential buy. You should then subject it to your own tests to see if it fits your personal investment strategy.

Although by regularly reading the recommendations and suggestions of analysts, and newspaper and magazine investment columns you will learn who gets it right more often than they get it wrong, there is an obvious flaw in following them blindly. Sensible investors should only rarely buy shares yet many of these publications suggest several share buys a week. The correct way to read them, therefore, is that they are suggesting general investment ideas or companies worth considering. Such publications are useful places to look for investment ideas, but buying a share solely because it is mentioned in a column is not an investment strategy.

Other Investment Strategies

Share perks

Enjoying returns from your shares does not just have to be about a rising share price and dividend income. You can benefit from your investment in other ways. If you own shares in a company you are entitled to attend the annual meeting, at which you are likely to get at least a cup of tea and some biscuits. Some companies even offer those attending a sample of their products. But for most companies this is as far as they go in offering rewards to their shareholders beyond the performance of their shares.

However, there are companies that offer shareholders incentives, which can provide an attractive bonus for investors. These bonuses are known as share perks and are generally offered by companies that like to view their shareholders as also their customers. They tend to be businesses that operate in consumer markets such as retailers and travel firms, and the perks can be highly valuable and are tax free.

More than 100 stock market-quoted companies offer perks and lists of those that do are available from firms such as Barclays Stockbrokers and Premier Asset Management. To qualify for perks most companies require shareholders to own a certain minimum number of shares and some companies stipulate investors must have held the shares for a stated period.

Some companies will only issue perks to shareholders who hold their shares in their own name. But others will also allow investors who hold shares in nominee accounts, where shares are held centrally by a stockbroker, to have access to perks. You will need to check out how a particular company distributes perks since some include vouchers with the annual report. Again, if you are in a nominee account you will not automatically receive this so you may have to contact your broker or whoever is operating the nominee account to ensure you are sent it.

Most perks are well worth having and will be readily used. High street stores such as Boots and Iceland offer discount vouchers worth just a few pounds, while retirement homes specialist McCarthy & Stone offers discounts on new homes that could save thousands of pounds. Channel Tunnel operator Eurotunnel offers discounted fares and ferry operator P&O offers ferry discounts to holders of its 5.5 per cent redeemable preference shares. Other company share perks include money off holidays and hotel rooms, magazines and even furniture.

Some companies are consistent in offering perks, while others change the terms and review them each year so it is always worth double-checking before buying shares. That said, you should not purchase shares merely because they offer perks. If you find that a company that fits your investment strategy and whose shares are worth buying also offers perks it is bonus. But do not use perks as an investment criterion. Although they may be valuable, they will never compensate for a poorly performing share.

Ethical investing

When choosing what shares to buy you are likely to use a number of criteria such as value, strength of management or even recovery prospects. All these factors are designed to identify shares that are likely to increase strongly in value. But there are other factors worth considering that do not put maximising profit at the top of the agenda. These include ethical investing where why you buy dictates what you buy. Ethical investing involves deciding what companies you will not invest in because you object to their activities and which companies have businesses that you are willing to back.

It therefore has both negative and positive elements. Some investors will simply not invest in certain companies that they consider unethical in their activities. Others will take it a stage further and only invest in companies they define as ethical. The negative criteria could cover areas such as animal testing, armaments, gambling, tobacco, alcohol, intensive farming and nuclear power. Ethical investors would spurn companies whose businesses involved these activities, but not limit their choice of other companies to invest in.

Some investors, though, will take a different approach and seek out companies showing a positive ethical approach whose activities provide basic necessities or socially important products and services. These could include power and water companies, healthcare services, public transport and education businesses. More generally, ethical investors searching for positive criteria may target companies that are committed to their local communities, have good equal opportunity employment and social responsibility records. Ecological considerations are important aspects of ethical investing and as a result it is sometimes known as green investing.

After defining your own ethical investment boundaries it is important to know that the companies you believe you are then able to invest in are truly ethical. A good source of information for this is the Ethical Investment Research Service (EIRIS). The organisation was set up in 1983 by a number of groups and charities including Oxfam, the Rowntree Trust and Quakers. Although its main function is to monitor the performance of collective investment funds such as ethical and environmental unit trusts, it also provides a screening service for direct investors. EIRIS will supply you with a list of companies that it has screened and that fit ethical investment criteria.

You must then decide how far you want to take your ethical investing and whether you will use a narrow or a broad definition to identify unsuitable and suitable companies. For example, you might not want to invest in brewers or pubs because they make and sell alcohol, but you may be willing to invest in supermarkets even though they also sell alcohol.

A broad approach is probably the most practical to take, since finding a company that is 100 per cent ethical and fits all environmentally friendly criteria can be very difficult. If you take too narrow an approach you may be sacrificing investment choice and be left with only a very few companies whose shares you can buy. If you take a broad approach you should be able to create a fairly large list of suitable companies that you can then scrutinise using more traditional investment techniques in order to identify the bargains among them. Even so, your list is likely to be overweight in smaller and mid-sized companies since these are the ones that are most likely to fit ethical criteria. It is harder for big companies, such as those in the FTSE 100 index, to measure up in ethical terms because of the scope and diversity of their activities.

Critics of the practicality of ethical investing view this as a major flaw since the performance of your investments is likely to suffer because of lack of exposure to larger companies and to focus on smaller businesses. They also point out that ethical investors may ignore entire stock market sectors such as pharmaceuticals, banks and chemicals – all of which could fail an ethical test – and therefore miss out on booms in these areas.

Although being overweight in smaller companies will mean that your portfolio is likely to see volatile share prices, ethical investing itself is not necessarily a poor strategy in terms of returns. Ethical companies have a good record of generating returns for shareholders and demand for the shares could increase on the back of recent changes affecting institutional investors.

Managers of pension funds are now obliged to consider the environmental, social and ethical implications of investing in companies, which should mean more investments being made on ethical and environmental grounds. While this should be a boost to the shares of ethical companies, it is unlikely they will ever prove to be a better investment in terms of profits than a diverse portfolio. Returns are about spreading risk across sectors and a narrow focus is never likely to be more successful in the long term.

If ethical investing does appeal to you, you are probably better off opting for a pooled investment product, such as an ethical unit trust, than trying to build your own portfolio. Because most ethical companies are small, only a fund can really give you the spread of investments needed to minimise risk.

If you insist on developing your own ethical portfolio there are certain measures you can take to minimise the problems associated with this type of investment. One is that you should buy and hold your ethical shares and look to invest for at least three to five years. As we considered in the last chapter, this strategy helps to iron out the peaks and troughs of volatile shares and is therefore particularly suited to ethical investing. Ethical investments are unsuitable as short-term trading buys. Another criterion to enhance your prospects of success is the one mentioned above that you should take a broad view of what makes an ethical company.

The whole point of ethical investing is that profit is not paramount, but it must still be an aim of your investment. Unless you subject your ethical investments to the same scrutiny and criteria as you would use for any share investment you may be better off simply donating your money to charity.

Indirect investing, options and warrants

Most of you will be content to limit your investments to ordinary shares. These can offer good returns and are easy to understand, and to buy and sell. But others may be interested in forms of indirect investing that will bring you into contact with options and warrants. A brief description of each was given in Chapter 4.

Both options and warrants do have a link with the ordinary share price, but they are only for more sophisticated investors. Their price is derived from the value of some underlying share and therefore this type of investment is called a derivative. The whole subject of derivatives is unnecessarily crowded with jargon, but once you get used to the terms they are easy enough to understand.

Derivatives have their origin in agricultural futures that were developed in the US in the mid nineteenth century. Farmers exported their produce to Europe, but because of the length of time taken to grow grain and rear livestock they were unable to predict accurately how much they would be able to sell and at what price. Their customers faced a similar problem in knowing how much they would be able to buy and what it would cost them. To overcome the problem, farmers and their customers agreed a price in advance for the delivery of produce on a certain date. Customers paid a small deposit up front and the balance on delivery. The system helped to cut the risk for both sides in the transaction and was termed hedging. Today futures have the same function, and while they are still used for agricultural products, since the 1970s they have been used for financial transactions including shares and currency dealing.

Although initially used just for hedging, futures were also picked up by speculators who realised that since the initial contract was secured with just a small deposit, many contracts could be bought at one time. If the price of the underlying product rose above the price agreed in the contract the holder of the contracts could make big profits. Of course, if the price fell they could also make big losses.

Speculators are important in a futures markets because they introduce liquidity into the market and that enables hedgers to buy and sell contracts as they need them.

Because of the potential for losses futures are suitable only for big companies and very wealthy and technically sophisticated investors.

For small investors **traded options** are a much more suitable device. This is because, unlike a futures contract, the buyer of an options contract can choose whether or not to buy the underlying product, perhaps a share, at a certain price (the exercise or strike price) on a certain date. If, for example, it is a share option and the share price is lower than the option price, meaning you would pay more for the shares than they are currently worth on the market and therefore make a loss, you simply let the option expire. All you would lose is the price you paid for the contract, which varies over time but can be about 10 per cent of the share price. If, however, the price is higher than the option you would exercise it, that is take delivery of the shares, since you will make a profit on the difference.

With options you can bet on both rising and falling share prices, although in both cases you would buy an option. If you believe the price of a share will rise you buy a **call option**, which gives you the right to buy shares at a predetermined price. But if you believe a share price will fall you buy a **put option**, which gives you the right to sell shares at a predetermined price.

There are several ways you can use traded options as a private investor and there are about 100 shares for whom they are available through the London International Financial Futures Exchange. You can speculate with them, use them to fix a future price at which you will buy shares and as an insurance policy for shares you already own. Traded options, as their name suggests, are able to be bought and sold and you can use them to speculate if you believe the underlying share is set to rise or fall. Because you only have to pay out a fraction of the full cost of the shares in the form of buying the contract you can gear up your investment. This means that for a relatively low investment you can return a much larger profit, while your loss is always limited to the amount you have paid for the contract. You do not even have to link the option to its underlying share since it is tradable in its own right.

If you want simply to buy and sell options, though, it is important to understand a little about the way in which they are priced. Suppose you bought an option in Widget & Co. You paid 10p for the right to buy a Widget share at 110p (the exercise price) within the next three months. If, after a month, the price of Widget's shares has risen from 100p to 115p the call option has an intrinsic value since it gives you the right to buy a share costing 115p in the market at 110p. As a result the option itself is worth more than the 10p you paid for it and could be worth 15p, so you could sell it and make a profit. In fact, you will have made a 50 per cent profit, far more than if you had bought the underlying share. Even if the share price had fallen below the option price you could still sell and at least not lose everything you had paid. When you initially bought your option it only had a time value: the hope that within three months it would be worth more than you paid for it. In the jargon of the market the option was said to be 'out of the money'. If, however, it was a call option to buy a Widget share at 110p when the share price was 115p it would have an intrinsic value of 5p and is said to be 'in the money'. If the share price and the option price are the same the option is said to be 'at the money'.

The time value of an option decreases through its life the nearer it gets to its expiry date. The odds of a share price rising over three months is much greater than over three days so as the option reaches its expiry date its market value will fall.

Another way a private investor can profit from options is to use them to fix a predetermined price at which you will buy an agreed quantity of shares at a future date. You could use this method to buy shares if you are convinced they will rise in value but you do not currently have the cash to purchase them.

But perhaps the most practical use of options is as an insurance policy for your existing share investments. You can use options to offset the risk of a fall in values in your portfolio or indeed in individual shares. If you think the stock market is set to fall and this is likely to drag down the value of your portfolio, you could take out a put option on the FTSE 100 index, for example. This would give you the right to sell the index at a certain price. The profit you make on the put option could help offset any losses on the value of your portfolio. If the market does not fall you could regard the cost of the option as an insurance premium. You could use the same technique to hedge against a fall in the price of an individual share in your portfolio.

There are several other ways in which investors can use traded options both for speculative gain and to mitigate risk in their portfolios and it really depends on the amount of risk they are prepared to take on as to which ones are suitable.

When considering options be aware that the costs involved in buying and selling can outweigh some of the advantages in using them as a hedging tool.

Finally, a word of warning. If you are considering using options as part of your investment strategy, steer clear of writing them. Writing options is extremely risky. Clearly, when you buy and sell options, someone, somewhere has written the option in the first place. They try to make money on pricing the option, but it is a risky strategy. Its riskiest form is called naked option writing where you sell options when you do not have an existing position to hedge. If you naked-write put options you could be exposing yourself to massive losses. You undertake to buy a share at a set price, but if that share slumps you will be buying the share at a price way above its market value. Even massive financial institutions have been caught out by writing options so the message for private investors is simple: don't do it.

Like traded options **warrants** may also appeal to investors seeking something a little different where a small investment can be rewarded with a large profit. Warrants can be bought and sold on the stock market and give the holder the right to buy shares in a company at a set price on a future date or dates. They are therefore little more than long-term options on a share, although if exercised the shares will come not from another shareholder, but from the company itself.

Their origin is usually as part of a fund-raising by a company and they are designed to make the exercise more appealing, but at no immediate cost to the company. Warrants are issued with a subscription price that will be above the current share price of the company so the warrant only has a hope value. For example, if a warrant gives the holder the right to subscribe for one share in Widget & Co at 150p at some point in the future and the current share price is 130p there is no intrinsic value in the warrant. But if Widget's share price rose to 180p the holder of the warrant could buy their shares at 150p, giving them a 30p-a-share profit.

Time is crucial to pricing a warrant. If a warrant is priced at 50p and carries the right to subscribe for shares at 200p the price would be 250p (200p + 50p). If the shares are currently 220p the premium is 30p (250p – 220p) although the intrinsic value would be 20p (220p – 200p). The reason the traded price of the warrant is at a premium to the current intrinsic value is the time value of the warrant. Investors are willing to pay more for the warrant because they believe that by the time it can be converted the future intrinsic value will be higher still. As time moves nearer to the exercise date of the warrant the traded price should move closer to the intrinsic price. The further away from the exercise date the greater should be the time value of the warrant.

Warrants also appeal to investors because they are a geared investment. Investors can buy into the movements of a share price for less than it would cost to buy the share itself and potentially enjoy greater returns. For example, suppose an ordinary share is trading at 220p and the warrant with an exercise price of 200p is trading at 50p. If the share price rises to 330p the shareholder will have made a 50 per cent return on their investment, but the warrant holder will have more than doubled their investment. Of course, it works in reverse and if the share price falls below the exercise price the warrant is valueless. In this way a warrant increases both gains and losses.

You can make money by trading warrants in two ways. Either selling the warrant when it goes up in value, normally when the shares in the company that issued the warrant go up, or wait until the conversion time arrives and convert if the underlying share price has risen. If it has not you simply do not exercise the warrant and lose whatever it has cost you.

Warrants have very long lifespans, some of 10 to 20 years, which can make them less risky than short-lifespan traded options since generally over time share prices do rise. But warrants remain a risky and volatile investment, and again one that beginner investors should leave to the experts.

Ofex

Although most people will associate share dealing with the London Stock Exchange other organisations have enabled investors to buy and sell shares.

In the past there has been the unofficial Over the Counter or OTC market. While this was a specific facility, OTC has become a generic term to describe trading in shares or other securities through a channel other than a recognised stock exchange.

In London the OTC market in shares used to be conducted by licensed dealers in shares over the telephone. It was hardly regulated and was not liked by the LSE, although the Exchange was powerless to stop it. What effectively ended the OTC market was the 1986 Financial Services Act, which make it difficult for firms to operate separately from a Recognised Investment Exchange such as the LSE.

But there does exist a share trading facility outside the LSE, although it is a member company of the Exchange, called Ofex. The Ofex OTC market was founded in 1995 by market-making firm J. P. Jenkins. Market-makers buy shares in the hope of finding someone to sell to and sell shares, that they may not even yet own, in the belief they will find a buyer. They make money on the difference in prices at which they buy and sell.

Jenkins set up Ofex as a home for companies that might previously have been dealt on the LSE before it abolished its Rule 4.2, which had enabled member firms to trade unquoted shares by matching buyers with sellers. When the rule was abolished companies that had previously had their shares dealt under 4.2 either joined the Alternative Investment Market or Ofex.

The Ofex market now has more than 200 companies on it with a combined value of more than £3 billion. Although many of the companies are tiny, others are very large and include well-known businesses such as household names Weetabix and Arsenal Football Club. Start-up companies and established businesses seeking funding are attracted to Ofex by its low costs and easy access. The companies tend to have sponsors such as accountants or solicitors. Information about the market is available on the Ofex website on www.ofex.co.uk, while share prices for some of the companies are listed in the *Evening Standard* and *Financial Times* newspapers.

For experienced investors looking for something a bit different, fishing in the Ofex pool could be lucrative. The market has enjoyed some spectacular successes with companies moving from it to AIM and the full market. Ofex also tends to plough its own furrow and its constituents are not affected by the vagaries of the main stock market indices.

But Ofex is only suitable for active investors who can take a long-term view. Since many of the companies are small and often in their start-up phase they are inherently risky, with little financial or trading history on which to base your investment decisions. The management is likely to be unknown to you and therefore you are often relying on your assessment of the merits of the company's business plan or idea to decide whether or not it makes a good investment.

Another problem with Ofex companies is lack of liquidity in their shares. The shares are often traded on a so-called matched bargain basis, which means that for every seller a buyer must be found. This means you could be unable to sell your shares when you want to.

Spread betting

Given the volatility of share prices and the potentially risky nature of investing in individual companies, many investors view the stock market as akin to a casino. The analogy has some merit, particularly because you should never invest money in individual shares that you are not prepared to lose.

But investing is different because provided you put in the research work, keep an eye on your investments and are prepared to hold shares for a reasonable length of time, the odds of success are better than a casino. Investing also differs in that the amount you are likely to spend on shares will be much more than you would probably stake on a bet. Some gambling investors have found a way of combining both methods of making money and they are helping to fuel the growth of spread betting.

Spread betting is a way of making money whether the stock market or a particular share is rising or falling. Small bets can produce big profits and these are free of capital gains tax. Financial spread betting was introduced by bookmaker IG Index in 1974, initially as a way to enable investors to bet on the price of gold. Since then IG has been joined by several other spread-betting firms and the range of sectors on which they take bets has multiplied manifold. It is a combination of types of investing and gambling, best understood by comparing it with traditional betting where you stake money on the outcome of a particular event at fixed odds. If your bet is right you win back your stake multiplied by the odds, but if your bet does not come off you lose your stake. With spread betting you do not have to predict the exact outcome of an event, you only have to pick the right side of a spread correctly and the odds are not fixed.

For example, a spread-betting company offers a spread of 500–505p on the price of ICI shares. The sell price is 500p and the buy price 505p. If you believe the shares are going to rise you make a buy bet at, say, £10 at 505p. If the share price does move higher and the spread quoted moves up to 520–525p you might choose to take a profit, which you do by making a £10 sell bet at 520p. Since you bought at 505p and sold at 520p your profit is the 15p difference multiplied by your £10 stake to make £150. Of course, the share price could have moved lower, in which case you would have lost the number of pence it dropped multiplied by your stake.

This is the leverage effect of spread betting, which means the more right you are in betting the correct side of the spread the more money you can make, but the more wrong you are the bigger your losses. The size of your profits or losses is determined by the size of your stake and the degree by which the price moves. But at no time do you ever own the shares; you are simply making a bet with the spread-betting firm.

Financial spread betting can be used to bet on a range of products including individual shares, stock market indices, currencies, interest rates, and futures and options. Because of the nature of the bet you can use spread betting not just to wager on shares you think will rise in value, but also those you believe will fall.

To take the ICI example again, with a spread of 500–505p you could place a £10 sell bet at 500p. If the share price then fell to produce a spread of perhaps 485–490p, you could place a £10 buy bet at 490p. This means you will have sold at 500p and bought at 490p a difference of 10p multiplied by your £10 stake to produce a profit of £100. As with the buy bet, if the sell bet moves against you because the share price actually rises rather than falls as you predicted you are faced with losses equivalent to the number of points the spread has moved above your sell bet multiplied by your stake.

The ability to make money out of falling share prices is alien to most investors. In bear markets making money from share dealing is very difficult, but spread betting provides a way of profiting even when share prices are dropping.

Since individual shares can be volatile and tricky for investors to call, most spread-betting beginners start with bets on stock market indices, for example, movements in the FTSE 100 index. With these you take a view on whether the FTSE 100 will close the day higher or lower than the spread and make your bet accordingly. The spreads are generally quite narrow compared with individual shares – the wider a spread the harder it is to make a profit – and indices are easy to understand and follow.

The main advantages for investors of spread betting are that it is free of commission and dealing costs, the spread-betting firms make their money on the spread, the difference between the buying and selling prices. There is no broker to deal with so bets can be made instantly and any profits you make are free of capital gains tax. Betting duty is paid on spread bets, but it is taken care of by the spread-betting companies.

Spread betting is suitable for short-term positions since most bets last only a day, a week or at most a couple of months. It can also be used to hedge against movements in shares that you already own. If you think a short-term situation that will affect your portfolio is likely to occur, you could sell the spread in an individual share or an index that closely matches your portfolio.

Spread betting can be fun and deliver quick returns on your judgements about individual shares or the stock market. But the biggest risk is that unlike normal betting your losses are not limited to your stake and unless you are very careful they can spiral into very large sums very quickly. Just as with individual share investing, it is important to cut your losses and you can place a stop-loss order on your bet. In theory these limit your loss, although in fast-moving markets the betting firms may be unable to close your position at the exact point you specified.

If you are interested in spread betting, be clear that it is not investing but gambling. You will need to open an account with one of the spread-betting firms and you will usually have to deposit a minimum sum of money in your account to start with.

Investing overseas

As we have discussed, successful investing involves spreading your risk and not putting all your eggs in one basket. You can achieve this by building a diverse share portfolio including individual shares from several stock market sectors. But even this will leave you exposed overall to the vagaries of the British stock market. If the British economy or stock market slides it is inevitable that the value of your shares will also fall.

The obvious way to mitigate against this risk is to invest overseas. As well as helping to spread your risk, it is also the only way to buy shares in some of the world's largest and most successful companies since most do not have a London Stock Exchange listing, although some do.

Investing overseas was once difficult and only really an option for sophisticated and wealthy investors, but now it is really no more difficult than buying British shares. Partly this is due to electronic settlement of share deals and increased use of the Internet to trade, which has helped reduce prices, as well as cutting across national boundaries. Plenty of British stockbrokers now deal in overseas shares and while the cost of dealing will be higher than when buying British shares it is coming down. You should watch out for additional charges on top of commission. These could include custodian fees, which are paid to a foreign broker or bank that acts as a nominee holding the shares and processing dividends.

Another cost to watch out for is the impact of currency movements on both the translation value of your shares and dealing costs.

Income and capital gains from overseas shares are subject to British taxation as normal. But where dividends have already been taxed overseas, British investors can claim a tax credit with the Inland Revenue to avoid being charged twice.

While exposure to overseas markets will help spread your risk from being totally exposed to British shares, many foreign markets are risky in their own right. Some foreign exchanges may not be as tightly regulated as the London Stock Exchange. Also, it is harder to get reliable information and keep track of companies and their businesses in foreign markets than in Britain. Certain market, such as the Far East, tend to be highly volatile and time zone differences can make trading problematic.

Although there are clear risks with ownership of foreign shares the rewards are spreading your risk, exposure to the world's leading companies and access to fast-growing economies in different parts of the world. Owning shares in overseas companies is not for everyone, but is certainly worth considering. More cautious investors might prefer to use a collective investment such as unit or investments trusts that specialise in overseas markets.

Conclusion

We have considered most of the traditional investment strategies that are pursued by both amateur and professional investors. But in practice the range and combination of strategies is limited only by your own imagination and the time you have to spend on investing.

Some of the strategies outlined will not appeal to you and some will seem to fit your risk-and-reward profile perfectly, but do not be afraid to experiment to find those that really work for you. No one strategy is the right one all the time and even if you are defensive by nature it can sometimes pay to take an aggressive course. While if buccaneering investment is for you be prepared occasionally to consider defensive moves.

The main thing to take away from this chapter is that there should be a pattern to your investing. It is important to develop strategies so you will know how to respond to changing stock market conditions and how to approach individual shares. A strategy should help you become consistent and remove the temptation to invest on emotional rather than rational grounds.

In the next chapter we will consider other ways to invest in shares that can offer a different perspective for investors from some of the strategies outlined above.

8
Tricks of the Trade and the Value of Information

Investors naturally want to make as much profit as they can with minimum effort in the shortest possible time. However, as we have seen, this is an unrealistic aim. Successful investing takes time and effort to develop a system that works for you and should keep working for you.

But there are some techniques which, though not exactly short cuts, will help you develop your investing method more quickly and ensure it is focused. We shall consider some of these trading tricks in this chapter.

A good understanding of how the City works in relation to companies and how businesses interact with their advisers is also useful for investors, so we shall examine these relationships as well.

Finally, one of the most valuable weapons an investor can have in his or her arsenal is information. We shall look at sources of information on companies and shares ranging from newspapers to the Internet and how to read between the lines of company statements to find out what is really being said.

Trading Tricks

Sorting the wheat from the chaff

Choosing which shares to buy is no easy matter and as we saw in an earlier chapter there are numerous investment techniques you can use to value one share against another. While you should always be searching for undervalued shares or growth opportunities, one of the hardest things is deciding to where actually to start your search. One obvious starting point for your research is to play to your strengths and stick with what you know.

Retail shares are popular with small investors for this very reason. Companies such as supermarkets are easily accessible on your local high street. In a few simple shopping trips you can determine how good they are at what they do, how efficient their service is and how competitive their prices are. This might seem very basic research, but supermarkets are very simple businesses. If you are convinced one has got the business right at the shop floor level it could provide a starting point for examining the company further. You could then undertake more detailed research at the corporate level, examining the company's profits record, its balance sheet, other businesses, management and strategic plans. It is these factors that are likely to convince you whether or not to buy the company's shares, but your initial shop floor research will also be an important factor. This kind of shop floor research is suitable for any company whose products or services you come into contact with.

Where do you work? Where do you shop? What washing powder do you use? What is your favourite pub? Where do you bank? Whose bus or train do you catch? What are your hobbies? Where do you live?

Answers to all these questions can produce potential investment opportunities based on your own particular expertise, often an expertise you do not even realise you have. In your daily life you will use the products and services of dozens of companies and you will know whether or not they do a good job and are therefore likely to be successful. American entrepreneur Victor Kiam famously liked the Remington razor so much he bought the company and his is a good attitude for investors to have. As a shareholder you are a part owner of the company in which you invest. Therefore it should be one you know well and trust, in addition to meeting the financial requirements of the investment equation.

You can extend this basic research function to include relatives, friends or even employees of businesses in order to widen the net of experience on which you can base investment decisions. If you want to know about a brewer why not ask your local pub landlord for his view of the company? If you are considering buying shares in a computer games company ask someone you know who plays these games so they can offer an assessment of just how good the business is at what it does.

You could choose to focus on a very narrow investment area – a strategy that can pay dividends but can also lead to poor returns unless you strike lucky with the right sector. But generally you will want to have as broad a knowledge of companies and sectors as possible and doing your own research and using other people to help can multiply the possibilities manifold.

Take an interest

As was mentioned above, through buying shares in a company you become a part owner of that business. Many shareholders pay little or no attention to this, simply keeping the shares in the expectation that they will rise in value and can later be sold for a profit. There is nothing particularly wrong with this attitude, but realising you have an ownership stake in a business is likely to provide you with many of the disciplines needed for successful investment. You will want to be sure the management who are running your business are sound, the company's strategy is good, its finances are strong and it is doing at least as well as other businesses in the same sector.

As a shareholder you may receive regular communications from the company such as copies of the interim and final results, and an annual report. Most important you will be able to attend the company's annual meeting and vote on various measures including the re-election of directors. You will also have an opportunity to raise any issues when the chairman asks shareholders for questions from the floor. At other times do not be afraid to contact directors either by phone or letter if you have any questions about the company.

Some shareholders take these rights very seriously and, with enough support, are able to put pressure on companies they do not think are behaving in the best interests of investors. It is a difficult area since for practical purposes shareholders cede day-to-day power to management with non-executive directors in theory providing the checks and balances on the board. But is it quite right that shareholders, who after all own the company, should be able to ensure management is acting in their best interests.

Although is it hard for small shareholders to ensure this is the case, many institutional shareholders are becoming more active investors. These so-called shareholder activists are often driven to shake up companies whose share price has underperformed relative to similar companies. Their success in instigating change to create value underlines that shareholders should not lose sight of the fact that they own the company.

Do not deal too often

Patience is a virtue and nowhere is this truer than when investing in the stock market. Instant returns are rare, so investors should always take a medium- to long-term view when buying shares. Such an investment horizon has traditionally been three to five years.

As we considered earlier, picking the right time to buy a share is always tricky and spotting its exact low point is a matter of luck as much as judgement, therefore holding shares for a three-to-five-year period is one way of smoothing out short-term fluctuations. Buying and holding can also work since it means you will not deal too often. Because buying and selling shares generally involves dealing costs, these can quickly eat into your profits if you are not careful.

If your investment strategy involves trying to make a quick return on an investment you should carefully bear in mind the costs involved in buying and then selling the share. Depending on the amount of money you are investing, this can be a large slice of any potential profits you might make.

Sit on the sidelines

It may seem strange for a guide to stock market investing to advocate not buying shares, but this can be a key investment decision. Once you have decided that buying shares in individual companies is for you, the temptation is to rush headlong into assembling a portfolio of stock market investments. While each share you buy should fit your investment criteria there is no guarantee that you will find ideal opportunities straight away. Therefore, as we suggested above, patience is an important strategy to pursue. Tempting though it is to buy shares that are nearly right and almost fit your criteria, you would do well to back off and sit tight. Waiting for the right opportunity is hard, but bear in mind that if it comes along it will repay your patience many times.

On a bigger-picture level it can pay to sit on the sidelines if the stock market or certain sectors within it are particularly volatile. Better to wait for things to calm down, then try to time your entry correctly.

Watch out for bad news

Bad news from a company such as a profits warning or the departure of a senior director will almost certainly knock the share price lower. In the short term this is a bad thing for investors, although if it is a temporary blip it could provide a buying opportunity. But be careful.

There is a saying in the City that profits warnings seldom occur in isolation and one warning is usually swiftly followed by another. It does very often prove to be true. So if you are tempted into buying because you think a company's share price has fallen too far on a piece of bad news that appears to be temporary, it could be worth holding off just a little longer to ensure there are no other skeletons in the company's closet before taking the plunge.

Know when to sell

Although you should always cut losses and run with profits, never forget the whole reason for investing in the first place is to make money. You have never actually made money, or indeed lost money, until you sell your shares. Only at this point will you crystallise a profit or incur a loss. Deciding when to sell is therefore crucially important, but it very much depends on the type of investment strategy you have chosen to pursue.

If you have adopted a buy-and-hold strategy, you will only sell if you need money or you have to admit that your picks were wrong. But if you have bought a share as a recovery play or because it looks fundamentally undervalued against its peers, you should consider selling once it has recovered or it has been rerated and is now on a par with its rivals.

Weighing up whether to sell a share that has performed extremely well and is now dominant in your portfolio as a result is a much harder decision. Generally, though, you should continue to run with the profits. Selling simply because it has been successful, as long as no other factors have changed, would probably be a mistake. Growth shares can continue to outperform for some time, although inevitably their growth rate will eventually start to slow and you should certainly consider selling at that point.

Cash is king

When you sell shares, do not be too eager to reinvest the proceeds into another share. Although over the long term investment in equities is far more lucrative than the interest to be earned on cash, in the short-term cash is a very powerful investment tool.

When first deciding how much money you have to invest in shares it is always wise to keep at least some of this money aside as cash. If you are fully invested in the stock market, that is all the money you have allocated for share investment has been used to buy shares, your freedom to pursue investment opportunities has been limited. It would mean that if you find an amazing investment opportunity, the only way you could buy shares in your discovery would be to sell an existing share to raise funds. Since ideally you want to choose the timing of share sales rather than have them forced upon you this is not a good investment strategy.

It is also worth keeping at least some of your investment money in the form of cash so that if the worst ever happened and the stock market slumped, lowering the value of your shareholdings, at least you would have some cash reserves. You could even make use of the cash to bargain-hunt shares that had been dragged down by the market fall. The amount of cash you should keep depends on your own risk-and-reward profile and the frequency with which you deal, as well as the underlying health of the stock market. A figure of about 20 per cent of the total amount of money you are prepared to invest in individual shares would not be a bad starting point. You will want to keep it somewhere handy where it can earn a reasonable amount of interest but is available instantly if you wish to invest it. Some Internet bank investment accounts or building society accounts pay a reasonable rate of interest and allow instant access to your funds.

The actual percentage of cash that you hold will fluctuate over time, depending on the number of investment opportunities you discover and also the general state of the stock market. If it is a bear market and share prices are tumbling you may want to keep a large amount of your investment funds in cash. If it is a bull market and share prices are charging ahead you may feel confident enough to use almost all your funds to invest in shares.

Keep records

There are two reasons to keep records of your investments. One is for tax purposes and the other is to monitor your performance.

We shall look at tax in a later chapter, but suffice it to say that you should file everything regarding your share purchases and sales and dividends and tax credits received. What you paid for shares and what you sold them for is important when calculating capital gains tax and dividend income, and tax credits have to be declared on your income tax return.

The second type of records that you keep are important for measuring how well you are doing in terms of investment return. These records not only give you a running commentary on how your portfolio is doing over time and relative to the wider stock market, but can also highlight where you might be going wrong and help you rectify mistakes.

At its simplest level keeping track of your investments can involve tracking share prices and therefore the value of your holdings over time. Just what time period you choose depends on how actively you invest. I would suggest for anyone who buys shares in individual companies that they monitor their shares at least once a week. But some of you will want to check on how your shares have performed every day, while others will be content to check once a month and true advocates of buy-and-hold strategies may feel once a quarter is sufficient.

Whatever time-frame you choose it is important to stick with it. The temptation in rising stock markets is to look at your portfolio regularly since your shares are also likely to be increasing in value and you get a psychologically warm feeling. There is nothing wrong with this, but it should not distract you from impartially monitoring your performance. The danger is in falling markets when the pain of lower valuations means investors are reluctant to check regularly on their portfolio. But you must try to overcome this psychological reluctance since falling markets are the very time when you need to be most vigilant about your investments.

To set up a simple record of your shares you can use a sheet of paper. Just write down the names of every company in which you have invested, the number of shares you own, the price you paid and the share price each time you check it. By multiplying the price by the number of shares you arrive at a value for your stake in each share. Add up all the values to give an overall value for the portfolio. You can also include another column comparing the values each time you check the prices with the previous time you did so. This will tell you how much each share and the portfolio as whole has risen or fallen in value over the period.

To get a feel for how your investments have performed against the wider markets you could measure the movement in an index such as the FTSE 100 over the same period. The easiest way to find share prices to use in your records is through daily and Sunday newspaper share listings, although you could also use Teletext on the television. You can play around with these simple tables by, for example, listing shares in order of performance with the best performers at the top of the list and the worst performers at the bottom. You could also draw a line to mark in percentage terms the index you have chosen as a comparison and see which of your shares are above the line and have outperformed the index and which below. In order to see the trends in your portfolio more easily you could graph the numbers. Graphs are a very quick and simple way to identify trends. For a more sophisticated method of keeping track of your shares you could turn to computer software or the Internet.

If you have access to a computer – and we shall consider later in this chapter how useful they can be – there are a raft of Internet websites that allow you to register your portfolio of shares and keep track of its value in real time. In addition you can purchase software that enables you to build up portfolios and track shares.

The practical use of keeping records of your investments is that it shows how good you are at investing and helps take the emotion out of the process. You might feel that a particular share has done very well, but if you compare it with the performance of the stock market you may find it has underperformed. If you consistently underperform the general market it might be worth changing your investment strategy. Keeping records is also a way to monitor stop-loss levels and ensure each share is still within its limits or if not, whether action should be taken.

Finally, keeping records is above all a good discipline and underlines the need to be aware of your investments and how they are performing on a regular basis.

Market lore

Timing is a crucial part of investment strategy, but it is also one of the hardest aspects to get right. Luck, and a good dose of it at that, is about the only way you will ever buy a share when its price bottoms out and sell it when it peaks. There is unfortunately no magic formula for telling investors when to buy or sell. At best, you should hope to buy on the way up and sell on the way down.

But none of this has stopped the elusive search for a solution. For individual shares it is a thankless task, but some theories have emerged concerning the stock market as a whole and the timing of investment. Really these theories are little more than market folklore and the health warning about them is strengthened by the fact that advocates tend to remember some of them in handy rhymes. But although scepticism is good thing for investors, some of these adages do stand up to scrutiny.

Perhaps the most famous is: 'Sell in May and go away. Don't come back till St Leger's Day.' The St Leger is a horse race run in early September. As well as being the most well-known adage about market timing, there is some evidence that it has proved broadly correct looking back over historical figures stretching back to the 1920s. The summer months do tend to be a lacklustre time for the stock market and historical research shows that returns in the second half of the year tend to be lower than in the first half.

There are several reason why this should be the case. The most obvious is the lack of financial information from companies for investors to react to. Another is that companies have issued their annual results for the previous year by May; indeed, most have published by the end of March, which means there are less financial figures post-May for investors to base their investment decisions on and most will prefer to wait until the interim reporting season in September. The autumn is also the time that cash dividends are paid out, giving investors cash to reinvest, while analysts begin firming up their financial forecasts for companies towards the end of the year and advise clients to buy. All these factors help lift shares at the end of the calendar year and into each new year.

There are more esoteric reasons why the summer is a dull time on the stock market. It is the holiday season as well as the social season that includes the Wimbledon tennis championships and horse racing at Royal Ascot, both of which are well attended by the movers and shakers of the City. With a reduced number of fund managers working in the City the volume of shares traded tends to fall and the stock markets tends to drift. The adage is not set in stone and indeed, August in isolation tends to be good month for shares, but it is useful for investors to know that if you intend to buy heavily during the summer as a whole the markets may be inclined to move against you.

Just as August on its own is good for shares, so can be the last half of December, summed up in the adage: 'Don't dally, here comes the Christmas rally.'

Investors should not get too carried away in the autumn and new year, though, according to the phrases: 'Bull market bashes end with October crashes.' and 'As January goes, so goes the year.'

Again, they may appear neatly to encapsulate investment strategy, but they do not really stand up under historical analysis. Although there have been some big stock market slumps in October only two of the twenty largest falls in the markets last century happened during the month. Over the long term October appears to be just an average month for investors. There is also little historical basis for suggesting that if the market starts well in January it will continue to rise for the rest of the year and if it begins the year by falling it will continue its downward path. A large fall of more than 3 per cent in the stock market in January more often than not will be followed by falls in the next 11 months but the times that a rise falls are enough to render it meaningless as a hard-and-fast rule. Small gains in January are often followed by increases in the rest of the year, but if the market rises by more than 4 per cent the chances of continuing increases are little more than 50–50.

Another old saying is: 'Sell on an election.' By definition this can only be tested about every five years, so it is not of much use to investors apart from during an election year and even then its merits are questionable. General Elections are often a vote on the economic success or failure of the government and it is easy to see how the stock market might have reacted strongly to an election when the Labour and Conservative parties' views on the economy were more polarised. Business would have thought Labour government bad and share prices would have fallen, whereas unless it was a surprise not predicted by opinion polls a Conservative victory would already have been discounted by the stock market.

The rise of wider share ownership has meant many share owners are normal voters and political parties have realised the importance of a stable stock market. Although General Elections do move stock markets, their impact is now unpredictable and relatively unimportant.

Another political event to have spawned an investment rhyme is the Budget, with the warning: 'Investors will pay come Budget Day.' In fact, historical data has shown share prices have risen on Budget Day three times out of four.

There is no cute rhyme to accompany the theory that investment timing can also be determined on a weekly or even daily basis, but some people do put forward such suggestions. One is: 'Up on Monday, down on Tuesday.' The implication here is that investors buy on Monday because they have been unable to deal for a couple of days and are reacting to newspaper reports and investment suggestions over the weekend. Shares that are tipped in investment columns also tend to be marked up on a Monday, so prices are higher in these stocks. The theory then suggests that a day later some of the predicted developments may not have happened, or if buyers did not emerge for the Sunday recommendations the prices are marked back down. Although common sense suggests there is merit in these arguments, again it can tell us that there are many good Mondays in the market that are followed by good Tuesdays.

Another piece of market folklore is that if you keep an eye on the stock market until mid-afternoon you should be able to call how it will close. The argument is that if the stock market opens strongly and stays strong until mid-afternoon it will close strongly. If it falls mid-morning and fails to recover after lunch it will close lower and if it falls mid-morning but recovers after lunch it will close up. The theory suggests market moves will work in reverse if the stock market opens weakly. While years ago the theory may have had some merits, the growing influence of the US stock market, which opens in the early afternoon London time, means what happens on Wall Street is far more important to the direction of UK shares than whether they have opened higher or lower. Even if the adage did hold water it is hard for small investors – other than devoted day traders – to exploit hourly changes in the stock market.

INFORMATION: THE MOST VALUABLE OF COMMODITIES

All investors need to respond to information of one sort or another when deciding which shares to buy. Even die-hard technical analysts need at least a company's share price over time in order to plot the graphs that indicate when to buy and sell. For investors information is the material that enables them to build up a picture of a company and consider the suitability of its shares as an investment.

There are several sources of information that all investors can make use of and they are examined later in this chapter, but it is also important to understand what this information tells you in the context of how listed companies operate and the relationship they have with their advisers.

Quoted companies and their advisers

Every stock market-listed company will have a raft of professional advisers, some of whom are kept on retainers for their services to be used as needed, while others are in full-time employ. A typical quote company will have a banker, a financial adviser, a stockbroker, an auditor, a solicitor and a financial public relations company.

Banks

Just as you have a bank account in which you deposit your income and from which you pay bills and sometimes run up an overdraft, so does a company. The banks favoured by companies are generally exactly the same high street giants that you bank with, although they will have accounts with the corporate rather than the retail arm of the bank.

Financial advisers

These tend to be investment banks. Some twenty years ago investment banks would have been known as merchant banks, but a series of takeovers and the increasing foreign ownership of the City have seen them become universally known as investment banks. They have few dealings with the general public and their prime role as far as companies are concerned is as deal makers.

Investment banks have corporate finance arms that advise companies on deals such as acquisitions and disposals, takeovers and bid defences, stock market listings and fund-raisings. They make their money from fees generated from deals and therefore have a vested interest in encouraging companies to do deals. Although many of their ideas and actions will be for clients, they also do a certain amount of speculative work in the hope of winning clients. Sometimes they will carry out research on potential deals, such as a merger of two companies, even though neither company is their client. They will take the idea to the companies in the hope of convincing them to do the deal and employ the bank to facilitate the merger.

Ideas are often generated by in-house analysts, although once a deal is active the banks operate a so-called Chinese Wall, which means the analysts do not know what the finance arm is doing.

Investment banks are an increasingly powerful force in influencing the strategies of companies and are powerful allies in situations such as takeover bids. Many top companies have several investment banks working for them.

Stockbrokers

There are so-called private-client retail brokers who cater for individuals who buy and sell shares and we shall consider who they are and how to choose them later. But there are also corporate stockbrokers who act for companies. These brokers are concerned with all aspects of a company's stock market listing and help ensure that companies meet Stock Exchange regulations. They also help with fund-raisings and stimulate demand for a company's shares by marketing the business to institutional investors, often with help from research by their own in-house analysts, and ensuring there is a market in the company's shares.

Corporate brokers play an important advisory role for companies and can have a crucial part to play in takeover activity by a company whether it is buying another business or defending itself against a bid.

Because brokers primarily buy and sell shares they are close to many institutional investors who are also their clients. This means they make a particularly good sounding board between their client companies and major investors. In this they tend to be closer to fund managers than financial advisers such as investment banks and are therefore vital for providing early warnings of any problems with the way the stock market perceives a particular company.

Although brokers do differentiate themselves from investment bank financial advisers the line between the two is becoming increasingly blurred.

Auditors

These are firms of accountants who are employed by the company and appointed by shareholders at the annual meeting. The auditors act on behalf of shareholders, the owners of the company.

While directors of the company prepare and sign accounts, it is the job of the auditor to certify that the accounts present a true and fair view of the company's profits and financial health, and to indicate if they do not.

Auditors are supposed to be independent of the company's management, although they will be open to persuasion about the presentation of certain items of the accounts and may accept it if management puts up a convincing case.

Auditors play an important check-and-balance role on behalf of shareholders and if their report says the accounts do not give a true and fair view or if they pass the accounts with qualifications, alarm bells should ring for investors.

Solicitors

Just as you will have a solicitor to advise you on legal matters, so do companies. Company solicitors advise on aspects of company law and are particularly used by companies during deals. Acquisitions and takeovers, or indeed anything requiring a contract, will see a company turn to its solicitor for help.

Financial public relations

In just twenty years or so financial public relations firms have become powerful players in the City. They are a link between companies and the media, analysts and investors.

At the most basic level PR firms help organise routine company announcements such as interim and final results. They ensure these are supplied to the media in the form of press releases that, as well as containing the financial facts, will highlight areas of the business that present the company in a favourable light. The firms will often also organise press conferences at which directors can be quizzed by the media on the company's results and these often follow earlier briefings for analysts run on the same lines.

PR firms also promote their clients by talking up the merits of companies joining the stock market, presenting deals in a positive light and helping to defend them when they are being bid for and bolstering their arguments when they are the bidders.

Just as the political world has spin doctors, so financial PRs are the spin doctors of the Square Mile. There are many financial PR firms in the City, although little more than half a dozen represent most of the major quoted companies.

At the highest level PR firms act as advisers to companies and are able to assess for them the public impact of deals and strategy decisions, and alert them to potential problems. A growing number of these firms are also involved in crisis management where they advise companies on the best ways to deal with unexpected or damaging events. In a world with a proliferation of media outlets the power of PR firms is increasing rapidly.

Many now act as gatekeepers and control the media's access to company directors, meaning they are able to keep a tight rein on stories and try to manage them to the advantage of their clients. While few journalists are willing to play along with the PR spin doctors, most realise they have to maintain some sort of relationship in order to do their jobs.

Most investors are unaware of the role financial PRs play, but one way or another these firms are responsible for much of the information available about companies. It is useful to bear in mind that PRs always have their client's interests at heart and therefore will try to present the company in the best possible light.

Other advisers

Although the above advisers are the most commonly used by companies, on occasion they will use other specialists.

Some companies such as supermarket groups often retain property consultants to advise them on their portfolio of stores and to help them acquire new sites. From time to time, other companies may employ such consultants perhaps when they are revaluing their properties.

Insurance agents are also retained by some companies on a permanent basis, particularly if they have a large number of assets or potential risks that need to be dealt with on a day-to-day basis.

Be advised

Small investors can learn a lot about a company by the advisers it has. Blue chip advisers such as well-known big City firms with solid reputations usually, although not always, can give investors confidence in a company. These firms would be unlikely to be involved with the company unless they were confident about its prospects. Certain stockbrokers and investment banks have gained reputations for being strong in particular fields – for example, technology – and their involvement with a company may give investors added confidence.

Equally, some brokers and advisers have less consistently successful reputations and these might make investors wary of companies they are involved with.

A particularly important signal for small investors can be provided by a company's appointment of new advisers. If a small company swaps its small broker and investment bank for much larger financial players it could indicate bigger ambitions by the business and hint at likely corporate activity such as acquisitions.

But changing advisers can also be a warning signal to investors, particularly if the company is unwilling or unable to explain why the changes have been made. If an adviser resigns it should ring warning bells for shareholders since it would indicate some disagreement that could harm investor confidence and hit the share price.

Investors should also be wary of a sudden surge in the amount of news flowing from a company, especially if it has a small market capitalisation. News flow is very important for these companies to draw attention to themselves and also keep investors regularly updated on their progress. But a sudden spate of information or coverage in the media could simply mean that the firm has just employed a new public relations firm that has been very active on its behalf, rather than any changes in its business fundamentals.

SOURCES OF INFORMATION

Changes in a company's advisers are just one of many facts about a business that are useful to small investors. There are plenty of places you can search to find out about such changes and other information about companies. These sources of information are worth considering in detail. They include the company itself, analysts, newspapers and other publications and, increasingly, the Internet.

Company

All shareholders who have their name on a company's register of shareholders will receive through the post certain documents published by the company. These include the annual report and accounts, and other notices of major events, particularly when they require shareholder backing in the form of a vote at an extraordinary general meeting. Such events include acquisitions, disposals and demergers, share splits and consolidations, and details of special dividends. Companies are also obliged to announce many of these events to the Stock Exchange, as well as their annual and interim results, dealings by directors in their shares and trading statements. These are all considered price-sensitive in that they are capable of moving the company's share price.

These announcements are made via the Regulatory News Service that is operated by the London Stock Exchange. RNS is currently only available in real time by subscribing to expensive information service providers such as Reuters or the LSE itself. The price of these dedicated computer terminals is prohibitive to small investors, putting them at a disadvantage against professional investors. But RNS is available, albeit currently with a delay of 15 minutes, on several Internet websites including the London Stock Exchange's site.

Small investors could also approach the company and its directors in order to find out information. The most obvious way of doing this is at the annual meeting, but you could write to or phone the company's directors. Although they will be unable to reveal price-sensitive information, they should be able to help with general queries and their availability is one way of gauging how seriously they take shareholder relations. If you want very general information only or a copy of the annual report you could try contacting the company secretary.

Analysts

Stockbrokers and investment banks employ analysts to examine companies and advise on whether their shares are worth buying, should be held or sold. The written research that analysts produce is available to these institutions and their corporate clients such as pension fund managers. It is also often made available to the media, so you are likely to read about analysts' recommendations in newspapers, magazines and on websites. It is still very hard, though, for small investors to get direct access to the research, often termed brokers' notes, although this is beginning to change with the growth of investment sites on the Internet.

Some analysts who are highly rated in the investment community for the accuracy of their views can have a powerful effect on a company's share price. If they rate a company's shares a buy, investors are likely to follow their recommendation and the share price will rise, while a sell note would have the opposite effect.

Most analysts research individual companies in specific stock market sectors and, depending on the size of the broker or investment bank they work for, they might be in teams as large as six people. So a banking analyst would cover the whole banking sector and do detailed research on its individual members such as Lloyds TSB and Barclays. While oil analysts look at the oil sector and in detail at companies such as BP Amoco and Shell.

Brokers rely on the advice of their analysts to tell them which shares are worth buying and which to sell for their clients, and they will also turn to their analysts to interpret particular company events such as results or how a contract win or an acquisition might affect the share price.

Analysts often talk to the clients of the broker or the investment bank but they also produce research notes, often as a result of visiting companies and talking to senior management. The research usually contains an overview of the sector and the company, some brief history and an outline of where the company is currently in terms of its businesses and strategy. It will also look back at its recent financial record and forecast ahead at least a couple of years in terms of earnings and dividends.

Analysts rely on information from the company and its advisers to draw their conclusions. They will utilise many of the investment techniques and strategies we examined in earlier chapters. They will use computer spread sheet models to input figures they know in order to help forecast future financial results. Inevitably, the results they obtain will depend on the quality of their information and the accuracy of their assumptions.

Taking all these factors into consideration the notes will offer a view on the company's shares. Analysts use a whole range of expressions to indicate how they feel about the company's shares. The terms used include buy, sell, hold, outperform, add and reduce, and each will mean something slightly different as used by different analysts.

Generally, a **buy** stance means the analyst expects the company's share price to outperform a benchmark index such as the FTSE Allshare by between 10 per cent and 20 per cent – the amount depends on the figures used by individual analysts – over a stated period. Some analysts include a target price of the shares.

A **sell** recommendation would imply that the analyst expects the share price to underperform the index by 10 per cent to 20 per cent over a given period.

If an analyst believes a share price will move ahead and outperform the index, but by less than 10 per cent to 20 per cent, they may rate the shares an **add**, or **accumulate** or **market outperform**.

If the share price is expected to underperform the index, but by less than 10 per cent to 20 per cent they will rate the shares either **reduce** or **market underperformer**.

An analyst who believes the shares will perform in line with the index will rate the share a **hold**, a **market performer** or **neutral**.

Although these descriptions are in general use, different brokers use different methods of grading shares. Some will use a number systems from 1 to 5 where 1 represents a strong buy and 5 a strong sell. Others make recommendations but also grade shares according to risk, making them either high, medium or low risk.

There is no doubt that some analysts are very good at what they do and their research into companies and the recommendations they make are extremely influential. But other analysts are less competent and their comments on shares are less informed.

It should also be remembered that analysts originated as a marketing service for stockbrokers to offer to clients who pay massive sums in commission. Today, analyst research is used by the sales department of a stockbroker to help stimulate interest in a company's shares. Stockbrokers make money on dealing commissions whether their clients are buying or selling shares, although since sell notes are only of interest to investors who already own the shares most clients are looking for buy advice. Cynics suggest this is a poor excuse for the predominance of buy notes over sell notes and suggest buy notes have more effect on stimulating business.

Buy notes tend to be particularly prevalent when the analyst's firm acts as stock market adviser, the house broker, to the company researched. You would be right to be sceptical about positive research produced by house brokers, but in the unlikely event that they out some negative research you should definitely take note.

Because of the problems of vested interest, when looking for analysts' research it is wise to put most credence on that produced by independent analysts. Getting your hands on such research is no easy matter and this tends to put private investors at a disadvantage against the professionals. But the situation is changing. Some newspapers and magazines will report analysts' views on a regular basis and many accounts of company results will often include quotes from analysts offering instant views on the figures.

Some private-client stockbrokers have their own analysts whose research they will send out to clients. But these teams of analysts are often small and while they may have good knowledge of some sectors they will be less reliable on others.

Traditionally, companies are keen to build close links with analysts since positive research is beneficial to their share price. It has meant that analysts have access and insights, which small investors are unable to match. Occasionally, some companies have given price-sensitive information to analysts to help them with their work.

But this situation is changing mainly because financial watchdog the Financial Services Authority is determined to ensure a level playing field for all investors. It is increasingly common for companies who have held meetings or site visits with analysts to issue a statement to the Stock Exchange detailing what was discussed. A few companies offer shareholders the chance to listen in to management conferences with analysts and some, such as BP Amoco, enable investors to do this via the Internet.

The Internet, as we shall discuss later in this chapter, is probably the small investor's best ally in trying to take on the professionals. Several sites regularly publish précis of analysts' research and some, including a few run by former analysts, offer their own company analysis and investment recommendations.

Newspapers and magazines

The cheapest and most easily accessible source of information for private investors is provided by newspapers and specialist investment magazines. For just a few pence a day small investors can keep up to date with developments on the stock market and what is happening to sectors and companies. You can also tap into analysis and investment suggestions, and find a wealth of raw statistics that you can use to make your own investment decisions.

There are daily newspapers whose bread-and-butter business reporting includes company results, takeover deals, board appointments and other so-called diary items. They are given this tag because they are reports of events such as announcements to the Stock Exchange where the information is available to all media and is simply reported. This is a useful service for small investors who cannot access this information in any other way. Most daily newspapers also have stock market reports that highlight particular share price movements and many have investment columns that consider the merits of particular shares that are currently in the news.

Daily newspapers will also include stories that their journalists have discovered, which could be anything from boardroom arguments to potential takeover bids. These exclusive offerings can provide real value for small investors since they are likely to be accessing them at the same time as their professional counterparts who are usually well ahead in the information race because of the sophisticated electronic services they can afford.

But for investors seeking stories that will not have appeared elsewhere on companies the financial and business sections of Sunday newspapers are the best port of call. Since Sunday journalists do not have to produce a paper every day they have more time to spend researching and chasing stories. As a result Sunday papers regularly carry stories that are likely to move a company's share price. They are also more likely to have a speculative feel than stories in the dailies. Sunday papers are also a favourite way for companies and more usually their PRs to place stories that are favourable to their clients. The paper gets a story and the company gets coverage. Sunday paper stories often move share prices on Monday mornings and as well as stories the sections often contain investment columns, personal finance pages, and interviews and profiles with prominent business people.

Statistics

Before examining the variety of publications available that offer good business and City coverage it is worth glancing at one piece of information that almost all newspapers offer: list of share prices. The *Financial Mail on Sunday*'s share price listing is typical of the format used and offers investors an instant snapshot of a company's financial situation.

		GENERAL RETAILERS						
650	443	Boots.........................615	5	0.8	5,535	13.5	4.1
560	232	Brown (N)...............260	-15	-5.5	761	22.4	1.8
238	144	Carphone................151	-13	-7.9	1,237	–	–
388	125	Debenhams.......381¾	12¼	3.3	1,413	16.2	2.8
400	176	Dixons.................258½	6½	2.6	4,950	26.9	4.3
565	334	Great Univ.........513½	12½	2.5	5,166	19.3	4
623	406	JJB Sports............616	63½	11.5	761	21	1.7
630	344	Kingfisher..............487	12	2.5	6,794	15.9	3
283	168	Marks & Sp...........246	13	5.6	7,073	18.6	3.7
805	348	Matalan...............518½	-12½	-2.4	2,178	52.9	0.8
837	430	Next...........................821	26	3.3	2,767	21.3	2.7
75	43	Signet.....................74½	4½	6.4	1,252	14.1	2
487	300	Smith WH...............475	5	1.1	1,191	11.8	4

The share price listings pages divide companies into their stock market sectors and then detail a range of information about them. For example, the General Retailers sector contains Boots.

In the Boots example the first two columns show the highest and the lowest that the company's share price in pence, has been in the last 52 weeks, in this case a high of 650p and a low of 443p. The next column shows the closing share price for Boots the previous week at 615p; on a daily paper this would be the previous day's close. The fourth column details the price change over the week in pence, 5p, and the fifth column puts this in percentage terms, 0.8 per cent. In the sixth column Boots's market capitalisation is detailed, which is its share price multiplied by the number of shares it has in issue making £5.535 billion. The seventh column provides a calculation of Boots's price/earnings ratio, which is the share price divided by the company's last reported annual earnings-per-share, which in this case is 13.5. So Boots's share price can be said to trade at 13.5 times earnings. The final column details the yield provided by the dividend last paid by Boots. The yield is the annual dividend divided by the share price expressed as percentage. Since the last total dividend paid by Boots was 25.2p and the share price is 615p the yield is 4.1 per cent.

From these simple figures alone it is possible to build up an investment picture of Boots. The company's share price is nearer the top of its trading range in the last 52 weeks than the bottom and its price moved ahead slightly last week.

By glancing at the other companies in the General Retailers sector you can see that most retailers saw their share prices gain in the last week.

Boots's market capitalisation figure tells you its size relative to other retailers, while the PE and yield figures are useful to compare it with other companies in the General Retailers sector. You can see that its PE is almost the lowest among all the companies listed, while its yield is one of the highest. This may lead you to conclude its share price is cheap relative to its peers, although you would then have to do further research to discover if it deserved to be on a lower rating than its rivals.

All papers with business sections will have some form of share price listings and while the order of the columns and the information given may differ slightly, they will all provide a useful snapshot of information for investors.

Newspapers

Britain has scores of newspapers all of which can be useful to small investors. The national press tends to follow and break the big stories, but regional papers can be useful for providing local insights into businesses.

Dailies: The main daily newspaper for anyone interested in the stock market and listed companies is the *Financial Times*, often referred to as the *FT* and printed on distinctive pink paper. Because it is almost entirely devoted to business it covers almost every company and economic story happening.

The paper has two sections: a main section covers major business stories, economic and political events; and a second company news section that focuses on company stories and is a journal of record for the previous day's stock market developments. This second section contains a wealth of statistics including comprehensive share price listings for the UK and many overseas markets, as well as commodity prices.

On the back of the main section is the Lex column, which comments on business issues, economic matters and individual companies. Its view is extremely influential, although it is seldom crude enough to say outright whether a company's shares should be bought or sold, so you will have to read between the lines to some extent.

For a view of the US markets investors could look at the *Wall Street Journal*. Its presentational style is very different from the British press but the paper has a good reputation for breaking stories and now has a European edition that contains more European news.

Although no other British national broadsheet matches the depth of business coverage of the *FT*, each has a business and City section. *The Times*, the *Daily Telegraph*, the *Independent* and the *Guardian* all provide slightly different slants on business coverage and some are particularly strong in certain areas. Most also have an investment column. For easily accessible company news and information, investors are increasingly turning to the popular tabloids. The *Daily Mail*'s business section has always been highly regarded but even the *Sun* and the *Mirror* have launched financial sections in recent years, while the *Daily Express* has a long-standing section.

Regional papers such as *The Scotsman* and the *Birmingham Post* give prominence to local companies including smaller businesses that the nationals may not follow closely. Therefore they can provide useful information for investors. Although not strictly a local paper, the *Evening Standard* in London is highly influential since it is read in the City on the same day as the companies it writes about present their results or announce their deals.

Sundays: The Sunday papers generally assume that small investors will have picked up most of their information during the week and are therefore either looking for analyses of the last week's news or new stories that might set the business news agenda in the week ahead.

The *Financial Mail on Sunday* has the largest circulation of any Sunday paper with a business section and is aimed at small investors and those interested in personal finance, as well as companies and City professionals and more general readers. Apart from business and financial stories, features and interviews, it has an investment column called Midas and at its heart a personal finance section.

The Sunday broadsheets – the *Sunday Telegraph*, the *Sunday Times*, the *Observer* and the *Independent on Sunday* – each have a business section, which follows a similar format and includes investment columns.

Magazines

Although newspapers offer extensive coverage of business and financial matters, there are a growing number of magazines that are aimed specifically at private investors. The doyen of investment magazines is the *Investors Chronicle* which, like the *FT*, is owned by media group Pearson. The *IC* is published weekly and offers detailed analysis of company results and the outlook for businesses. It also offers recommendations on companies it analyses, as well as six share tips a week. In addition it runs portfolios of shares using different investment criteria.

The Economist is also a weekly publication and though it does contain UK business and company news it is international in its outlook.

In recent years a raft of new investment magazines have hit the news stands ranging from publications aimed at beginners to stock market investing through to subscriber share tip sheets. With these you very much pays your money and takes your choice, but it is worth checking out at least a few to see if you find them useful. Some tip sheets have a good track record, but others are less solid. Either way, only use their advice to point you in a general direction and always do your own research as well.

If your investment focus is on a particular sector it could be worthwhile buying one of the many trade publications that cover that area. The trade press often has an interesting perspective on a company and has stories that may not yet have made it into the wider media.

THE INTERNET

Without doubt the biggest boon to small investors in recent years has been the growth of the Internet and the wealth of information on companies and the stock market that it offers. While access to the Internet can be achieved through some television services and limited access is available through mobile phones, the most common means of going online is by using a computer. Although you can use a computer in an Internet café or library to check out information, if you plan on becoming an active investor you will find life a lot easier if you own a computer. The help it can give you not only in accessing the Internet, but also in keeping records on companies and your own trading means it could pay for itself in a short time.

Equipment

To become an online investor you will need a computer, a modem through which the computer connects to the Internet, a phone line, software and an account with an Internet service provider (ISP).

Broadly speaking there are two types of computer: a personal computer or PC and computers made by Apple. Although the Apple products are stylish and well marketed, there is a greater choice of investment software available for PCs.

You will need to spend £600 to £1000 to buy a new PC, while a laptop version will cost about £1500. Many computers will include a modem, but if not this could cost up to about £100. You can use your home phone line to access the Internet, although if you are a heavy Internet user you might consider installing a second line.

Software varies in price and in quality, with many financial websites offering free services. An account with an ISP can be free, although if you want unlimited access at no charge as you use it you can pay over £100 a year.

Your choice of computer should be determined by your budget and the demands you will put upon it. Technology gets cheaper each year and the power of computers in terms of speed and memory increases likewise. Therefore you should spend as much as you can afford in order to get the highest-specification computer you can. Although cheaper computers will do a job the limitations of their technology will become more obvious in a few years' time than a more sophisticated system.

The basic requirements of any computer you choose is that it should be fast – computer speed is measured in megahertz and you should target a machine with at least 350 MHz. Your computer should also have a temporary memory – known as RAM – of at least 64 megabytes and a permanent memory – on the hard disk – of at least five gigabytes. The computer should also have both a floppy disk drive and a CD-ROM drive for loading software and enabling you to make back-up files.

A modem is simply a device that connects the computer to the phone line through a lead and the specification of your modem will determine how quickly you can download web pages. You should try to buy a modem with a top speed of at least 56.6 kbps.

The specification of other computer peripherals will depend on how much use and what other things you want to use your computer for, but a screen is essential and colour with a sharp image is preferable. In addition a printer can be useful.

Although you can buy separate computers, screens and printers, most high street electrical stores and mail-order computer companies will offer all the components as part of a package. So-called multimedia computers, which feature speakers and DVD players, are very popular and usually have the necessary specification to use them as an investment tool.

All ISPs will enable you to surf the web and send and retrieve e-mails, while many now allow you to create your own web pages.

Your choice of ISP will depend on how important service reliability, cost and access are to you. Free ISPs – that cost nothing to join but charge a local-rate call to use – sound good but reliability can be a problem and helplines can be expensive to dial. ISPs that charge may be more reliable and offer freephone access at certain or even all times, but you must decide whether the charges are justified.

Whichever ISP you use, they will provide the software you need to get online such as dialling and connection software and you will use an Internet browser such as Microsoft or Explorer of Netscape Navigator to explore the web, and these are usually already installed as part of the software you receive when you buy a computer.

Exploring the web

The amount of information available on the World Wide Web is awesome. As a private investor there are many sources you can turn to for information, each with its own advantages and disadvantages. These sites are constantly changing in terms of what they offer, as well as new sites coming into existence and others closing. Most are free of charge, although you may have to register as a member to gain full access. Some sites charge for membership and access to their services. The websites referred to below were all active at the time of writing.

Overview

Financial author Peter Temple has a site at www.cix.co.uk/ ~ptemple/, which lists a series of websites with links including individual companies, share price providers, brokers and newspapers, and is a useful starting point if you have a general idea of what you are looking for. If you do not, then try the University of Strathclyde's financial site at www.dis.strath.ac.uk/busienss/, which has many links but also includes a search facility to help you find what you are looking for.

Individual company sites

These are websites set up by listed companies themselves. They vary in quality, but at best provide an overview of the business and its directors, financial figures, regular news updates and a means of contact, usually via e-mail. Some company sites enable you to download copies of the annual report and accounts. Others show the company's share price. Company reports and accounts can be viewed or ordered from www.carol.co.uk and www.annual reports.ft.com.

General company sites

These sites offer information on quoted companies including an outline of their businesses, financial statistics and share price histories. Useful sites are www.hemscott.net, which also contains directors dealings, and www.hoovers.co.uk. For a sideways look at investing try Motley Fool at www.fool.co.uk. A good site is www.companyrefs.com, although this charges a subscription.

Share prices and stock market news

Currently only subscription sites allow investors to access share prices in real time, but most provide prices with a delay of about 15 minutes. Many of these sites also provide stock market news and regulatory announcements, brokers recommendations, and offer you the chance to set up and monitor a portfolio of shares. Among useful sites are www.market-eye.co.uk and www.iii.co.uk.

Company financials and personal finance

These sites offer some stock market and company facts and figures, as well as personal finance information. They include www.thisismoney.com, www.moneyunlimited.co.uk and www.moneyextra.com.

Exchanges and markets

All exchanges and markets have their own websites and they include the London Stock Exchange at www.londonstockexchange.com, NASDAQ at www.nasdaq.com and Ofex at www.ofex.co.uk.

Newspapers and other media

All newspapers and magazines now have a web presence, with some simply recycling stories that have been in print but others adding further services and information. Some interesting sites are the *Mail on Sunday/Daily Mail* and *Mail on Sunday* alone www.thisismoney.com, the *Financial Times* at www.ft.com/, the BBC at www.bbc.co.uk, *Bloomberg News* at www.bloomberg.co.uk and *Investors Chronicle* at www.investorschronical.co.uk.

Government departments and regulators

Useful addresses include the Inland Revenue at www.inlandrevenue.gov.uk and the Financial Services Authority at www.fsa.gov.uk.

Education and advice

Numerous websites offer new investors introductions to the subject, as well as advice and information on specifics such as investment trusts and shares clubs. A very good site is ProShare's at www.proshare.org.uk and others include the Association of Investment Trust Companies at www.aitc.co.uk, the Association of Unit Trusts and Investment Funds at www.investmentfunds.org.uk and the AAA Investment Guide at www.wisebuy.co.uk. A good educational site is www.stockacademy.com.

Caution

While the Internet will open up a powerful research medium to you and should make you a more efficient investor, its use comes with several notes of caution.

One is that the facts and figures available on websites may not always be totally up to date. Brokers' notes may have been on a website for a while and the forecast figures for a company may have been rendered obsolete by changes such as profits warnings. So if you are relying heavily on figures from a website it is probably best to double-check them elsewhere.

But by far the biggest note of caution regarding the Internet is the proliferation of so-called chat rooms or bulletin boards that enable anyone to post messages on financial websites. In an ideal world these enable investors to swap ideas and pass on their own experiences to each other. Unfortunately, they can also be hijacked by unscrupulous individuals who spread rumours in order to inflate or deflate the share prices of certain companies. Bulletin boards can be little more than rumour mills and at worst are used by investors deliberately to talk up or down a share they may wish to sell or buy. This caution is not designed to warn you away from reading or even participating in bulletin boards, but do so with a healthy scepticism for some of the content.

Other online services

Although some websites do provide basic charting online and many offer you the ability to register a portfolio of shares and keep track of their performance, there is also dedicated investment software available that you can load on your computer.

The cost and complexity of this software varies greatly, but it can be a useful tool as you develop your investing techniques. Some packages download share prices and information via the Internet, while others have their own dial-in database or use information provided by television's Teletext service for which you will need specialist hardware installed in your computer. Others use disks that are sent to you weekly and some rely on you manually entering share prices.

At the cheaper end of the scale a simple financial software package such as Microsoft Money or Quicken enables you to set up a share portfolio and download share prices from the Internet. Once you have bought and installed the software there is no additional cost. You can monitor the performance of your shares and the whole portfolio, but its use in detecting potential investments is limited.

Further up the price scale are software packages that combine fundamental and technical analysis. These offer financial figures on companies such as reported and forecast earnings and dividends, together with historic share prices that enable you to generate graphs on to which you can superimpose various technical indicators. Some of these packages require an upfront fee and then monthly payments. Examples are Sharescope and The Analyst from Winstock.

If you are an investor who intends to deal regularly and perhaps even daily you will want a software package or information system that gives you real-time share prices. Once you move into this realm the cost of such products will be out of the reach of most investors who are happy to operate a small portfolio of shares and deal only occasionally. However, if you intend to day trade, up-to-the-minute prices are essential. The sort of systems you might consider range from software for your PC such as products provided by Updata Software to dedicated terminals supplied by Reuters or Bloomberg, which offer real-time prices, the Regulatory News Service, charts and historic information.

OTHER SOURCES OF INFORMATION

There are a number of other ways in which you can find out about share prices, company results and statistics, and investment information.

One of the simplest methods of checking share prices, company results and market movements is through your television set. Ceefax on BB2 and Teletext on Channel Four provide a rudimentary financial news service but also comprehensive share price listings that are regularly updated during the day.

There are a number of dedicated business television channels available on satellite or cable, while among the offerings of the traditional broadcasters is the BBC's *Working Lunch*, an early-afternoon business and personal finance programme.

You can use the telephone to access information and the

Monday edition of the *FT* includes an *FT* Cityline code number after each share listing that can be used in conjunction with a phone number that it publishes to check on the price of the share. The *FT* also operates a free annual reports service for investors covering about 1200 major listed companies. The companies that offer the free reports are indicated in the *FT*'s share price listings and there is a general number for you to ring to request the report.

A growing number of specialist publications also exist to cater for investors' hunger for information. They tend to be produced either in print form or on CD-ROM for use with a computer. While the information they offer is extremely useful, these publications are not cheap on a subscription basis and therefore may be out of the practical price range of some investors. It is usually possible, though, to buy a single copy and it is also worth checking with your local library to see if they can get hold of one.

Some of the most useful sources of company information are produced by HS Financial Publishing which was formerly called Hemmington Scott. The firm's publications include *Company REFS* (Really Essential Financial Statistics), which was devised by investment expert Jim Slater and explains the main financial ratios used by analysts, provides historic and forecast figures for individual companies and ranks them against their peers. The company also produces the *Hemscott Company Guide*, which offers detailed financial and general information on more than 2300 UK stockmarket-listed companies. It also publishes the *PricewaterhouseCoopers Corporate Register* which contains information such as addresses, directors, advisers and shareholders of stock market-listed companies.

CONCLUSION

In this chapter we have considered some tricks of the trade designed to give you an edge when investing. While they are not short cuts, they should help you avoid some common errors when buying and selling shares.

We have also discussed the importance of understanding how

companies interact with their advisers and that whom they appoint or sack as advisers can send important signals to investors.

We have examined sources of information that are the lifeblood of investors. Without accurate information it is impossible to make a reasoned judgement about the investment potential of a share. We have shown how to access and interpret this information.

Finally, we have looked at the wealth of information available on the Internet. While a computer and the Internet are not essential in order to buy and sell shares, the amount of free information available and the speed at which it can be accessed means they are extremely useful tools for investors. Another reason to get an Internet-enabled computer is that many brokers now allow you to trade online. We shall consider this in the next chapter, which advises on how to choose a stockbroker.

CHAPTER **9**

Choosing a Stockbroker

The previous chapters have equipped you with a number of skills you will need when investing in shares. You now know what shares are, how to read company accounts and use the information to conduct fundamental analysis to judge whether or not a share is worth buying. You can also use technical analysis where the shape of a share price graph may help you judge the merits of investing in or selling a share. We have considered, too, a raft of strategies ranging from defensive to risky methods of investing, as well as sources of information to give you the facts and figures you need to make investment decisions. Armed with this knowledge you will be keen to put it into practice, but while you are almost ready to start dealing you need just a little more patience.

In this chapter we shall consider how you can apply what you have learned by actually dealing in shares. We shall look at the process of dummy or paper trades before you do the real thing; how to choose a stockbroker to enable you to deal, other ways of buying shares without a stockbroker and what to do if it goes wrong.

DUMMY TRADING
Investing your own money is not something to be done lightly and you should be confident in your methods before doing so.

Fortunately, with share trading there are several ways of testing your investment theories before you need actually to part with cash.

The simplest method of trying out different investment techniques is to paper trade. This involves deciding on a strategy, perhaps investing by value looking for low PE ratios and high yields, and then building a portfolio of shares. Draw up a list of perhaps half a dozen shares that fit the investment criteria and add their current share prices, which will be the theoretical prices at which you bought. Add stop-loss limits, then regularly update the progress of the share prices. It is useful to make a note of why you picked a particular share and why you chose to sell it. This process will enable you to track the progress of the shares you picked and help you determine the efficiency of the method you chose to help pick them. Since you should probably track the progress of the shares for several months it is quite a laborious process and one requiring great patience. But, of course, its best feature is that any losses will only be theoretical, although so will any profits.

A quicker method for checking out how well certain investment strategies fit your own risk-and-reward profile and how effectively you can put them into practice is to use historical share price data. You could get information about past share prices over the last couple of years by visiting your local library for back copies of newspapers or publications such as *Company REFS*. Some financial websites, including www.finsight.co.uk, offer historical prices. Online subscription and other subscription services offer historical prices as a matter of course. Using past share prices, you can track how a share that may have fitted your investment criteria perhaps two years ago has performed since and therefore conclude whether your method works or not.

While you should always keep a record of your dummy trades, they do not have to be written down and if you have a computer you can make use of the portfolio facilities offered by many investment websites.

One way that you may be able to test your strategies and make money without actually investing any cash is to take part in one of the many fantasy share trading games promoted on the Internet and in national newspapers. However, a word of warning about these competitions. Although they appear to replicate real share dealing by offering prizes for the best-performing share prices, they tend to favour contestants who buy and sell on a frequent basis, a strategy which, when trading for real, would incur large dealing charges that would eat into any profits.

Whatever dummy method you choose to test out your investment strategies, it is worth the effort. You will discover that you are better suited to some techniques than others and all it will have cost you is time. Once you have discovered which investment methods fit your profile and are most effective when you pursue them, you are ready to start dealing for real and you will need to choose a stockbroker.

STOCKBROKERS

What stockbrokers do

To buy and sell shares you will have to employ a stockbroker, a name that is often shortened to broker. At the simplest level buying and selling shares is what a stockbroker does. They make their money from charging commission on customers' orders to buy and sell shares. The amount they charge will depend on the type of broker and the size of the deal. It is usually based on a percentage of the order size of perhaps 0.5 per cent to 1.75 per cent, although flat-rate prices are now common. The main type of broker you will have contact with is known as a retail or private-client broker, to differentiate them from corporate brokers who act for companies, although some do both jobs.

Traditionally, brokers were stand-alone companies, but today many high street banks and building societies offer broking services. This choice is good for investors, although it does mean there are a range of different charges and services, and therefore, once you know what type of service you require, it pays to shop around. As well as several different types of brokers, there are many ways of accessing their services including by post, telephone and the Internet.

Stockbrokers are members of the London Stock Exchange and were regulated by the Securities and Futures Authority until its responsibilities were taken over by the top City watchdog, the Financial Services Authority. Free lists of brokers and the services they provide are available from the private-client stockbroker trade body, the Association of Private Client Investment Managers and Stockbrokers, ProShare and the London Stock Exchange.

Types of stockbroker

There are three main types of broker: discretionary or portfolio management, advisory and execution only. Which type you choose will depend on how experienced you are as an investor, how much you have to invest and how much you can afford in charges.

Discretionary

A discretionary broker manages your portfolio of shares at their own discretion. They have the authority from you to buy and sell shares without needing to ask you each time they do so. But you can set ground rules as to what type of shares you want them to buy or not. For example, you could specify you want your portfolio of shares to yield a high income or that you do not want unethical investments such as tobacco companies included.

Suitability: If you have not got the time or inclination to buy and sell shares yourself a discretionary broker will make all investment decisions for you. You will have a large amount of money to invest in shares, probably at least £50,000.

Good points: Discretionary brokers take the effort out of share dealing. They provide a point of human contact to discuss investments and will offer a host of benefits such as tax planning, keeping you up to date with corporate developments at the companies you invest in and advise you on what action to take with events such as bid situations. If you travel abroad a lot they will be able to react quickly to situations that you might otherwise miss. If you have a large portfolio of shares it is very difficult to keep a check on it and discretionary brokers have the staff and facilities to do so. **Bad points:** Although discretionary brokers offer a wide range of services and take the responsibility for buying and selling shares away from you, they obviously charge for the service. The commission or dealing charges will be high compared with other types of brokers and there will probably be a quarterly or annual management charge. Obviously the performance of your portfolio will depend on the skills of the broker. If they are good you have nothing to worry about but they cannot offer a guarantee of performance and remember that as well as investing in shares you are investing in their skills. Although the whole idea of using a discretionary broker is to avoid the need to keep tabs on your investments you should keep an eye on their performance. Watch out also for churning, a technique whereby brokers buy and sell shares regularly to generate commission rather than necessarily to improve the performance of your portfolio.

How to choose one: If you have decided a discretionary broker is the best type to look after your investments you will need to narrow down the choice from the hundreds in the marketplace. One of the best methods to achieve this is to ask friends or colleagues for a personal recommendation. They will be able to tell you how efficient and helpful the staff are and what the broker charges.

If you do not know anyone who uses a discretionary broker you should compile a short list from the comprehensive list available from APCIMS, perhaps based on geographical criteria since you will certainly want to meet regularly whomever you choose. You should then write to or phone the broker and get details of their charges and services. You might even like to test their investment prowess and ask them for a couple of investment ideas that you could then follow to see if they are any good. Remember that discretionary brokers want your business and firms should pull out all the stops to impress you. If they do not work hard to win your business that they are not worth giving it to.

Advisory

An advisory broker will give you investment advice on request, but a final decision on what shares to buy and sell is down to you. The broker does not have the authority to trade on your behalf. Your investment decisions would therefore be a combination of the suggestions of your adviser, based on their research expertise, and your own risk-and-reward profile. There are several different types of advisory service ranging from advice on which shares to buy and sell to advice on tax issues.

Suitability: You should consider using the advisory service if you have the time and inclination to keep control of your investments but are unsure about how to research shares and want ideas as to how you should invest. Advisory brokers are a halfway house between discretionary brokers and execution only. You should probably have a portfolio of shares worth at least £20,000 for such a broker to make economic sense and trade frequently.

Good points: Using an advisory broker will give you access to valuable professional advice and research facilities that you are unlikely to be able to afford to replicate. An advisory broker will be available at the end of the phone when you want to ask them advice on your investment ideas and, if you agree, they are likely to contact you with shares they consider worth buying. Since the broker will have met you and know your financial circumstances the suggestions they make should be tailored to fit your particular investment needs.

Bad points: An advisory broker's charges will be higher than execution only and in some cases the service costs more than a discretionary service since they have to contact you before they can deal. The fact that they must get in touch also means that an advisory broker cannot act as quickly to buy or sell shares as a discretionary broker. As with discretionary brokers, you are depending on their advice being right, although with an advisory broker you can choose to ignore it. Watch out for churning and recommendations of their own clients, although they must tell you if they are recommending such shares.

How to choose one: Just as with discretionary brokers, a personal recommendation is probably the most efficient way of finding a good advisory broker. After that, get some names from one of the lists and contact them to find out which you feel most comfortable with. Again, you could ask them to recommend some shares and see how good their advice is. Then consider their charging structures and dealing requirements since some firms only deal in minimum amounts starting at perhaps £10,000 and others will require you to deal a certain number of times during the year.

Execution only

An execution-only broker buys and sells shares as you instruct them without giving any investment advice. They are so simple they are often referred to as share-dealing services. There are plenty of execution-only brokers to choose from and you can give them your instructions using a variety of channels including by post, in person, by telephone and using the Internet. Although their basic function is to provide a medium through which you can buy and sell, many also offer administrative help such as summaries for your tax return, although they may charge extra for this.

Suitability: If you are the sort of person who has the time to take full control of his or her investments and trust your own judgement in deciding when to buy and sell shares, execution only is for you. Although execution only is suitable for regular traders, it is also useful in one-off situations such as stagging a privatisation issue.

Good points: Execution-only brokers are simple and cheap. Many high street banks and building societies offer share-dealing services and there are a raft of other companies including many on the Internet. They offer a variety of ways of buying and selling shares and commissions, through which they make their money, are low compared with discretionary and advisory brokers. They are able to keep prices low because they have no research departments to support and they handle large volumes of business, while competition – there are more brokers in this type of business than any other – also keeps charges down. One of the best points for regular traders is that they offer online share dealing whereby you can deal instantly over the Internet using the broker's website, which often also contains company data and news.

Bad points: As their name suggests, execution-only brokers will not be able to offer you any advice, therefore you must be sure of your own judgement. Although the service levels of many brokers is good, do not necessarily expect the same standard of personal service as you would get through a discretionary or advisory broker, both of whom want to retain your business. Occasionally things can go wrong with the systems of an execution-only broker, which means you may not be able to buy or sell at exactly the time you want to.

How to choose one: Yet again, use the route of personal recommendations to find an execution-only service. If this is not practical, consider candidates from lists of brokers or even advertisements since many execution-only brokers advertise their services. You want a firm with a reputation for good service and reasonable charges. Once you have produced a shortlist of potential brokers you should ask them a series of questions. If you want to buy shares you will need to open an account and you will want to know if a minimum deposit is needed and what rate of interest is paid on any cash in the account. You should find out what markets the broker covers, particularly if you are interested in trading AIM shares as well as shares listed on the main market. Check out dealing charges and find out if there is a discount if you deal regularly. Ask if there are ongoing charges if you keep your portfolio of shares with the broker and be clear about methods of dealing such as telephone and the Internet, as well as how you can contact them if things go wrong.

Opening an account

Once you have made your choice of broker you will need to open an account. Your broker will provide you with application forms or if the broker has an Internet service you should be able to apply online. Although you will not always need an account if you plan to use an execution only-broker very occasionally, if you intend to deal regularly you should open one.

Most brokers will require a banker's reference and will want you to deposit cash into your account, which will pay a rate of interest, before they allow you to trade. This provides the broker with security, since they know that when they execute an order you have the funds in your account to pay for the shares, rather than having to wait for you to post a cheque. But it also gives you greater flexibility as it enables you to buy shares quickly and it is a useful way of separating your share-dealing cash from your other monies.

Once you have set up your account the broker will give you a client number and a password, which again is a security device both when contacting them by phone or when using an Internet connection.

Dealing

Once you have opened your account you are ready to start dealing in shares. There are several ways you can do this, although the most common methods you are likely to use are the telephone and the Internet. Dealing by post is a cheap method of selling shares, but beware because the delay means you will have little control over the price at which you sell. Using the telephone and the Internet means you will know the price at which you buy and sell.

Although in theory you can trade at any time, you will most probably choose to deal when the London Stock Exchange is open for trading between 8 a.m. and 4.30 p.m. Monday to Friday. Trading during the stock market's opening times should ensure the prices you are quoted are current market prices. You can place orders to buy and sell outside market hours but you will need to specify a maximum price at which you are prepared to buy and a minimum price at which you will sell.

Telephone dealing

Buying and selling shares over the telephone is quite straight-forward. You will phone your broker, give your name and account number, and ask for a price at which you can buy or sell shares in a particular company. The broker can quote two prices. One is the price at which they will buy your shares, which is known as the bid price, and the other is the price at which they will sell your shares, known as the offer price.

The bid price will be the lower of the two and the difference between the two prices is called the spread and represents the profit of the market-maker who sells the shares to or buys the shares from the broker. Usually a small company with only limited demand for its shares will have a wider spread than a large company whose shares are actively traded. Market-makers are obliged by the London Stock Exchange to quote firm bid and offer prices based on a minimum number of shares, known as the normal market size (NMS). NMS for shares in a company is determined every three months and based on 2.5 per cent of the share's average daily turnover, the number of shares bought and sold, in the preceding year.

If you are buying shares you are interested in the broker's offer price. If you consider the figure quoted too high, you will choose not to pay it. But if you are willing to pay the figure quoted you must decide whether you want to buy at best or place a limit. If you place the order at best, the broker will endeavour to get you the shares at the price they quoted, although if they cannot secure them in the market at that price they may have to charge you slightly more. If this is unacceptable you can always place a limit order by telling the broker the maximum price you are prepared to pay for the shares. Be careful, though, since not all brokers allow you to place limit orders and some of those who do impose restrictions such as the limit being within 10 per cent of the current share price. They may also charge for the service.

If you are selling shares the whole process works in reverse. You will be interested in the broker's bid price. If it is too low, just ring off. But if you want to accept it you can choose to sell at best or set a limit for the minimum price you will accept for your shares.

Once your call to buy or sell shares is completed you are deemed to have made a contract with the broker and you cannot change your mind. For their part the broker is required to effect timely execution, which means they must contact a market-maker and fulfil the order to buy or sell as quickly as possible. If they cannot fulfil the limit order they will contact you to let you know.

Online dealing

If you plan to buy or sell shares online you will need to call up your broker's Internet website, which will have a trading screen that will display the current bid and offer prices. There will also be a trading form for you to fill in stating the number of shares you wish to buy or sell. You will be able to say whether you want to do this at best or put a limit on the price.

You will then be asked to confirm the deal and, once you have, you should receive online confirmation that the deal has gone through, and the relevant share price.

Different online brokers have different systems, with some using computers to transact the entire deal and others using the Internet only to register their order and then manually executing it. As part of the health check you use to pick your broker you should find out how automated their systems really are.

Prices

The examples we have used for telephone and Internet dealing reflect the traditional method of buying and selling shares where investors ask brokers for a share price and use them to buy or sell. This is called a quote-driven system since the price the broker quotes drives the transaction.

But there are currently two systems by which shares are bought and sold and as well as the quote-driven system there is an order-driven system for the FTSE 100 index of the largest 100 listed companies and an increasing number of the next 250 largest in the FTSE 250 index. The order-driven system is known as the Stock

Exchange Electronic Trading Service (SETS). It allows you to place an order with a broker to buy or sell shares at a price that you decide. Your order is posted on an electronic order book and matched automatically with someone willing to sell you or buy from you shares at the price you stipulated. Eventually the order-driven system should drive down costs since it effectively removes the need for a middleman enabling investors to deal directly with each other.

Contract notes

After your broker has dealt on your behalf they will post to you a contract note detailing the deal. It will name the company whose shares you have bought or sold, the date of the deal, the number of shares traded and the price. It will also detail the commission charged by the broker and the stamp duty paid. Stamp duty is a government tax that is charged when you buy shares and is levied at a rate of 0.5 per cent of the value of your purchase.

If you buy or sell shares worth more than £10,000, your contract note will also detail a £1 flat fee to the Panel of Takeovers and Mergers known as the PTM Levy.

You should check all the details on the contract note to make sure they tally with the figures you expected in terms of price and number of shares bought and sold. You should then keep the note somewhere safe since it will be important for your trading records, as well as helping you fill out your tax returns.

Settlement

Until recent years the Stock Exchange operated one- two- and three-week accounting periods, which meant no matter how many times you bought or sold shares during the period no money was actually paid until the second Monday after the accounting period. This meant you could buy shares and sell them again without actually ever coming up with the purchase price and if you sold them for more you made a profit.

But in the 1990s the Exchange introduced an electronic share-dealing settlement and registration system called CREST, which works on a rolling settlement basis. This means each transaction is handled separately and must be settled a set number of days after dealing, in other words settlement is happening every day. A settlement period is the time you have to supply your broker with money if you are buying shares or proof of ownership, such as a share certificate, if you are selling shares. Although some broking firms operate settlement periods of ten days or even more, the standard settlement period has been a working week of five days or T (for trading day) +5. In February 2001 a faster T+3 system was introduced, requiring settlement within three days.

Although many brokers will still offer extended settlement periods, the move to T+3 turned the spotlight on the traditional way in which investors held their shares – through a share certificate – and the increasing use of nominee accounts as an alternative.

Share certificates

Traditionally, the buying and selling of shares involved the transfer of a share certificate, which proved ownership of those shares. After buying shares through your broker they register the fact with the company which then issues a share certificate to the new owner. If you sell shares you must send your certificate to your broker. The advantages of this system are that you have positive proof of share ownership and as a registered shareholder you are entitled to receive an annual report and accounts, attend the annual meeting, vote on resolutions put by the company and you are also entitled to any perks that accompany ownership of the shares. The disadvantages are that you must keep the certificates safe, since they are as valuable as your shares, and with faster settlement times you have only a limited time to send off your certificate when selling shares. Some brokers may also charge more if you want shares in certificated form. Most brokers will still enable you to trade using share certificates but increasingly they are promoting the use of nominee accounts. If you have only a few shares and deal infrequently, however, keeping share certificates is probably best for you.

Nominee accounts

You can choose to hold your shares in a broker's nominee account, which means the broker's name rather than yours will appear on the company's share register. You are still the beneficial holder of the shares and you are entitled to dividends paid by the company. Your broker will send you regular statements and valuations of your holdings.

A nominee account has several advantages over holding share certificates and the biggest single one is that it speeds up transaction times. This means if you are selling shares you get your money quicker. It also makes life easier for the broker, which should translate into lower dealing charges, and for you, since your entire portfolio can be held in one place. Nominee accounts are also the future for share dealing and in the case of Individual Savings Accounts, tax-free investments that we shall consider in the next chapter, all shares have to be in nominee accounts.

There are disadvantages with nominee accounts, not least that you do not normally get shareholder benefits such as perks and attending the annual meeting, although some brokers can make special arrangements to ensure you do get these things.

Many brokers will require you to open a cash account linked to the nominee account. This can be both good, since it means you can instantly pay for shares and it is a depository for cash raised from share sales, and bad, since it means you must leave money on deposit with a broker when it could earn more in interest elsewhere. You are likely to be charged for the nominee account and you must also make sure your broker is well insured in case of problems such as fraud, since they hold all your shares. If you have large portfolio of shares and deal frequently, a nominee account is probably the most efficient way for you to hold your shares.

There is another option, though, and that is to become a personal member of CREST. Personal membership of CREST allows you to keep legal ownership of your shares, as well as benefiting from the speed of CREST settlement. You will still not have a share certificate, but you will receive all the shareholder benefits of owning the company's shares. Your broker will carry out the necessary settlement and transfer arrangements. To become a member of CREST you need to be sponsored by a broker who will be charged £20 a year by CREST and is likely to pass the charge on to you.

OTHER WAYS OF BECOMING A SHAREHOLDER

Although you are likely to use a stockbroker for most of your share dealings, there are ways of becoming a share owner that do not use a broker.

New issues

When a company sells its shares on the stock market for the first time to raise money it is called a new issue. Most new issues are bought through a stockbroker either when they start trading or, if you are able to gain access through your broker, when the shares are being allocated ahead of flotation. But large new issues such as privatisations and some that are likely to be popular with retail investors – for example, companies with strong consumer brands or high street retailers – are often marketed directly to the public. In this case adverts will be carried in newspapers and magazines, or information posted on the Internet, which enables you to register for the share issue and receive a prospectus. At this stage there is no obligation to buy the shares, but the prospectus will contain an application form for you to apply for shares. If you decide to buy the shares you will post this, along with a cheque for the value of the shares you wish to buy. Depending on the demand for shares, there may not be enough available to satisfy everyone who has applied and the issue is said to be oversubscribed. Therefore, as already mentioned, companies adopt several methods to ensure that at least some investors receive shares. The fairest and most popular technique is to scale back applications so that every shareholder receives a minimum number of shares and those who apply for large amounts receive a proportion of what they applied for. The investors receive the shares plus a refund of the difference between the value of the shares they are allocated and the amount they subscribed. The danger with scaling back is that it can leave all investors with just a minimum handful of shares that is an uneconomic holding since dealing charges if you sold them would be disproportionate to the value of the holding.

Some new issues that are oversubscribed use a ballot procedure to allocate shares whereby applications are drawn at random and investors who are chosen receive the shares they subscribed for until all the shares are gone.

Another method of allocation is to introduce a cut-off point, which means those applying for a very large number of shares are excluded from the allocation.

The main advantages of buying shares when they are first issued is that you will not have to pay a dealing charge and the share price, particularly in the case of privatisations where the government is keen to ensure they are a success, is usually pitched as low as possible. There can also be other incentives with new issues such as a discount for small investors over the price that institutional investors have to pay and bonus shares if you hold on to your shares for a certain period of time.

Although new issues are a popular way to buy shares, they do carry risks. The fact that the company is unlikely to have been listed before, for example, means it should be valued at a discount against similar quoted companies with track records of trading on the market.

Demutualisations

In recent years millions of people have become shareholders through the trend for demutualisation. This is a movement whereby mutual organisations such as building societies and insurance companies that were owned by their members decided to become companies and list on the stock market. Once members approved the change of status the organisations gave them shares, based on a series of different criteria. Most gave a minimum number of shares to each of their members and additional shares based on the value of their mortgages, savings or policies. Some organisations gave members the chance to buy further shares in their flotation. Many of the companies then set up low-cost dealing services to help shareholders who wanted to sell their shares.

Although demutualisation shares cost members nothing, since they already owned the company, pro-mutual groups claim the change in status of these organisations to quoted companies that are focused on making profits have led to higher charges and lower levels of customer service.

Employee share schemes

Most quoted companies offer their employees the opportunity to purchase shares in their company in-house through various schemes. It encourages employees to invest in the company, which employers like because it aligns their interests with those of shareholders. Governments are also keen on such schemes since they encourage wider share ownership and they offer tax concessions on some schemes.

At the top end of these arrangements company directors are often incentivised with option plans that enable them to buy shares at a certain predetermined price at some point in the future. These option schemes can be highly controversial, with critics suggesting they can be too generous to management, while companies defend them as a valid way to link management bonuses to one form of shareholder value – the share price.

But there are also a raft of ways in which ordinary employees can buy shares in their company.

Priority on flotation

Often companies that are joining the stock market will reserve some shares for employees. Although companies are unable to offer discounts to employees from the price paid by other shareholders, such preferential treatment ensures they get the shares for which they apply.

Save as you earn (SAYE)

This scheme has to be open to all employees who have worked for the company for a certain length of time. It gives employees the right to buy shares at a discounted price – 20 per cent off the market price when you started saving – on a future date, which is three, five or seven years after the grant of the option.

Employees agree to save between £5 and £250 a month from their after-tax pay into an SAYE plan run by a building society or bank on behalf of the company. After the three- five- or seven-year period you will receive an interest bonus on your savings and can then choose to use the money to buy shares. If the share price is below the discounted price you would just take the money, although you would be liable for tax on the bonus. But if it is higher you can use the cash, without paying tax on the bonus, to buy the shares and make an instant profit. You may then choose to sell them, often through a low-cost dealing service provided by the building society or bank, or to hold them. If you sell them you may be subject to capital gains tax (which will be explained in the next chapter) depending on the amount of profit you make, but it should also be possible to avoid this by transferring them into a tax-free wrapper such as an Individual Savings Account. In exceptional circumstances you may be allowed to exercise your option early if you leave the company and the options may be triggered if the company is taken over.

SAYE schemes are almost always worth taking up if you can afford to because they are risk free. At worst they are cash savings schemes, although you should make sure the bonus rates are attractive, but at best they can offer big rewards if your company's share price has performed well.

Company share option plan (CSOP)

These allow a company to grant employees options to buy shares worth a maximum of £30,000 per person on the day of the grant, at a future date, but at today's stock market price. The option usually runs for three to ten years and you would obviously only exercise the right if the share price rose.

There is no income tax to pay on the paper profit – the difference between the original option price and the price on the day you exercise – but profits may be subject to capital gains tax.

All-employee share ownership plan (AESOP)

This plan has several aspects and enables companies to give employees free shares as a reward for performance and also encourages employees to buy shares in their company. Companies award free shares worth up to £3000 to all employees each year free of tax, provided they are held for at least five years after the award.

Under the partnership shares aspect of AESOP employees can buy, free of income tax and National Insurance, shares at the stock market price worth up to £125 per month or 10 per cent of their salary, whichever is the smaller. Employers can then award up to twice the number of partnership shares to employees who have bought them up to a maximum value of £3000 per year, free of tax and National Insurance.

WHAT IF IT ALL GOES WRONG?

Hopefully, you will enjoy trouble-free trading in shares but unfortunately problems can arise. If they do there are a number of avenues of complaint and also compensation available to you. While in general there is no compensation if your shares simply fall in value, regulatory systems do exist to prevent you suffering because of dishonesty or incompetence.

Regulatory systems and the watchdogs that enforce them have changed greatly in recent years, but are now evolving into a more simple structure.

Financial Services Authority

A new super regulator called the Financial Services Authority, known until 1997 as the Securities and Investments Board, was given powers to regulate the financial service industry under the Financial Services and Markets Act 2000. Its objectives are to maintain market confidence, promote public understanding of the financial system, protect consumers and fight financial crime.

By the end of 2001 the FSA is set to become the single statutory body for financial business in the UK. It will regulate and authorise all financial businesses, unit trusts and open-ended investment companies. It will also supervise investment exchanges and clearing houses.

The FSA aims to protect consumers by requiring firms and advisers to be honest, financially sound and competent. It can take action against firms that operate illegally. In addition it makes sure there is a proper system for dealing with complaints and that there is a compensation safety net if a financial firm goes bust.

How to complain

You must be sure you have a complaint and that the situation is not simply a misunderstanding. If you are confident you do have a genuine grievance you should follow a three-step procedure by first contacting the firm, second taking your complaint to an independent complaints scheme and finally taking the case to court.

Contact the firm

You must give the firm the chance to put right any wrongs you believe it has done you. Most firms will have a formal complaints procedure that you can follow. Start by contacting the person you dealt with and only if they fail to satisfy you take your case to their superior or the most senior person in the organisation such as the chief executive. If the firm is no longer trading call the FSA public enquiries helpline on 0845 606 1234.

Independent complaints scheme

If the firm fails to help you with the problem you can go to an independent complaints scheme, which is a body set up to resolve disputes between you and a financial firm. Nearly all financial firms belong to an independent complaints scheme, some because they are obliged to by law and others on a voluntary basis.

There are two types of scheme: an ombudsman scheme and arbitration scheme. Both will look at your case, decide whether the complaint is justified and, if so, will order the firm to put it right. They can also order the firm to make a financial reward of up to £100,000. In the recent past there have been a number of ombudsmen covering different financial firms such as banks and insurance, but under the new FSA there is a single Financial Ombudsman Service.

Arbitration schemes differ from the ombudsman service in that they work in a way set out by law and an arbitrator's judgement will be based on the legal responsibilities of you and the firm. Usually both you and the firm must agree in advance to accept the arbitrator's decision and in doing so you give up your right to go to court.

Details of the ombudsman and arbitration schemes can be obtained from the FSA Complaints Unit, South Quay Plaza, 183 Marsh Wall, London E14 9SR, tel: 020 7964 0474.

Court

This should only ever be a last resort since taking a firm to court can be an expensive and lengthy process. If possible, use a Small Claims Court for claims of up to £5000 as it is usually fast and relatively cheap.

Investors Compensation Scheme

You should always check that your financial adviser or stockbroker is authorised by the SFA to conduct investment business. This will give you some protection. Additional protection could come from special insurance carried by many stockbrokers, which pays out to clients in the event of major problems. If you choose to hold your shares in nominee accounts and leave cash on deposit with a broker it is important to make sure the broker has such insurance.

If an adviser or broker has been fraudulent and goes bust, you may still be able to get some of your money back under the Investors Compensation Scheme. The scheme steps in when an authorised investment firm goes out of business and cannot repay money it owes to clients. Under the scheme the first £30,000 of a valid claim is paid in full and 90 per cent of the next £20,000, up to a total of £48,000 per investor. The Investors Compensation Scheme can be contacted at Cottons Centre, Cottons Lane, London SE1 2QB, tel: 020 7367 6000, website: www.the-ics.org.uk.

London Stock Exchange

Although most of your complaints about stockbrokers and problems such as not receiving a share certificate from a company following an allocation of shares should be addressed to the FSA or the company itself, the London Stock Exchange does have some power to deal with certain problems. For example, you should contact the Exchange if you wish to complain about the way it operates its markets or if you believe a company whose shares are traded on the Alternative Investment Market is in breach of AIM rules.

You should address your complaint to Regulatory Complaints and Enquiries, Market Operations, London Stock Exchange, Old Broad Street, London EC2N 1HP, tel: 020 7797 3523.

Prevention is better than cure

While it is useful to know how to complain effectively, it is preferable not to have to complain at all. There are few simple rules worth following before you sign up with a broker or buy a financial product or service to ensure that you have done all you can to protect yourself.

- Read all the information you are given in detail including the small print.

- Don't be afraid to ask questions about anything you do not understand.

- Be wary of claims about the returns on investments. Often these may be based on historical returns, with no guarantee they will be repeated in future. The simple rule is that if something sounds too good to be true it is.

- Make sure you understand the risks and charges involved.

CONCLUSION

In this chapter we have looked at applying your investment skills in the real world by first experimenting with dummy trades, then choosing a stockbroker to deal for real. Although a stockbroker is likely to be your most regular route to buying and selling shares, we have also considered a few other ways to own shares without using one. Finally, we looked at what to do when things go wrong, and the organisations and schemes that exist to help you.

In the next chapter we shall consider a subject that makes all investors groan: tax. We shall look at what you have to pay, but also ways to pay less and in some cases pay nothing at all.

10
Tax and Your Investments

There are big profits to be made from investing in individual shares and it is something not lost on the Inland Revenue, which can hit investors with a variety of taxes. The taxation of investments underlines the importance of keeping records of your share purchases and sales, and any dividend income you receive. You will be taxed on your dividends and each time you buy shares, and you also face being taxed on profits when you sell shares. But before you despair totally, there also exist tax-free wrappers for your investments, which enable you to hold shares and sell them free of tax.

In this chapter we shall consider all aspects of taxation as it affects investors and the methods by which you can keep as much of your profit as possible. But bear in mind that rules on taxation and allowances change each year and therefore for an accurate understanding of your own tax position you must check it with a tax adviser.

Stamp duty

As we saw in the last chapter, stamp duty is a charge the government levies on share purchases. It is currently 0.5 per cent of the value of the transaction. In Europe only the UK, Denmark and Ireland have stamp duty, which makes the cost of share dealing comparatively higher in these places than other European countries. There is a growing lobby for abolishing stamp duty, but the government generates a large revenue from it and has been reluctant to end the practice.

Income tax

For investors this means tax on the income earned from their investments, which comes in the form of share dividends normally paid out twice a year after a company's interim and final results. Tax is already deducted at a rate of 10 per cent from dividends before they are paid to you. If you are a non-taxpayer you cannot reclaim this tax. If you are a basic-rate taxpayer you will have nothing more to pay. But if you are a higher-rate taxpayer you pay tax on dividends at a rate of 32.5 per cent. So you will have to pay tax at 22.5 per cent in addition to the 10 per cent rate.

The same position holds true for income from unit trusts and open-ended investment companies. Dividend income needs to be declared on your tax return whether or not you must pay extra tax.

Tax on scrip dividends and bonus shares

Sometimes, instead of paying a cash dividend, a company will offer shareholders extra shares, called a scrip dividend. These shares are counted as income by the taxman. When there is a choice between receiving cash or shares the value of the shares for tax purposes is equivalent to the amount of cash that would have been paid in dividend. When there is no cash alternative the market value of the shares is used instead. If you are a basic-rate taxpayer you will not have to pay tax on the value of the shares received, but if you are a higher-rate taxpayer you will have to pay extra tax.

If you receive bonus shares, which are a popular way of

attracting initial investors to a privatisation, they are treated as a dividend and there may be additional tax to pay on them.

Capital gains tax

CGT is a tax on assets you own that have increased in value and which you sell at a profit. The tax is levied if the profit is in excess of an annual capital gains tax allowance which, for the tax year ending 5 April 2002, is £7500. This means you can realise profits of up to £7500 on your investments during the year without having to pay tax on them. Even for active investors in shares this is quite a high level of profits before you have to pay tax, but it is easily attainable if you have a large portfolio or your shares perform particularly well.

The rate of CGT that you will pay will depend on your personal tax position, but will be 10 per cent, 20 per cent or 40 per cent. However, you are able to deduct the cost of buying or selling shares such as stamp duty and stockbroker commission from your profit. You are also able to offset any losses, including expenses, that you may have realised on your shares against any profits you have made. This means that if you have sold shares at below the price you paid for them and incurred a loss, you can use this to offset any profits to the same amount that you have made above your capital gains tax allowance in any one year. If in a tax year your losses exceed your gains you are allowed to carry over net loss to reduce chargeable gains in later tax years. Until 5 April 1998, if you sold shares at a profit you could add in any percentage increase in inflation, the Retail Prices Index, since you bought the shares. This is known as indexation. But it does not apply if you made a loss on the shares.

To help with your calculations the Inland Revenue publishes a table that tells you the indexation factor for every month from March 1998 back to March 1982, the month when indexation began. To work out your CGT liability you should multiply the amount you spent on the shares by the indexation factor. The table below provides all the indexation factors you will need to make your calculation.

	Jan	Feb	Mar	Apr	May	Jun	Jul	Aug	Sep	Oct	Nov	Dec
1982			1.047	1.006	0.992	0.987	0.986	0.985	0.987	0.977	0.967	0.971
1983	0.968	0.96	0.956	0.929	0.921	0.917	0.906	0.898	0.889	0.883	0.876	0.871
1984	0.872	0.865	0.859	0.834	0.828	0.823	0.825	0.808	0.804	0.793	0.788	0.789
1985	0.783	0.769	0.752	0.716	0.708	0.704	0.707	0.703	0.704	0.701	0.695	0.693
1986	0.689	0.683	0.681	0.665	0.662	0.663	0.667	0.662	0.654	0.652	0.638	0.632
1987	0.626	0.62	0.616	0.597	0.596	0.596	0.597	0.593	0.588	0.58	0.573	0.574
1988	0.574	0.568	0.562	0.537	0.531	0.525	0.524	0.507	0.5	0.485	0.478	0.474
1989	0.465	0.454	0.448	0.423	0.414	0.409	0.408	0.404	0.395	0.384	0.372	0.369
1990	0.361	0.353	0.339	0.3	0.288	0.283	0.282	0.269	0.258	0.248	0.251	0.252
1991	0.249	0.242	0.237	0.222	0.218	0.213	0.215	0.213	0.208	0.204	0.199	0.198
1992	0.199	0.193	0.189	0.171	0.167	0.167	0.171	0.171	0.166	0.162	0.164	0.168
1993	0.179	0.171	0.167	0.156	0.152	0.153	0.156	0.151	0.146	0.147	0.148	0.146
1994	0.151	0.144	0.141	0.128	0.124	0.124	0.129	0.124	0.121	0.12	0.119	0.114
1995	0.114	0.107	0.102	0.091	0.087	0.085	0.091	0.085	0.08	0.085	0.085	0.079
1996	0.083	0.078	0.073	0.066	0.063	0.063	0.067	0.062	0.057	0.057	0.057	0.053
1997	0.053	0.049	0.046	0.04	0.036	0.032	0.032	0.026	0.021	0.019	0.019	0.016
1998	0.019	0.014	0.011									

On 6 April 1998 the situation changed and the Inland Revenue replaced indexation with the tapering of CGT. The idea behind this was to reduce the amount of tax to be paid on profits from selling shares in proportion to the number of years you held the shares since 5 April 1998. The longer you hold the shares the lower the percentage of the gain that will be taxed.

The table below shows how the Inland Revenue has set the taper.

	Gains on non-business assets	
Number of complete years after 5.4.98 for which asset held	Percentage of gain chargeable	Equivalent tax rates for higher/basic-rate taxpayer
0	100	40 / 20
1	100	40 / 20
2	100	40 / 20
3	95	38 / 19
4	90	36 / 18
5	85	34 / 17
6	80	32 / 16
7	75	30 / 15
8	70	28 / 14
9	65	26 / 13
10 or more	60	24 / 12

The upshot of the introduction of tapering of capital gains is that if you bought shares before 5 April 1998 and sell them now you will have to make two calculations to work out how much CGT you owe.

The first part of the calculation involves using indexation to work out the cost of buying shares before 5 April 1998 so that it includes the effect of inflation. The second part involves taking the period from 6 April 1998 until the shares are sold and the profits realised, and using the tapering system to work out your entitlement to relief. This system is all very well for shares bought between 1 April 1982 and today, but what about shares that were bought on or before 31 March 1982?

If you owned shares on or before 31 March 1982, only the profit since that date is liable for capital gains tax. Any gains made before 1 April 1982 are tax free. Therefore the starting value of your shares for CGT purposes is considered to be the market value of your shares on 31 March 1982, although expenses incurred on or before that date cannot be used for CGT purposes.

A problem arises, though, since you may have bought shares before 31 March 1982 that fell in value up to 31 March 1982 and then increased in value. Using the 31 March 1982 value in this case would mean increasing your liability to CGT. To solve the problem the Revenue allows you to consider two calculations for gains or losses incurred on shares held prior to 1 April 1982. The first is the chargeable gain using the market value on 31 March 1982, not counting any costs incurred on or before that date. The second is the actual gain, using the original price you paid plus any allowable expenses. Once you have calculated the gain or loss under both methods, you use a so-called 'kink test' to decide on the final figure. If both calculations produce a gain, the smaller one is used to work out your CGT bill. If both produce a loss the smaller loss is used. If one produces a loss and the other a gain the disposal is deemed to produce no gain or loss. It is clearly a complicated matter, but the Revenue does allow you to make a so-called rebasing election, which means you can agree that all shares owned on or before 31 March 1982 will be based on their market value on 31 March 1982. Once you have made the election you must stick to it.

Although for most investors their annual CGT allowance will more than outweigh any profits you may make on shares during the course of a year there are ways of avoiding CGT. The most obvious, if you are married, is to transfer some of your shares to your spouse to use up his or her annual allowance. Transfers between married couples are tax free.

Until 1998 investors could take advantage of a system call bed-and-breakfasting whereby you sold shares one day and bought them back the next in order to realise a capital gain, which could then be offset against your annual CGT exemption. This loophole was closed in the 1998 Budget and you now have to wait a month before you can repurchase the same shares if you are doing it in order to crystallise a profit to offset against CGT. Given the potential changes in share price over the month, it has become a risky method of reducing CGT exposure.

Tax on demutualisation shares

Free windfall shares from demutualised building societies or insurance companies are classed as a pure capital gain when they are sold. So unless you keep them in a tax-free wrapper such as an Individual Savings Account the full amount you realise from the sale will eat into your CGT allowance.

Tax efficient investment in shares

There are a number of ways to invest in shares without incurring tax or at least minimising the tax, you may have to pay. Among them are the employee share schemes we considered in the last chapter and pension schemes. Investing in non-listed stocks, including shares on the Alternative Investment Market, can also qualify for tax relief in areas such as inheritance tax and roll-over relief if shares in one qualifying company are sold and the proceeds invested in another qualifying company. In addition, CGT taper rules for AIM shares are also attractive. For a higher-rate taxpayer who sells AIM shares after four years the CGT liability on any profit falls from 40 per cent to just 10 per cent.

But for the majority of investors the best and most accessible tax-efficient method of investing in shares is via an Individual Savings Account or ISA.

Individual Savings Account

This replaced two existing tax-free investment products: Personal Equity Plans and Tax Exempt Special Savings Accounts, for new customers in 1999.

ISAs are effectively tax-free baskets into which you can place several types of assets. You could just use them to hold cash that can generate interest free of tax or you can shelter an insurance product such as life assurance.

But most relevant to investors is that you can also use an ISA as a tax-free wrapper for your ordinary shares, fixed-interest bonds issued by companies, unit trusts, investment trusts, OEICS and UK government gilts with at least five years to maturity. No matter how large the profits you generate from your shares, in an ISA they will be free of capital gains tax.

At present ISAs also offer a 10 per cent tax credit on any dividend income, but from 2004 tax credits will cease to be payable on dividends paid on shares held in an ISA. This means that while currently you earn more from dividends paid by ISA-held shares, by 2004 you will get the same dividend whether the shares are held in an ISA or not. Any individual over the age of 18 can start a new ISA each tax year and invest up to the current limit of £7000. You do not have to declare that you have an ISA on your tax form.

There are different types of ISAs called mini-and maxi-ISAs. If you choose a mini-ISA you can invest up to £3000 a year in shares, £3000 a year in cash and £1000 a year in insurance. The advantages of mini-ISAs is that you can buy each one from a different provider, so you can shop around for the best deal.

But if you are a serious investor you are probably better off choosing a maxi-ISA since this allows you to invest your full allowance of £7000 a year in shares. You do not have to invest the full amount and you can choose to invest a lump sum or a regular monthly amount, which is probably preferable for investors seeking to smooth out the effects of the peaks and troughs of the stock market.

There are various funds you can invest in through an ISA or you could use it to track a particular index such as the FTSE 100 or simply put individual shares, either new or those you already own, into the tax-free wrapper.

While cash ISAs should be free of charges from the provider, the charges on equity ISAs vary considerably depending on what funds you choose and how you buy. You can expect to pay an initial charge of between 1 per cent 6 per cent of the amount invested, plus an annual management fee of up to 1.75 per cent. Rates can change during a year, particularly as fund managers try to sell more towards the end of a tax year.

Deciding the suitability of particular equity ISAs is a judgement for yourself, based on your risk-and-reward profile, but the government does offer some help in ensuring the ISA meets certain standards. There is a government-approved CAT standard – standing for Charges (which should be low), Access (which should be easy) and Terms (which should be fair). Equity ISAs can only carry the CAT mark if the total charges are 1 per cent a year or less. But beware since CAT standards are no guarantee of performance and anyway, the standard is a purely voluntary code.

CONCLUSION

Tax is a complicated subject and you should seek professional advice to fully understand your own position. The first port of call should be the Inland Revenue itself, which operates a network of tax enquiry centres and most are open Monday to Friday from 8.30 a.m. to 4.30 p.m. You can also call the Revenue's Self-Assessment Helpline on 0645 000 444 or visit its website on www.inland revenue.gov.uk. In addition there are several computer software packages available to help you work out your tax liabilities.

Or you could get a qualified tax adviser, accountant or an independent financial adviser to help you. There are several professional bodies that should help you find advisers suitable for your needs. They include the Institute of Chartered Accountants in England and Wales, the Association of Chartered Certified Accountants and the Chartered Institute of Taxation and Association of Tax Technicians.

CHAPTER # 11

Investment Gurus

Every investor is unique since each of you will have your own risk-and-reward profiles, favourite investment techniques and different goals.

Hopefully, this book has given you some ideas as to your tolerance for risk and your craving for reward, as well as suggesting a number of techniques you might want to try. Ultimately, how you invest in shares is down to you, but there is no harm in considering how great investors of the past and present have come to their own conclusions of what works for them.

In this chapter we shall consider how some of the most successful stock market investors have honed their techniques and put their theories into practice. The list is far from exhaustive, but it does provide some thumbnail sketches of leading investment gurus.

There is a heavy bias towards US investors because they have come to dominate investment thinking. This is no real surprise since the United States has a long-standing culture of wide share ownership and wealth creators are admired. But the prominence of US investors is doubtless also because they are more adept at self-promotion than their European counterparts.

VALUE INVESTORS

Benjamin Graham

Widely regarded as the grandfather of investment gurus and the founder of value investing, American Benjamin Graham came to prominence in the wake of the 1929 Wall Street Crash. His place in the history of investing was secured when he wrote a textbook for professional investors called *Security Analysis*, first published in 1934, and a popular investment classic called *The Intelligent Investor*, first published in 1949.

Security Analysis, which Graham co-wrote with David Dodd, took an academic approach to explaining the financial characteristics of industries, establishing financial ratios for evaluating companies in those industries and assessing those companies performing best in their sector and whose shares were therefore worth buying.

The Intelligent Investor distils some of the early book into a more accessible format for private investors, stressing the advantages of operating a portfolio of shares, and is also concerned with the psychology of investing.

Central to Graham's investment philosophy was the development of his theory of value investing together with a formal structure to investment analysis. He differentiates between investment and speculation. Investment is different because it is based on analysis, is designed to protect your original investment and produces an acceptable return.

Graham believed in investors holding both shares and bonds in their portfolios, with the balance reflecting the strength or weakness of the stock market. He suggested sticking with a strategy and ignoring stock market fashions, although he also cautioned that you should not rely on the same investment theory in all market conditions. He gave growth stocks a wide berth because there were no acceptable methods of selecting them. He also cautioned on relying on the same investment theory for all market conditions.

Graham split investors into two groups: defensive and aggressive.

Defensive investors should opt for a portfolio of 10 to 30 companies each of which is large, well-financed and has a strong position in its market. It should have a lengthy record of continuous earnings and dividend pay-outs, and should only be bought if the price-to-earnings ratio is 'modest', which Graham described as not more than 15 times average earnings in the past three years.

Aggressive investors should target value companies that are out of favour with the stock market and Graham described these as bargain issues. He said a bargain issue should be bought for less than two-thirds of its net quick assets – which is working capital minus all debt. It should then be sold when its price is equivalent to its net current assets. Graham also stipulated that a bargain share company should owe less than it was worth, so its gearing – the ratio of debt to shareholders funds – should be less than 100 per cent.

He also proposed two measures in relation to the yield on top-rated bonds such as gilts. The first is that the earnings yield on a bargain share should be twice the prevailing gilt yield. By earnings yield he meant the PE ratio expressed as a percentage, so if a share sold for ten times earnings it would have a 10 per cent earnings yield and if it sold for five times earnings the yield would be 20 per cent. The second is that a bargain share should have a dividend yield no less than two-thirds of the gilt yield. Roughly summed up, Graham was hunting for shares that sold on low price-to-earnings ratios and high dividend yields.

Graham also helpfully suggested when such shares should be sold. He recommended selling after the share price had risen 50 per cent or after two years, whichever came first. He also advised selling if the dividend was passed or if earnings fell to the extent that the stock market price was 50 per cent higher than the buying price suggested by the fallen earnings figure.

Graham was not just a theorist and he managed funds through his business, Graham-Newman Corporation, which grew by 21 per cent a year on average between 1936 and 1957.

Warren Buffett

The world's most famous investment guru, Buffett has become an idol for investors because his straightforward investment techniques have made him one of the world's richest men. A down-to-earth American, his devoted followers point out that despite his great wealth he lives a simple lifestyle in his hometown of Omaha, Nebraska.

Buffett studied under Benjamin Graham and adopted and adapted many of his techniques as he developed his investment vehicle Berkshire Hathaway. Between 1956 and 1999 Buffett produced a compound growth rate on his investments of 25.8 per cent, which would have turned an initial investment of $1000 into $19 million.

Investors watch out each year for Buffett's chairman's letter in Berkshire's annual report and his sometimes homespun and common-sense wisdom has earned him the title the Sage of Omaha.

Buffett follows many of Graham's techniques to identify shares and buys undervalued companies that have fallen out of favour with the stock market. But he contrasts with the strategy of his mentor in that he then holds on to his investments permanently. With major stakes in companies such as Coca-Cola, Gillette, Walt Disney and American Express, he is the ultimate buy-and-hold practitioner. In addition Berkshire also owns several businesses outright such as insurance company Geico and jewellers Borsheim. In this respect Buffett's real investment strategy is not to buy shares, but to buy companies or large enough stakes perhaps to influence businesses.

He sticks to businesses he understands, which tend to be in manufacturing, retailing and services with well-known brands or franchises and strong market positions. He wants businesses with good management and sound long-term prospects. Buffett has no interest in technology companies – which he readily admits he does not understand.

The most important factor for Buffett is determining the value of a business and paying a bargain price for its shares. He is quite prepared to wait for the right opportunity to appear and seems to have little interest in the wider machinations of stock markets or the economy at large. He looks for businesses with a good return on capital, which have their profits in cash, strong market positions and are therefore unlikely to see margins squeezed by competitors, which have easily predictable earnings, are not a target for regulators, carry low levels of stock and have a high turnover of assets.

Although his value strategy and long-term investing techniques would appear to mark him out as a defensive investor, his core portfolio of just a half-dozen or so shares suggests quite an aggressive risk-and-reward profile. But Buffett reduces risk by showing great patience in selecting and then holding shares for a long time. He only buys shares when they are good value, which allows him a certain safety margin.

Buffett has outlined six qualities that he believes you must have to succeed as an investor.

1   You must be greedy, although you need to keep control of your greed and be fascinated by the investment process.

2   You must be patient in your investments.

3   You must make your own decisions and stick with them.

4   You must be confident in your actions based on your own research and not be influenced by external factors such as a falling stock market.

5   You must accept there are some things you do not know.

6   You must be flexible when considering investments and only pay what a business is worth.

Buffett's investment strategy came in for stick at the end of the 1990s when stock markets soared on the back of technology shares, which he had avoided, and Berkshire's returns looked pedestrian. But the strength of his strategy was underlined when the tech bubble burst and investors flooded back to value shares that he had never abandoned. The Sage of Omaha had lived up to his name yet again.

GROWTH INVESTORS

T. Rowe Price

Although no one person can be crowned the originator of growth investing in the same way as Benjamin Graham can claim to have founded value investing, American T. Rowe Price has as good a claim as any.

Author of *Principles of Growth Stock Valuation*, Price argued that investors should pick companies with growth potential and hold them for a long time. The earlier in the life of the growth company you can buy the shares the better the return.

Price's hunt for growth stocks began by identifying an industry that was enjoying a growth phase and picking the most promising company or companies in that industry.

The characteristic of a growth industry was one where volumes of unit sales and net earnings were both growing. To identify the most promising companies within such industries Price believed they must have proved their qualities by raising unit growth and profits through a downturn in the business cycle – a characteristic he described as stable growth – or show higher earnings during several business cycles – which he termed cyclical growth. Companies that demonstrated this ability had qualities such as good management, patented products, strong finances, outstanding research and a favourable location.

Price's growth investment approach led him to focus on its price/earnings multiple rather than the company's assets when picking a particular share to buy. He looked for shares with a record of earnings growth, but warned against extrapolating that level of growth too far into the future. The best time to buy a growth stock, according to Price, is when it is out of fashion and therefore its PE ratio is close to that of the market rather than higher as it deserves.

Although primarily interested in capital growth, Price recognised that blue chip shares with a record of improving dividends were worth more than secondary shares that showed no dividend growth. He said, too, that companies with stable growth were worth more than cyclical shares.

The level of interest rates was also important for Price's investment strategy and he suggested you should pay lower earnings multiples for growth shares when interest rates are high than when they are low.

Taking all these factors into account, Price would work out the high and low PEs for a share over the last few market cycles and buy at up to a maximum of a third higher than the lowest PE.

Although the idea behind a growth share is to buy, sit tight and enjoy the ride as the share price rises higher, Price did include sell signals in his theory. He said that if you saw a decline in the return on your investment this could be a signal that the growth company was reaching maturity and therefore no longer qualified as a growth investment. When Price did decide to sell in a rising share market he adopted a scale system to exit a share. He would wait until the share price had risen 30 per cent above his target level for buying and sell 10 per cent of his holding. He would then sell a further 10 per cent of his shares for every 10 per cent increase in the share price. This may be termed selling into strength since the rising price meant there would always be willing buyers for the shares. It is a strategy of booking profit and the follows the City saying of always leaving something for the next guy.

But if the scale strategy was not possible because the bull market had petered out, or the share price seemed to be falling sharply, or there was bad news from the company, Price would simply sell his entire holding at the market price.

Although advocates of the Price investment approach stick solidly with his growth investing criteria, the man himself subtly changed his approach in the 1970s, after deciding there were few genuine growth opportunities around, and adopted a more flexible attitude to investment. As the bull market ran out of steam in the early 1970s Price favoured splitting his investments into bonds and shares, and targeted companies in natural resources and inflation-resistant sectors such as property and gold.

Peter Lynch

Although ranked as a great growth investor, American Lynch was really a hugely successful trader who used several investment approaches but did extremely well from buying growth shares. His prominence is based on his management of Fidelity's Magellan mutual fund, which is the US equivalent of a unit trust. In the 13 years that he managed the fund, between 1977 and 1990, he grew it 30-fold. He also wrote several investment books including *One Up on Wall Street* and *Beating the Street*.

Lynch uses fundamental analysis to pick shares, but also invests in large numbers of shares, hoping to increase his chances of finding a successful investment. He looked at shares that he described as stalwarts, cyclicals, turnarounds and asset plays. But he was also interested in growth stocks, which he termed 'fast growers' and his target was to find what he termed a 'ten-bagger' – a share capable of rising in value tenfold. Fast growers were small businesses growing at 20 per cent to 25 per cent a year, which had to have a winning and repeatable formula and a healthy balance sheet.

Lynch wanted simple businesses that anyone could run. His famous quote was: 'I choose a company which can be run by an idiot because you can be sure that one day it will be.'

He also looked for companies in out-of-fashion industries, rather than hot sectors, which many investors were targeting, and suggested buying as early as possible to get in before the growth story was fully out and long before the growth slowed. He also said the PE ratio should be at or near the growth rate, which should still be accelerating. So if the earnings-per-share were rising by 25 per cent a year, the PE ratio should be around 25.

Although Lynch admitted he never had an overall investment strategy, he did follow a series of rules, many of which were simply common sense, as he went about picking shares. Among these was that you should stick to companies and sectors you know about in order to give yourself an edge over other investors. He was also a fan of lone investment and advocated ignoring the investment herd.

Although he said that if you could not find anything to invest in you should put your money in the bank and wait.

He suggested keeping a small portfolio of shares, perhaps as few as five, since that made it easier to keep track of companies. He believed in the importance of research before you buy and also sticking to your buy decision, as long as the reasons still remained, rather than being swayed by outside forces, other investors or stock market changes.

Lynch emphasised that you should not be buying shares unless you are prepared to take the downs as well as the ups, and stressed that you should never be complacent and should always worry in order to stay sharp.

A very successful investor, Lynch's rules of engagement are well worth being taken on board by the private investor.

OTHER INVESTORS

Anthony Bolton

An Englishman who has made his mark running funds for Fidelity Investments, Bolton is one of the most respected British investment gurus.

Although he does favour value investments, he also looks for growth shares and, as well as fundamental analysis, uses some technical analysis in evaluating shares. His skill lies in marrying together different investment techniques and not getting hung up on one particular style.

Bolton targets recovery plays that are not cyclical shares, but rather companies where something has gone wrong, such as a change of management. This special-situations approach is core to his investment strategy, nor is he afraid of smaller companies. He also buys undervalued and under-researched shares, as well as unrecognised growth shares or growth shares suffering a temporary setback.

His quest for unfashionable and undervalued shares leads him to look for a variety of characteristics that might mark out a company as a worthwhile investment. Among those features are companies that have fallen on hard times but are capable of internal recovery, those that trade at a discount to assets, are vulnerable to takeover, have an industry niche, and businesses where supply and demand of their product is transparent.

Once he has identified potential investments he subjects them to fundamental analysis, although he does not over-rely on earnings-per-share measurements. One ratio Bolton is fond of is enterprise value to gross cash flow, which he defines as the company's stock market value plus net debt divided by the operating profit plus depreciation.

As well as fundamental analysis, Bolton differs from most investment gurus in that he is happy to use technical analysis and share price charts too. Although he does not overplay their importance, he views charts as a screening tool to help him arrive at shares worth buying since they offer a clue as to what other investors are thinking in terms of whether they are buying or selling a share.

In addition to running numbers and viewing charts, Bolton believes in the importance of meeting companies face to face both to find out about them and their managements, and what they think of their competitors. He also talks to customers, reads trade journals and considers anything that can add to his insight on a particular business.

Once he has selected shares worth buying he runs a portfolio heavily weighted towards his favoured picks, rather than a balanced portfolio approach.

Bolton has clear rules as to when he will sell a share. First, he will sell if he needs to raise cash to buy something better. Second, a sale may be triggered if something changes, either internally or externally, and the reasons for buying the share no longer hold. Third, he will sell once the share becomes fully valued relative to his target when he bought it.

Bolton does not buy and hold shares and although some may stay in his portfolio for many years, he tends to turn over about 75 per cent of the portfolio each year. This does not necessarily make him a trader rather than an investor, but it does mark him out as someone who believes there is always additional value to be found if you look hard enough.

George Soros

This Hungarian émigré rocketed to fame in 1992 when his Quantum Fund made $1 billion betting that the pound would fall out of the European Union's Exchange Rate Mechanism. Soros's claim to fame as the man who bet against the Bank of England and won is therefore as a speculator rather than an investor, but there is no doubt that he has won a place in the hearts of many admiring students of investment. Speculators have earned a fair amount of criticism in some quarters for being short-term gamblers with little regard for the longer-term economic consequences they may profit from. However, they do perform an important function in providing liquidity to financial markets.

Although Soros's modus operandi is to take massive high-risk positions in financial markets, some of his theories do have a potential relevance for small investors in the stock market.

Soros is concerned with markets and in his book *The Alchemy of Finance* he considers their characteristics. He has developed what he terms a 'theory of reflexivity' to explain some aspects of their behaviour. The theory suggests that markets tend to get out of control at their peaks and at their troughs. In stock market investment terms this would mean that the final phases of bull markets see share prices running away unjustifiably, while the depths of a bear market see share prices fall too far below fundamental values. Central to Soros's theory is that markets are never efficient, but if you can second-guess them you can profit by timing your investment ahead of a change in the market. The trouble with the theory is that if your prediction is wrong you could lose heavily and indeed, Soros has made loss-making calls, although he has suggested that these have been useful learning experiences.

Small investors seeking to follow the Soros market position approach, perhaps in terms of timing investment in an index tracker fund, are unlikely to receive a unique insight into which direction the stock market will next move. However, Soros is a useful reminder that sometimes the bigger picture is important and he underlines the need to understand what and when to buy.

CONCLUSION

Remember that gurus are teachers not prophets. Investment gurus can teach you some valuable lessons, but you should never follow them slavishly. Times and situations change and what was right in the stock market conditions of Benjamin Graham's day, for example, may not have quite the same relevance today. Also, no matter how great the guru, none has a totally unblemished record.

What they do show is that their theories have worked and that you should generally take a long-term view of investment, but never be afraid to take profits and cut losses. As this book makes clear, when considering the wisdom of investment experts you should try to take what makes sense to you and fits with your investment profile, and use it to develop your own investment strategy.

The stock market can be a hostile place, but armed with your own approach to investment you stand a better chance of making progress than by following strategies or techniques you feel uncomfortable with.

Although you might decide that day trading is for you and you therefore have a very short investment horizon, the time you take to decide on that particular strategy should be as long as you spend deciding you are better suited to pursue a buy-and-hold strategy. To begin with take your time. Learn to walk before you run and do not be afraid of making mistakes. They may seem expensive in the short term, but in the long run losses from mistakes you learn from will turn out to be sound investments.

Good luck, good investing and have fun.

Useful Addresses

Association of Investment Trust Companies (AITC)
Durrant House, −13 Chiswell Street, London EC1Y 4YY
Telephone: 020 7282 5555
Website: www.aitc.co.uk

Association of Private Client Investment Managers and
Stockbrokers (APCIMS)
112 Middlesex Street, London E1 7HY
Telephone: 020 7247 7080
Website: www.apcims.org.uk

Association of Unit Trusts and Investment Funds (AUTIF)
65 Kingsway, London WC2B 6TD
Telephone: 020 7831 0898
Website: www.investmentfunds.org.uk

Financial Services Authority
25 The North Colonnade, Canary Wharf, London E14 5HS
Telephone: 0845 606 1234
Website: www.fsa.gov.uk

FTSE International
St Alphage House, 2 Fore Street, London EC2Y 5DA
Telephone: 020 7448 1800
Website: www.ftse.com

IFA Promotion
2nd Floor, 113–17 Farringdon Road, London EC1R 3BX
Telephone: 020 7833 3131
Website: www.ifap.org.uk

Investors Compensation Scheme
Cottons Centre, Cottons Lane, London SE1 2QB
Telephone: 020 7367 6000
Website: www.the-ics.org.uk

London International Financial Futures and Options Exchange
1 Cousin Lane, Cannon Bridge, London EC4R 3XX
Telephone: 020 7623 0444
Website: www.liffe.com

London Stock Exchange
Old Broad Street, London EC2N 1HP
Telephone: 020 7797 1372
Website: www.londonstockexchange.com

NASDAQ
Website: www.nasdaq.com

Ofex
Website: www.ofex.co.uk

ProShare
Centurion House, 24 Monument Street, London EC3R 8AQ
Telephone: 020 7220 1730
Website: www.proshare.org.uk

Stockbrokers

Execution only

Abbey National Sharedealing Service
Capstan House, One Clove Crescent, East India Dock, London
E14 2BH
Telephone: 0845 601 2201
Website: www.sharedealing.abbeynational.co.uk

Barclays Stockbrokers Limited
Murray House, 1 Royal Mint Court, London EC3N 4HH
Telephone: 0845 777 6776
Website: www.barclays-stockbrokers.co.uk

Charles Schwab Europe
Telephone: 0870 601 8888
Website: www.schwab.Europe.com

DLJDirect Limited
Telephone: 0800 358 4477
Website: www.DLJdirect.co.uk

E*TRADE UK
Mount Pleasant House, 2 Mount Pleasant, Cambridge CB3 ORN
Telephone: 0800 525 050
Website: www.etrade.co.uk

Halifax Share Dealing
Trinity Road, Halifax HAX 2RG
Telephone: 0870 241 1114
Website: www.halifax.co.uk/sharedealing

Lloyds TSB Stockbrokers Limited
48 Chiswell Street, London EC1Y 4XX
Telephone: 0870 608 8600

NatWest Stockbrokers Limited
55 Mansell Street, London E1 8AN
Telephone: 020 7895 5609
Website: www.natweststockbrokers.co.uk

TD Waterhouse Investor Services (Europe)
201 Deansgate, Manchester M3 3TD.
Telephone: 0161 819 6000
Website: www.tdwaterhouse.co.uk

Discretionary and advisory (many also offer execution-only service)

BWD Rensburg
Has offices in major cities across Great Britain including London
(tel. 020 7638 0033), Manchester (tel. 0161 832 6868) and
Glasgow (tel. 0141 333 9323)
Website: www.bwd-rensburg.co.uk

Brewin Dolphin Securities
Has offices across Great Britain including London (tel. 020 7248
4400), Aberdeen where it trades under the Bell Lawrie White name
(tel. 01224 589 345), Edinburgh where it has an execution-only
arm called Stocktrade (tel. 08457 090 919) and Manchester where
it trades as Wise Speke (tel. 0161 839 4222)
Website: www.brewindolphin.co.uk

Charles Stanley & Co Limited
Offices across Great Britain including London (tel. 020 7739
8200), Bath (tel. 01225 335 616), Bournemouth (tel. 01202 317
788), Chelmsford (tel. 01245 267 345) and Manchester (tel. 0161
828 0200)
Website: www.charles-stanley.co.uk

Gerard

Offices across Great Britain including London (tel. 020 7002 4000), Birmingham (tel. 0121 200 2244), Bristol (tel. 0117 943 4600), Edinburgh (tel. 0131 225 2171), Manchester (tel. 0161 834 2040) Newcastle (tel. 0191 260 4000)

Website: www.Gerard.com

HSBC Investment Management

6 Bevis Marks, London EC3A 7JQ

Telephone: 020 7336 9195

Website: www.im.hsbc.com

Killick & Co.

Offices in London

Telephone: 0870 606 1444

Website: www.killick.co.uk

Rowan Dartington & Co. Limited

Offices in the South West of England

7th Floor, Colston Tower, Colston Street, Bristol BS1 4RD

Telephone: 0117 925 3377

Website: www.rowan-dartington.co.uk

Index